NEW YORK CITY FIRSTS

NEW YORK CITY FIRSTS

Big Apple Innovations That Changed the Nation and the World

Laurie Lewis

Guilford, Connecticut

Globe
Pequot

An imprint of Globe Pequot, the trade division of
The Rowman & Littlefield Publishing Group, Inc.
4501 Forbes Blvd., Ste. 200
Lanham, MD 20706
www.rowman.com

Distributed by NATIONAL BOOK NETWORK

British Library Cataloguing in Publication Information available

Library of Congress Cataloging-in-Publication Data available

978-1-4930-6303-1 (paper)
978-1-4930-6304-8 (electronic)

∞™ The paper used in this publication meets the minimum requirements of American National
Standard for Information Sciences—Permanence of Paper for Printed Library Materials, ANSI/
NISO Z39.48-1992.

CONTENTS

CONTENTS

INTRODUCTION

When I was studying to become a New York City tour guide, I was struck by the many firsts that New York could claim. Some of them were logical given the city's size compared with other cities and its pre-eminence, even in its early days, as the commerce capital of the country. But other facts came as surprises. As I recall, the initial time I exclaimed to myself, "That's fascinating! I had no idea!" was when I read that New York City passed the first zoning law in the nation. After I discovered that, I started to look for other firsts. The list kept growing. Many of the firsts were engaging stories, and I thought a collection of them would make an interesting book.

More and more firsts emerged as I started to research each fact. A source about one first would mention another innovation, and as I researched that I might find yet another. It was like my experience using a dictionary. I look up one word, which suggests another, which prompts me to check out yet another, until an hour has passed and I don't recall how I had started the session. Only instead of using a single dictionary, I was now researching with the books in my personal library and especially with the wide world of the web.

Initially I assumed that this book would be of interest mainly to New Yorkers. Later I realized that this is more than a book about the city. It is a history of some of mankind's most spectacular achievements. I chuckled when I realized that I was writing a history book, because history was my least favorite subject in school. But this book skips the type of history I found boring: wars, politics, and the like. Rather, this book is a social history, an account of changes and innovations that originated in New York but often affected lives elsewhere in America and sometimes around the globe.

The first of its kind is not necessarily the best. Just the opposite; the first is often a rough cut that subsequent renditions hone to perfection. But the first is a window on the people and the times. What problems of the day cried out for solutions by daring individuals with bold ideas? How difficult was it for the innovator to promote the idea? How did life change because of the achievement?

Indeed, some of these innovations were life-changing: air conditioning, credit cards, and elevators, to name a few. Others reflect the changing social attitudes of the country: the first suburb, the first breadline, and the first bat mitzvah. Other firsts are somewhat amusing: the introduction of starlings in America, cronuts, and my personal favorite, safety pins.

Have these teasers made you want to read this book? Good! But before you dig in, let me tell you about some decisions that I had to make when writing the book.

The first decision was the meaning of *first*. Some of the entries in this book are the first of their kind in the world. Other innovations had already occurred elsewhere, usually in Europe, but were the first instance in the United States. I give credit to the original in the latter case.

Strange though it may seem, I had to decide how to define New York City. Until 1898, New York meant Manhattan. After that, the city officially expanded to include the five boroughs of Manhattan, Brooklyn, Queens, the Bronx, and Staten Island. I chose to present innovations that occurred in the so-called outer boroughs even if they predated 1898. Manhattan may seem overrepresented, but that is because it was the most populous area for most of the city's history. More people meant a larger pool of creative individuals.

In addition, I had to decide who would be considered a New Yorker. Some of the most accomplished people are citizens of the world; they do not claim a particular city as home. I determined that an individual who was born or raised in New York but who did not live or work in the city later, especially during the period of achievement, and did not profess strong ties to the city would not qualify for inclusion in this book.

A medical writer and editor for many years, I know how to research. I know that some sources are more trustworthy than others, and I know how to tell the difference. I was prepared for that aspect of research but not for another. Conflicting, reputable sources often made reasonable claims that more than one city was the first to do or have something. In many cases, I eliminated the disputed claim from the book. In other cases, when the story was just too good to omit, I acknowledged the controversy in my coverage. My goal was to make this book both accurate and interesting.

As I delved into the social history of New York, I realized how entrenched division is in this country. From the earliest days, an unofficial class system has separated the haves from the have-nots. Black Americans have always been denied opportunities to succeed. Emotionally loaded terms like *slave* and its opposite *free Black*, *impoverished* and a sometimes equivalent adjective *immigrant*, appear in this book more often than I would like. But they reflect the reality of New York, and the United States, through much of history.

As important as source notes are in literature for professionals, I don't know many people who read them in books for the general public like this one. I must admit that I rarely read them. I think source listings in this type of book look pretentious and serve no real purpose except to inflate the word count, so I have not included them. But rest assured, I have checked out all facts in this book. I included firsts only if I could verify them in at least two independent, reliable sources. (Sorry, Wikipedia fans. That's not a reliable source.) I have documentation to back up all facts.

By the time I had assembled all the innovations that merited inclusion in this book, I had identified about 325 firsts. Wow, have New Yorkers ever been inventive! The stories of these accomplishments fall into nineteen broad categories, presented here alphabetically from Art to Women Who Led the Way. Within each category, the stories appear more or less chronologically, unless logic dictates otherwise; for example, entries in the Religion section group the faiths, so that all Christian entries come together. Reading each section, you'll get a feel for New Yorkers' ingenuity over time in a given field.

Readers who like a more general understanding of an era, across multiple disciplines, will enjoy the appendix called New York City Firsts by Year. This list presents all the firsts mentioned in this book in chronological order.

As great as reading a book may be to understand a city, walking it is even better. I have included four walking tours that, like the chronological appendix, cut across multiple fields. Even if you can't take a walk, read this section. You'll find out more about some of New York's most beloved places. Do you know, for instance, what the Empire State Building was called in its early years and what was previously in its location?

Recognizing that the outer boroughs often play second fiddle to Manhattan, I have included an appendix that lists the unique accomplishments in the other four boroughs and several islands that are part of the city. If you love Queens, check the Beyond Manhattan appendix to see what happened there before it occurred anywhere else.

A final note: I completed this book during the coronavirus pandemic that began in 2020. Because of the devastating effect of the pandemic on the city's economy, some places that I mention as if they're still there, especially in the walking tours, may no longer be in operation or at the same location.

Art

NEW YORK HAS ALWAYS ATTRACTED ARTISTS AND OTHER CREATIVE PEO-
ple. In the first half of the nineteenth century, some of these men (they
almost always were men) came from prominent families, and they did
not have to worry about mundane matters like putting food on the table.
Later, having established itself as a city where artists could thrive, New
York beckoned to creative people of a different sort, the type for whom
the epithet "struggling artist" applies. Whether rich or poor, native born
or transplants from another city or country, artists in New York, especially
those living and working in Greenwich Village, found like minds among
other creative individuals—artists
as well as writers and musicians.
Together, the artists established
new genres, such as the Hudson
River School in the mid-1800s and
abstract expressionism and several
postmodern genres a century later.
Because the artists were working at
the same time, it's sometimes difficult to identify the one individual

Diana, by Augustus Saint-Gaudens, c.
1900, atop Stanford White's Madison
Square Garden. The snake-like object to
her right is the fabric that was supposed
to cover her nudity.

who was first on the scene with these new genres. But it certainly was a New Yorker.

Pioneering work in the New York art scene is not distinguished by unique genres alone. Several individual sculptures were the first of their kind in America. A New Yorker chiseled the first marble statue made in America, and a prominent New York artist sculpted the first female nude made in this country. The city also claims the first statue of a physician in America.

Search the internet for "most artistic cities in America," and New York almost always comes up at or near the top of various ratings. No surprise, then, that New York can claim quite a few firsts in the art field.

HUDSON RIVER SCHOOL

The United States was undergoing a sort of identity crisis in the early nineteenth century. With only a short history, relatively speaking, America turned to Europe for its cultural models and inspiration—until a group of New York–based landscape painters realized that they had awe-inspiring scenery right in their own backyard. Later, their style was dubbed the Hudson River School of Art. It was **the first uniquely American genre of painting**. The artists became a tight-knit professional and social group.

The first Hudson River School artist was Thomas Cole, an English-born painter. Shortly after arriving in New York City in 1825, he headed upstate to the Catskill Mountains, which border the Hudson River. There he sketched the dramatic, untamed mountain scenery. Returning to the city, Cole developed his sketches in oil paint on large canvases. The finished works reflected both the realism of the landscape and the imagination and idealism of the artist.

By the time of Cole's premature death in 1848, he had formed close friendships with other landscape painters, including Asher Durand and Frederic Church. They followed his approach and style, cementing the Hudson River School as an American genre. Like Cole, these artists sketched along the mountainous banks of the Hudson River, then returned to New York City to paint large-scale, emotive works of American scenery. Many Hudson River School artists lived and worked in the

Tenth Street Studio Building in Greenwich Village, the first live-work space for artists in the country (*see* Tenth Street Studio Building in the Residences and Residential Areas section).

Later artists who worked in this style often traveled and depicted scenes far from the Hudson, especially the wild American West. Although territory along the Hudson did not appear in their paintings, the genre kept the name.

HAMILTON STATUE

Imagine taking almost two years to carve a fifteen-foot-tall statue from a nine-ton block of marble. Now imagine seeing that statue crumble into pieces as the building where it was unveiled just eight months earlier collapses to the ground.

That happened to sculptor Robert Ball Hughes. The Great Fire of 1835 destroyed his statue of Alexander Hamilton that graced the rotunda of the New York Merchants Exchange. Praised for its perfection and an immediate favorite of city dwellers, the Hamilton likeness was **the first marble statue made in America**.

The Great Fire of 1835 was the worst fire in New York City history. It destroyed seventeen blocks of the financial and business district of Manhattan, including the last remnants of the Dutch and British colonial periods. The fire spread rapidly because most buildings were made of wood. Water to extinguish the flames turned to ice on this December night. Even the East River was frozen.

When Ball Hughes, as he was generally known, awoke to the sound of fire alarms, he rushed to the Merchants Exchange. He arrived just in time to see his masterpiece crash. A group of incredibly strong men had managed to lift the massive structure off its pedestal and were trying to carry it out to safety when the dome of the building came tumbling down, taking out the statue as it fell.

After this devastating experience, the outdoors seemed a safer place for a replacement statue of Alexander Hamilton. The Founding Father's youngest son hired sculptor Carl Conrads to create a statue for Central Park in 1880. This statue is made of granite—not an easy stone to carve but more durable than marble.

3

A few plaster models of Ball Hughes' *Hamilton* still exist. Two are in New York, at the Museum of the City of New York and at the New-York Historical Society.

DIANA

Late nineteenth-century Americans could be such prudes! They were so shocked by **the first nude female statue made in America** that it had to be draped with fabric. Not that anyone could see the intimate details of *Diana* that clearly, because the statue was high off the ground—more than forty feet higher than the Statue of Liberty's torch.

Diana graced the tower of Madison Square Garden (*see* Walking Tour 3), the second structure by that name and the masterpiece of preeminent architect Stanford White. He engaged his friend and frequent collaborator, the well-known sculptor Augustus Saint-Gaudens, to create the statue. It was meant to be a weathervane, but at 1,800 pounds the 1891 creation was too heavy to rotate in the wind. After just a year, this *Diana* came down, and a lighter version took its place in 1893. The second *Diana* weighed 500 pounds less than its predecessor and stood thirteen instead of eighteen feet tall. Saint-Gaudens' use of thin sheets of hammered copper, as well as the smaller size of the new *Diana*, enabled the sculpture to move as a weathervane should. The fabric drapery moved too—so much that it floated away, leaving behind a nude goddess of the hunt.

During the daytime, the gilded *Diana* shined so brightly that it could be seen for miles. It gleamed at nighttime too, because *Diana* was **the first statue in the world lit by electricity at night**.

Both versions of *Diana* had a life beyond Madison Square Garden. Shortly after being taken down from its perch high above New York City, the first *Diana* went to the top of the agricultural building at the World's Fair in Chicago. The second *Diana* came off Madison Square Garden in 1925, when the building was leveled for a high-rise office tower. After seven years in storage, the statue found a new home in the Philadelphia Museum of Art, where it remains today.

Incidentally, Hiram Powers is sometimes credited as the first American to create a female nude statue. Technically, that is correct. The Vermont-born sculptor created *The Greek Slave* in 1843, when he was living in Italy, his home for most of his adult life. Although Augustus Saint-Gaudens was born in Ireland, he came to America as an infant and lived here most of his life. Without question, his *Diana* was the first female nude statue made in America.

FATHER OF MODERN GYNECOLOGY

How times change! Shortly after the death of J. Marion Sims, MD, his professional colleagues spearheaded a drive for a monument in his honor. Unveiled on October 20, 1894, it was **the first statue of a physician in the United States**. In the early twenty-first century, mounting protests led to the removal of that very statue from its site in Manhattan.

Dubbed "The Father of Modern Gynecology," Sims was hardly a familiar name outside the medical community until recently. In the early 2000s, the statue of Sims, like those of other one-time American heroes with a dark side, such as Christopher Columbus and Thomas Jefferson, became the subject of controversy: should it go or should it stay? The debate reflects a look backward at history through a twenty-first–century lens.

In the 1840s, Sims practiced medicine and surgery in Alabama. He was particularly interested in the medical care of women. In addition to creating several medical instruments, Sims perfected an operation to cure a common and embarrassing wound that is the result of giving birth. He is condemned today for the way he developed the procedure: by experimenting on slaves without anesthesia (which was just then being cautiously introduced in the operating room).

Sims moved to New York City in 1853 and made it his home until his death thirty years later. He founded a women's hospital in New York and lectured and practiced both in this country and in Europe. In 1875 he became president of the American Medical Association. Well respected among his colleagues, it is no surprise that they wanted to honor him after his death.

The statue of Sims, created by Ferdinand von Miller, originally stood in New York City's Bryant Park. In 1934 it moved to the Fifth Avenue perimeter of Central Park, opposite the New York Academy of Medicine. In 2018, amid demands to dismantle statues of one-time heroes who exploited vulnerable groups, the statue moved again to Green-Wood Cemetery in Brooklyn, where Sims is buried.

Abstract Expressionism

While a battle-scarred Europe was recovering from World War II, the center of artistic innovation shifted to New York City. Here, a group of artists pioneered a movement called abstract expressionism. It is often considered the last type of modern art; genres that emerged afterward may be classified as postmodern or contemporary art.

Like the artists of the first uniquely American art movement, the Hudson River School (*see* Hudson River School in this section), the abstract expressionists were a close-knit community whose home base was Greenwich Village. Clyfford Still is usually credited as **the first abstract expressionist.** Other artists whose works in this genre also debuted in the late 1940s and early 1950s included Jackson Pollock, Willem de Kooning, Barnett Newman, Mark Rothko, and Franz Kline.

The question "Yes, but is it art?" may have first been uttered by someone viewing an abstract expressionist work. Abstract expressionists did not try to create recognizable subjects. Rather, they filled large canvases with bold colors and abstract forms that conveyed or inspired emotions. Masters of this color field painting style included Still, Newman, and Rothko. For another group of abstract expressionists, action painters like Pollock, de Kooning, and Kline, the physical act of creating the work was as important as the finished product. Who can forget the 2000 film *Pollock* depicting the artist throwing paint on canvases and watching it drip?

Familiar Subjects, Unusual Media

Trendspotters might have predicted that the reaction to abstract expressionism would be a swing of the pendulum in the opposite direction, to the recognizable rather than the abstract. Two genres that began to dominate the postmodern art scene in the mid-1950s—Neo-Dadaism and pop art—were anything but abstract. Rather, they depicted familiar subjects, but like abstract expressionism, they evoked the question "Is it art?" The artists of this era often used a variety of media. Although these genres had roots in Europe, New York artists firmly established these postmodern art forms.

The first Neo-Dada artists emerged in the mid-1950s. Robert Rauschenberg began to create "combines" that incorporated found objects, print, paint, and sculpture. His friend Jasper Johns is famous for *Flag,* an encaustic and oil painting mounted on a collage of newsprint. The Neo-Dadaists felt that the viewer's interpretation of their work was at least as important as the artist's intent, a distinct departure from the attitudes of artists expressing their feelings in abstract paintings.

It was a short step from Neo-Dadaism to pop art, which drew its inspiration from mass media, consumer goods, and popular culture. **The first pop art exhibitions** were in the early 1960s. The person probably most synonymous with pop art is Andy Warhol, who used silkscreen techniques to create repetitive images of pop culture icons like Marilyn Monroe and everyday objects like Campbell's soup cans. Fellow New Yorker Roy Lichtenstein mimicked the bold, primary colors and characters of comic strips in his paintings.

Earth Art

Several ironies surround the movement variously known as earth art, land art, or earthworks. It's mainly an American movement, but it originated in England. The creations often are site specific, are created and remain on large tracts of land, and change over time as natural elements wear them away. Yet for their creations to be seen by more than a few people, artists have captured the work on film in a single or series of moments and brought it indoors. And the first gallery to exhibit earth art was in a place with little open land, New York City.

The earth art movement began with Richard Long's 1967 creation *A Line Made by Walking.* Long strode back and forth in the British countryside until he wore a track distinct enough to photograph.

Earth art and the use of natural materials like rock, soil, sand, and water have especially appealed to American artists. They usually work at the site of the materials and leave their creations there. Land art is ephemeral, but the artists don't worry that their creations will change and maybe even disappear; that is the purpose of this art form. The creations will not be lost forever, though, thanks to photographs and other documentation.

In 1968, the Dwan Gallery in New York City mounted **the first exhibition of earth art**. The show, called Earth Works, featured samples of material and photographs, maps, and drawings documenting the works of Robert Smithson, Walter De Maria, Michael Heizer, and other land artists.

At least two masterpieces of earth art continue to intrigue New Yorkers and visitors to the city. De Maria created *The New York Earth Room*, a thick spread of soil, in a Soho gallery in 1977. The next year, Alan Sonfist planted a forest on a Greenwich Village street in an earthwork called *Time Landscape*. Rather than erode like most outdoor land art, the forest grows more mature every year.

Buildings and Bridges

THE IMAGES ASSOCIATED WITH SOME CITIES INCLUDE NATURAL FEA-
tures, such as mountains or beaches. Not so with New York. The iconic
images of New York are man-made: buildings and bridges. Think the
Empire State Building, Rockefeller Center, and the Brooklyn Bridge.

Walk around New York City,
and you'll see several distinctive
styles of architecture: brownstone
townhouses, cast-iron façades,
"wedding-cake" or tiered skyscrapers, Art Deco buildings, and glass
curtain-wall high-rises. These
styles may have originated in New
York, although other cities were
experimenting with some of these
materials and genres around the
same time. Often, the style became
popular so quickly that it is almost
impossible to identify with certainty the first building of its kind.
But some firsts are clear enough to
merit entries in this book.

Chrysler Building, c. 1930. An Art Deco
masterpiece, the skyscraper was the first
building in the world taller than 1,000
feet.

9

Not just buildings but also bridges distinguish New York, and for good reason. New York is a city bordered by water, and its five boroughs are also separated by water. Bridges connect the parts into a cohesive whole. This city of innovation introduced some unique features with these river-spanning connections.

This section of the book focuses on architecture. You'll find more about New York buildings throughout this book, especially in the section Residences and Residential Areas. The walking tours toward the end of the book offer opportunities to see some New York buildings up close and to read interesting facts about them, including about buildings that no longer exist.

Cast Iron

In the mid-1800s, a revolutionary construction material became popular: cast iron. Previously, brick or stone masonry supported the weight of a building, and these heavy materials limited both the height of the building and the potential expanse of windows. Now, metal could carry the weight and allow for more window glass, which was important in the days before good artificial lighting. Not only was cast iron strong; it was also relatively inexpensive, attractive, and easily mass-produced to create façades of repeated motifs. Cast iron also was thought to be fireproof, a belief later proven wrong.

Although which cast-iron building came first—various sources list different addresses—all the contenders were the work of the same man. **The first building with a cast-iron façade** was the creation of James Bogardus. The building went up around 1848 (the exact year depends on the source consulted and the specific building). With patents to protect his innovation, Bogardus mass-produced prefabricated, interchangeable, cast-iron parts in his New York City factory. Builders and building owners could select designs from a catalogue, and the parts were then bolted into place.

The cast-iron era lasted only about fifty years. The Soho area of New York was developing at the time, and that remains the cast-iron district of the city. Another good place to see cast-iron construction is on Broadway between Union Square and Madison Square, in the once-fashionable shopping district known as Ladies' Mile. The survival of so many cast-iron buildings for 150 years or more is testament to the durability of the material. With cast-iron an accepted building material, the development of skyscrapers was just around the corner.

AIR RIGHTS

An idea floated more than a century ago has allowed New York to create structures where no buildable land exists and to go higher and higher. The idea didn't come from an architect designing buildings but from an engineer creating a railroad station.

The Grand Central Terminal of today replaced a railroad station in the same location. That depot served steam-powered trains, which had to run on open-air tracks so the steam could escape. Grand Central engineer William Wilgus proposed electrifying the trains, which meant that the tracks could be covered. Think about the shape of covered tracks: long and narrow, like a street. Wilgus suggested making the railroad's air rights—a term that he coined—available for purchase so that buildings could go up on these newly constructed streets. The streets were not on solid ground but were essentially bridges on pylons over the tracks.

The first structure built on air rights was a twelve-story apartment hotel called the Marguery. Opened in 1917, the elegant hotel was designed by Grand Central architects Warren & Wetmore. It filled a full block between 47th and 48th Streets on Park Avenue. Other hotels quickly followed, later to be replaced by office buildings. (*See* Walking Tour 4 for more about this stretch of Park Avenue.)

A few interesting points about this story are worth repeating. First, Park Avenue in Midtown and nearby cross-streets are basically bridges over railroad tracks. Also, those who profited most from the earliest use of air rights already had an inside track (sorry about the pun): the New York Central Railroad and Grand Central's architects and engineer.

A concept that enabled buildings to go up on new "land" later evolved into a way to make mega-skyscrapers. Starting in 1961, New York City zoning laws have allowed developers to purchase unused air rights from shorter neighboring buildings so they can make the new structures taller than would otherwise be allowed.

Art Deco

Miami has sometimes jokingly been called New York's sixth borough or New York City South. Besides sharing residents during different parts of the year or at different phases of their lives, the two cities have a common architectural style. Both Miami and New York boast great Art Deco buildings. New York's romance with Art Deco came earlier, and the buildings rose taller.

The American Radiator Building, erected in 1924 and now the Bryant Park Hotel, is often considered **the first Art Deco building**. The creation of Raymond Hood, one of the masters of the genre, the American Radiator Building has a distinctly gothic look but also incorporates many features of Art Deco: bold colors (in this case, gold contrasting dramatically with black bricks); a verticality to the windows; sleek lines, suggesting modernity; geometric ornamentation; and repetition of decorative elements.

Art Deco became popular during the Midtown building boom of the 1920s and 1930s. It is the style of many of New York's most iconic structures, including the Chrysler Building, the Empire State Building, and Rockefeller Center. The movement was short-lived, fizzling out by World War II. Art Deco buildings can be found in all five boroughs and far beyond New York's borders. As in Miami.

Once you know how to recognize Art Deco, you can estimate the age of a New York City building. If it is in the Art Deco style, it probably was built in the 1920s or 1930s. Now take a walk in Midtown with a friend or two and impress them with your architectural smarts! (*See* Walking Tour 4 for a route that will let you observe famous Midtown Art Deco buildings, including the Bryant Park Hotel, the Empire State Building, and the Chrysler Building.)

Skyscrapers

One would think that New York, a city famous for its tall buildings, would lay claim to the first skyscraper. Not so; that honor goes to Chicago. (A native of Chicago, I can confirm that the Windy City has a magnificent skyline.) However, New York developers aggressively fought the Race for the Tallest and therefore can boast of several height-related firsts for skyscrapers.

The Chrysler Building, completed in 1930, was **the first building in the world taller than 1,000 feet**. Topping out at 1,048 feet, the seventy-seven-story building was the tallest in the world—for a short time. After less than a year, that honor went to the Empire State Building, which at 1,250 feet was not only the tallest but also **the first building in the world with more than 100 stories**.

The Chrysler folks should not have been surprised at losing the "tallest" distinction, because they had recently pulled off a similar coup, snatching the title from the Bank of Manhattan at 40 Wall Street. Chrysler architect William Van Alen and Bank of Manhattan architect Craig Severance were one-time partners turned arch-rivals and fierce competitors in the Race for the Tallest. Severance completed his Wall Street structure in 1929, topping it out at 927 feet, which he thought would make it the winner. He did not know that Van Alen was secretly assembling a spire inside the empty shell of the Chrysler Building.

It's hard to take a picture that shows the entire Empire State or Chrysler buildings because they are so tall. Most photos focus on their distinctive tops. You may not even recognize the buildings on the street level, where they are big and boxy like so many other Midtown structures. A 1916 zoning law (*see* Zoning Regulations in the Government and Law section)—the first in the nation—mandated that buildings cannot keep a boxy profile all the way to the top; setbacks are necessary at designated intervals to let in air and light. The setback rule created a unique style of tiered skyscrapers, called wedding-cake architecture. As a variation on the tiered look, creative architects designed buildings with narrow, memorable tops, leading to the city's spectacular skyline. (*See* Walking Tour 4, which offers views of the tops of the Empire State and Chrysler Buildings.)

BRIDGES

The East River separates Manhattan and Brooklyn, two boroughs of New York City. They are connected by three suspension bridges, each of which was a marvel in engineering.

The oldest of the three is the Brooklyn Bridge, which was the longest suspension bridge in the world when it opened in 1883. The Brooklyn

Bridge took fourteen years to build and cost many lives, including that of the designer, John Roebling. His son Washington then took charge. The younger Roebling had to supervise the construction from his Brooklyn home, with the aid of his wife Emily, after he suffered—as did so many others working on the bridge—from what was then known as caisson disease (also called decompression sickness or "the bends"). Huge caissons sunk into the river were fundamental to construction of the bridge. Workers descended into the caissons and excavated until they hit bedrock. Then the caissons were filled with cement, anchoring the bridge. Deep in the East River, these engineering feats are invisible. What catches the eye are the shiny steel cables coming from the granite towers. The Brooklyn Bridge was **the first suspension bridge in the world with steel cables**.

Sometimes the Brooklyn Bridge is erroneously called the first steel suspension bridge. The granite towers belie that title. **The first all-steel suspension bridge**—cables and towers—was the Williamsburg Bridge, which surpassed the Brooklyn Bridge as the longest suspension bridge when it opened in 1903. The Williamsburg Bridge has huge stiffening trusses to support the rail lines on its deck.

Even before the Williamsburg Bridge opened, work was underway on the Manhattan Bridge. Relying on a novel design concept, it was **the first suspension bridge based on deflection theory**. According to this theory, forces on the cables and deck render suspension bridges stronger than previously thought, so they can be built with less material. Unlike the other two East River crossings, the deck of the Manhattan Bridge does not have massive stiffening trusses; the stiffening system is incorporated into the cables. The Manhattan Bridge, which opened on the last day of 1909, is often considered the forerunner of modern suspension bridges.

Business and Commerce

F<small>ROM ITS EARLIEST DAYS</small>, N<small>EW</small> Y<small>ORK WAS A CITY OF BUSINESS AND COM-</small>merce. While other colonial cities prided themselves on religious tolerance, New York was the destination of settlers who wanted to make money. One early resident became America's first multimillionaire. He

A. T. Stewart's "Marble Palace," the first department store in America. With an expansion in 1870 (seen here), the building filled an entire square block.

and other successful New Yorkers formed the first chamber of commerce, even before America became the United States.

In the mid-1800s, a new concept in retailing debuted here: a department store carrying an array of goods at a fixed price. The subsequent opening of the first central power plant to generate electricity forever changed how people lived and worked.

The business mindset continued well into the twentieth century and beyond. Certain amenities that the modern American cannot live without—the credit card and automated teller machine—made their trial runs in New York. What better way to use that cash or credit than to eat out? Although New York has fewer chain restaurants than many other cities—just ask a tourist looking for familiar fare—several restaurants that began locally have proven so successful that they went on to become international chains. As the working world started to morph from the office setting to the gig economy, New York introduced a new concept: a shared workspace.

People often associate business in New York with Wall Street. As this section demonstrates, the New York business world has always been multifaceted. And highly innovative!

CHAMBER OF COMMERCE

You may not know exactly what a chamber of commerce does, but you have doubtless heard of it and perhaps used its services, for example, by seeking information about a locale you are visiting. A chamber of commerce is an organization of local businesses that jointly promote their community. Thousands of towns, cities, states, and regions in the United States have a chamber of commerce.

The first chamber of commerce in the United States formed in New York City in 1768—when America was still a British colony. It was a reaction to the hated Stamp Act, a tax that Britain had imposed on the colonies three years earlier. (*See* Stamp Act Congress in the Government and Law section.) On April 5, 1768, twenty-four leading New York merchants and business leaders met at Fraunces Tavern at the southern tip of Manhattan. (*See* the site on Walking Tour 1.) The group included John Jacob Astor, J. Pierpont Morgan, Peter Cooper, and former mayor John

Cruger, Jr. Their main goal was to promote New York businesses. You might say they were the first to urge residents to buy American.

After the Revolutionary War, the New York Chamber of Commerce became especially active. Its greatest foresight was the proposal for the Erie Canal. When completed in 1825, the Erie Canal connected New York and other eastern ports with the Midwest states and beyond. The Erie Canal was perhaps the single most important development in solidifying New York City as the business capital of the United States.

DEPARTMENT STORES

In the 1820s, Irish immigrant Alexander Turney Stewart operated a small dry-goods store on Broadway near City Hall. In a way, this store was his laboratory. It gave him an opportunity to observe how people shopped and what might entice them to spend more time and money in a store. A.T. Stewart turned these observations into a new venture in 1846, opening **the first department store in America** across the street, at 280 Broadway.

From the outside, the store was like no other. Marble cladding of the Italianate palazzo earned it the nickname the Marble Palace. Large plate glass windows teased shoppers with glimpses of the merchandise inside and filled the store with natural light.

Shopping at the Marble Palace was a unique experience. Every item had a fixed, clearly marked price—no haggling with the proprietor! If the shopper thought the price was too high, she could wait for a sale (nearly all shoppers were women, often ladies of the leisure class). Much of the clothing was ready-to-wear, another novelty in that day, and ladies could try on the garment and admire themselves in a full-length mirror on the second floor. Even the ability of shoppers to go off the main floor was unusual at the time.

The shopping and browsing public loved these innovations. They flocked to A.T. Stewart's store. Other retailers took notice and copied his architectural and merchandising styles. The Marble Palace set the standard for what a department store would look like, inside and out.

A.T. Stewart made a fortune, which explains why grave robbers dug him up in 1878, two years after his death, and demanded $250,000 for the return of his body. Family and friends refused to pay the hefty sum. Eventually, his widow offered $20,000, which the body-snatchers accepted—probably thinking that something was better than nothing. In the dark of night, a sack of money was swapped for a sack of bones; they were never proven to be Stewart's.

The building once known as the Marble Palace still stands, just north of City Hall in Lower Manhattan. Long after Stewart moved his store to a more fashionable neighborhood uptown, a morning newspaper called the *Sun* (*see* Penny Press in the Media section) moved into the space; its clock still hangs on the corner of the building. City offices are among the current occupants. The building's landmark status assures that it will have a long life.

Another New York department store, Macy's, also was an innovator. The original Macy's, on Sixth Avenue just south of 14th Street, hired **the first department store Santa** in 1862 (*see* Christmas in the Religion section). Promotion of a Macy's employee, Margaret Getchell, in 1866 made her **the first woman in an executive position in retail** (*see* Retail Executives in the Women Who Led the Way section). When Macy's moved to its flagship location in Herald Square in 1902 (*see* it on Walking Tour 3), it was **the first building in the world with modern wooden escalators** (*see* Elevators and Escalators in the Inventions section). A few wooden escalators still carry Macy's shoppers to higher floors, although the mechanics have been upgraded over time.

BRINGING ELECTRICITY TO BUSINESSES AND HOMES

Much of the work of one of the geniuses in electricity, Thomas Edison, was done in his Menlo Park, New Jersey, laboratory. So why does this Jersey boy merit mention in a book about innovations that occurred in New York City?

Let's start with Edison's invention of the incandescent light bulb in 1879. He developed, improved, and demonstrated it in Menlo Park. Seeing this marvel in a demonstration, J. P. Morgan, one of Edison's biggest financial supporters, decided to illuminate his New York City home with the new-fangled lights. Edison installed incandescent bulbs throughout Morgan's home and put a steam engine and dynamo in the yard to power them. In 1881, Morgan's home became **the first electrified residence in the world**.

With this and other small-scale, single-customer experiments proving successful, Edison was ready for a broader rollout. His goal was to create a complete power system that would generate electricity for multiple homes and businesses. Because he was using direct current, the geographic reach of the system was rather limited. To maximize his customer base, Edison chose an area of New York City bordered on the south by Wall Street that was packed with businesses and residences. The inventor and his crew built a steam-powered station in two adjacent buildings, at 255 and 257 Pearl Streets. When it opened for business on September 4, 1882, the Pearl Street Station was **the first central power plant in the world**. (*See* the site on Walking Tour 1.)

One of the eighty-five original customers was the *New York Times*. Amazingly, the life-changing significance of the electric power station escaped the newspaper editors. The paper did report on the opening of the power plant, but the story was buried on an inside page under miscellaneous city news.

Those in the service area who saw how much better lit the world was with electricity quickly connected to the power grid. In about a year, the Pearl Street Station boasted more than 500 customers. Edison's company soon built electric power systems in other areas of the country.

On January 2, 1890, a fire severely damaged the Pearl Street Station. It was rebuilt but served only a few more years. By then, the advantages of alternating current, associated with other great names in electricity like Tesla and Westinghouse, had become clear.

MILLIONAIRES

Fur was so important to the early economy of New York City that a fur-bearing animal, the beaver, is on the official seal of the city. **The first multimillionaire in the United States**, John Jacob Astor, made his initial fortune in the fur trade. Astor soon discovered what other wealthy New Yorkers, to this day, know about the city: the real money is in real estate. Purchasing and then selling property in the rapidly growing city, Astor parlayed a small fortune into a sizable one. When he died in 1848 at the age of eighty-five, John Jacob Astor was the wealthiest man in the country, with a fortune estimated to be about $20 million.

Astor's assets are peanuts compared with those of John D. Rockefeller, Sr., who was **the country's first billionaire**. The Rockefeller fortune came mostly from oil, as in the Standard Oil Company. Early on, the businessman lived in Cleveland to be near his refineries, but he soon set up an office in New York City. He bought a home here on 54th Street just off Fifth Avenue in 1884, and it remained his residence until his wife died in 1915. The next year, his assets topped the billion-dollar mark. Despite giving away huge amounts to various educational institutions, medical initiatives, and his namesake foundation, John D. Rockefeller, Sr., had assets estimated to match one and a half percent of the nation's total economic output when he died in 1937 at age ninety-eight.

In the early twentieth century, business was still the province of white men. Yet a Black woman known as Madam C. J. Walker was extraordinarily successful promoting hair care products to people like herself. Her work made her itinerant; she traveled around the country and to Latin America, giving lectures and demonstrations. Her company's headquarters were in Indianapolis, but she made her home in Harlem and managed her business from there starting in 1916. She died in 1919 at just fifty-one years of age. We'll stretch the facts a bit and call Madam C. J. Walker, **the first Black female millionaire in America,** a New Yorker.

Credit Cards

Do you remember scenes from old movies when a customer would shop at a local store and tell the owner, "Put it on my tab"? Those tabs evolved into credit cards issued by a merchant, such as a department store or gas station, that were good only at the company's outlets. Then a Brooklyn banker decided to take it one step further by creating a credit card that could be used at many different types of businesses within an area.

John C. Biggins, who worked for Flatbush National Bank, created the Charg-It card in 1946. This was **the first universal bank-issued credit card.** Well, universal is perhaps an overstatement. Only businesses and shoppers in the vicinity of the Brooklyn bank could participate in the program. The stores would deliver their sales slips to the bank, which in turn would deduct money from the shoppers' accounts. It was a small-scale proof-of-concept experiment, and it was so successful that today a wallet without a credit card or two is almost worthless.

A variation on the theme came a few years later, when Frank McNamara, head of the Hamilton Credit Corporation, was dining in a New York City restaurant with a couple of associates. At the end of the meal, McNamara reached for his wallet and came up empty. Vowing never to face such an embarrassment again, he had an idea for a credit card that could be used at multiple locations. This "First Supper," as it is sometimes known, led to the creation of the Diners Club card in 1950. Although considered **the first multipurpose credit card**, most businesses accepting it initially were restaurants; hence the name Diners Club. It was a humble cardboard card, but was it ever popular! Many of the early cardholders were salesmen who often entertained clients and prospects and didn't want to fumble for cash.

The story that McNamara being short of cash led to creation of the Diners Club card may be just that—a story. In 2016, sixty-six years after the card first appeared, *The Saturday Evening Post* published an article by Matty Simmons, a public relations pro, business associate of Frank McNamara, and holder of the third Diners Club card issued. Simmons claimed that he made up the story of the First Supper. McNamara, he said, actually thought up the charge card concept while on a commuter train. Believe what you will. Either way, the Diners Club card was a New York innovation.

AUTOMATED TELLER MACHINE (ATM)

Chances are you wouldn't have wanted to use **the first ATMs** when First National City Bank of New York (now Citibank) installed them in a few bank lobbies in 1960. The inventor himself, Luther George Simjian, reluctantly admitted that the main users of the ATMs turned out to be gamblers and prostitutes, who preferred the anonymity of a machine to face-to-face encounters with live bank tellers. Perhaps it was the presence of the unsavory characters that kept other customers away. At any rate, the bank jettisoned the devices after only six months.

Simjian, a prolific inventor, had been tinkering with automated banking technology for about twenty years. He hoped to create a hole-in-the-wall device that would enable customers to do their business at any hour of the day or night without entering the bank itself. He called his first completed machine—the one Citibank introduced—the Bankograph. It took deposits in the form of cash or checks but did not dispense money.

Meanwhile, other banks around the world were toying with similar devices. In all probability, the first machine to dispense cash, an invention of John Shepherd-Barron, was installed in a Barclays Bank in England in 1967. However, Japan and Sweden also developed cash dispensers around the same time. In the United States, the first cash-giving ATMs appeared in 1969 in a Long Island branch of New York's Chemical Bank.

COWORKING SPACE FOR WRITERS

Writing can be a lonely profession. In New York City, where apartments are cramped, often bombarded with noise from neighbors and street traffic, and sometimes cast in shadows by surrounding buildings, writing from home can be especially challenging. The Writers Room helps meet the needs of New York authors for space to work and a sense of community. Founded in 1978, The Writers Room was **the first shared writing workspace in the country**. It's moved around but has always called New York City home. (*See* Walking Tour 2 for its present location.)

The Manhattan outpost for writers differs from other coworking spaces, which encourage interaction among work-at-home professionals in multiple fields. Everyone here is a writer. The Writers Room has a strict no-talking, no-phone, no-noise policy in the communal work area. But writers can schmooz in the kitchen and take workshops together. Should a writer's inspiration fizzle, the napping area might provide just the right boost. In a city that never sleeps, The Writers Room is open 24/7.

Apparently, this formula works. The Writers Room boasts that members have written more than 1,000 books since the facility opened. The model has been copied in other cities in America and elsewhere.

By the way, The Writers Room predates the coworking space trend by decades. That term didn't even exist until 2005, when a coworking space opened in San Francisco.

CHAIN RESTAURANTS THAT STARTED IN NEW YORK CITY

New York City is not particularly friendly to chain restaurants. Real estate is expensive, and the square footage of a typical New York eatery may be too small for a standard corporate layout. City laws, such as the posting of calorie and sodium content, add burdens and may force a restaurant to depart from practices of the parent company. Many New Yorkers would rather support mom-and-pop operations than eat in the outlet of a corporate giant, adding to the challenge.

Although New Yorkers may shun imported chains, a number of restaurants that began here became so popular that they evolved into local mini-chains and then expanded to national and international locations. The business model varies. Some of the expansions are owned by the parent company, whereas others are franchises.

Often, chains that began in New York are textbook examples of immigrants living the American dream. Consider the mall favorite Sbarro. In 1956, not long after they moved here from Naples, Gennaro and Carmela Sbarro opened an Italian grocery in Bensonhurst, Brooklyn. Neighborhood workers often stopped in to grab a quick bite, and Mama Carmela's pizza was a big hit. Soon the family opened another Brooklyn location just for pizza, **the first Sbarro**, and then other restaurants under the same name. Sbarro took space in the city's first large shopping mall, in Brooklyn, in 1970 and kept expanding far outside the city's borders.

Another immigrant success story is Benihana. A young man from Tokyo, Hiroaki "Rocky" Aoki, moved to New York and opened a restaurant in 1964 in Midtown Manhattan. An Olympic-qualifying wrestler, Aoki knew little about the restaurant business, except that he wanted to have teppanyaki tables, where cooks prepare the food in front of guests. He named his establishment after his parents' coffee shop back in Japan. This was **the first Benihana** (*see* it on Walking Tour 4). After the restaurant proved successful, Aoki opened another Benihana in New York and then one in Chicago. Today Benihana has more than seventy locations in the western hemisphere.

Around the same time that Aoki was introducing New Yorkers to Japanese food prepared with fanfare, Alan Stillman was wondering how to meet girls. He decided to start a bar that would appeal to women and chose his own neighborhood, the Upper East Side of Manhattan, as the location. This was **the first singles bar** (*see* Singles Bar in the Food and Drink section) and **the first TGI Fridays**, which began operations in 1965. Five years later, Fridays started to expand outside the city. The chain now has more than four hundred locations in the United States and even more in other countries.

Why would a celebrity chef want to have a hot dog cart? To support a park. The chef was Danny Meyer, and the park was Madison Square in the Flatiron District of Manhattan. The seasonal hot dog cart drew huge crowds to the park, and soon Meyer built a permanent food kiosk in the same location; this was **the first Shake Shack** (*see* it on Walking Tour 3). Opened in 2004, Shake Shack became known not just for hot dogs but especially for hamburgers and, of course, milkshakes. Six years later, Shake Shack started popping up all over Manhattan, and it went beyond the city in 2011 with a Miami venue. The upscale burger joint is now global.

Looking for healthy alternatives, Nick Kenner opened **the first Just Salad** in 2006 in Manhattan (*see* it on Walking Tour 4). With many locations in the New York area, the salad server has moved into other markets in the United States and overseas. The company emphasizes not just its healthy food choices but also its commitment to sustainability—focuses that likely will keep it growing.

Bareburger is another company that emphasizes sustainability. **The first Bareburger** opened in Astoria, Queens, in 2009. A year later, another Bareburger appeared in Manhattan. Like all the restaurants mentioned here that began in New York, Bareburger now has outlets in cities throughout the country and in locations worldwide.

See, it's not true that New Yorkers shy away from chain restaurants. They like chains that are New York originals. As do food lovers elsewhere.

Food and Drink

SOMETIMES IT'S SURPRISINGLY DIFFICULT TO VERIFY THE CREATOR OF A dish. Two or more individuals or restaurants may make recipes with similar ingredients or names, and then both claim to be the original, authentic version. Recipes often are trusted to memory. When they are written down, many years may have passed since their creation, and details may have been forgotten or embellished in the meantime. The origin story may cross into the realm of urban legend or local folklore.

Delmonico's, 1898. The epitome of fine dining, Delmonico's is considered the first restaurant in America. It may be where eggs Benedict was created.

Most of the entries in this section have a fairly certain New York start. Some tales of questionable origin, though, such as the invention of the Reuben sandwich, were just too good to omit. I did skip a few New York staples for lack of detailed information. For example, we know that East European Jews who settled in New York in the late nineteenth century made and sold two favorites from their homeland: bagels and kosher dill pickles. But we don't know the specific who, when, and where of their introduction to America, so neither bagels nor kosher dills have an entry in this book.

Besides introducing some foods and beverages, New York also premiered certain types of eating and drinking venues. This section tells the stories not just of what people ate and drank in New York before the item spread to other cities but also new places where they enjoyed refreshments.

Hot Dog

Some people say that the hot dog isn't an American creation, merely an adaptation of German sausage. That's like saying that knockwurst, liverwurst, and Jimmy Dean breakfast sausage are all the same.

When an individual is credited as inventor of the hot dog, the honor goes to a German immigrant named Charles Feltman. In 1871 he opened **the first hot dog stand** in Brooklyn's Coney Island, calling his food Coney Island red hots. Wanting to avoid plates and silverware, Feltman put the meat on a bun, establishing the way Americans should eat their version of sausage. At ten cents a pop, Feltman sold thousands of red hots in the first year. His business was so successful that he was able to expand into a huge food and entertainment empire over subsequent decades. With nine restaurants, a roller coaster, and a carousel, among other attractions, Feltman was a principal player in the movement that made Coney Island synonymous with amusement park.

In 1916, one of Feltman's employees, Nathan Handwerker, opened his own hot dog stand a few blocks away, pricing his dog-in-a-bun at just five cents. This was the start of Nathan's, the name usually associated today with Coney Island franks and the sponsor of an annual hot-dog–eating contest every Fourth of July weekend.

By the late nineteenth century, America's favorite food was standard fare at America's favorite pastime. In 1901, sports cartoonist Tad Dorgan was at a baseball game at the Polo Grounds in Upper Manhattan, where the New York Giants baseball team played. Hearing vendors hawk red hots, which many people called dachshund sausages, Dorgan supposedly drew a cartoon of a dachshund in a roll. Uncertain how to spell the breed name, he captioned his cartoon "hot dog." Some claim that this was the origin of the name. The cartoon has never been found, however, calling the story into question. Furthermore, according to the National Hot Dog and Sausage Council (there actually is such an organization), the term "hot dog" was already in use about a decade before the nonexistent cartoon.

The same source states that Germans had always eaten sausages with bread, so putting a hot dog in a bun was nothing new. Do you suppose that New York's claims to selling the first hot dog, putting it in a bun, and naming the food just might be exaggerations?

English Muffin

English muffins don't hail from England. They originated in a bakery in Manhattan in the late nineteenth century.

Samuel Bath Thomas immigrated to New York from England in 1874. Six years later he opened a bakery, where he produced **the first English muffins**. Thomas didn't call the yeasty concoction that initially; he called them toaster crumpets. By cooking them on both sides on a griddle before baking them in an oven, Thomas made his muffins crisp on the outside and soft on the inside. They could be toasted just before eating so they would be nice and hot.

The English muffins were so popular that Thomas soon opened a second bakery, at 337 West 20th Street. Once a foundry, the building already had large brick ovens. In the ever-repurposing saga of Manhattan real estate, the building is now a small co-op apartment house. In 2006, the owner of one of the co-ops discovered the original ovens under the rear courtyard, earning the edifice a nickname: The Muffin House.

In this country, Thomas' English muffins remain the big seller in the category. Incidentally, English muffins are not very common in England.

There, what we think of as an English muffin is called an American muffin, a more accurate description of the place of origin of this breakfast bread.

Eggs Benedict

Two restaurants claim to have created eggs Benedict. Whichever claim is correct, **the first eggs Benedict** was served in New York City.

According to one story, sometime in the 1860s Mr. and Mrs. LeGrand Benedict were having a meal at one of their favorite New York restaurants, Delmonico's (*see* First Restaurant in this section). In those days, patrons could ask the chef, Charles Ranhofer, to prepare a dish of their liking. Mrs. Benedict asked him to make something with a toasted muffin, ham, and poached eggs covered with Hollandaise sauce. Voila! Eggs ala Benedick, as Ranhofer called the dish in his 1894 cookbook *The Epicurean*.

The same year that Ranhofer's cookbook was published, a man with a hangover, Lemuel Benedict (no relation to Delmonico's Benedicts), stopped by the Waldorf Hotel for breakfast. He ordered buttered toast, crisp bacon, two poached eggs, and Hollandaise sauce. That is not exactly eggs Benedict, but the Waldorf's famed maitre d', Oscar Tschirky (who previously worked at Delmonico's), made the necessary substitutions when he put the dish on the Waldorf's menu.

By the way, both of these establishments are famous for dishes that bear their name. Delmonico steak has always been a favorite at that restaurant. For the Waldorf, Tschirky created the namesake salad, which originally had only three ingredients: apples, celery, and mayonnaise. Walnuts were a later addition to this classic salad. (*See* the site of the original Waldorf, where Tschirky worked, on Walking Tour 3 and the present Waldorf on Walking Tour 4.)

"Chinese" Food

Two standards on Chinese restaurant menus in America did not originate in China. They started in New York. Probably.

As is true for so many foods, the exact origin of chop suey is vague. New York City often is seen as the place where **the first chop suey** was eaten and where the dish became popular.

But first comes the San Francisco tale. In that urban legend, set in 1849, a group of intoxicated miners went into a Chinese restaurant near closing time. Anxious to go home and assuming the men were too drunk to care what they ate, the proprietor threw together whatever he could find and called it chop suey.

Another story that receives as much credence took place almost fifty years later. In 1896, a Chinese diplomat was visiting New York and wanted to entertain some Americans. Concerned that they would not find authentic Chinese fare palatable, he instructed his chef to prepare something that resembled Chinese food but that would appeal to Americans. The result: chop suey.

By the early 1900s, restaurants in the Chinatown areas of major cities, particularly along Mott Street in New York, began to attract customers who were not Asian. They loved the steaming servings of tasty, inexpensive fare called chop suey. Whether or not it was invented here—we'd like to assume it was—chop suey was a hit in New York.

General Tso's chicken is such a standard dish among lovers of Chinese food that you may be surprised to learn it is a mid-twentieth century invention. You'll also hear echoes of the chop suey stories in the origin of General Tso's chicken.

In 1952, when a U.S. naval official was visiting Taiwan, chef Peng Chang-kuei prepared traditional Hunan food for him. One time the chef improvised, creating a dish so tasty that the visiting admiral asked what it was called. Peng responded with the first thing that came to mind: General Tso's chicken.

Fast-forward two decades. The latest culinary craze in America was spicy Hunan food. The very same chef Peng was now living in New York City. He opened a restaurant—called Peng's, of course—in Midtown Manhattan in 1973. One of his signature dishes was the one he had created years earlier: **the first General Tso's chicken served in America**.

Pizza

I've often heard that pizza is not an Italian dish, that it was invented in America. That simply is not true. Europeans and Middle Easterners ate versions of pizza, or flatbread with toppings, long before the first intrepid seamen crossed the Atlantic. The ancient Romans, Greeks, Egyptians, or others in that part of the world probably were the first to consume pizza.

By the sixteenth century, pizza became especially popular among the working class residents of Naples. Toppings often were similar to those we associate with classic pizza, including tomatoes, herbs, and cheese.

In 1905, an Italian immigrant, Gennaro Lombardi, opened **the first pizzeria in the United States**. It was on Spring Street in a section of New York City with a large and growing Italian population. Lombardi previously had a grocery store nearby, where he sold tomato and cheese pies that workers could pick up for lunch and eat on the job, without need for utensils—the way New Yorkers eat pizza today. Lombardi's pizzeria was an instant hit among *paisanos*.

After a while, other customers were attracted to the tasty, inexpensive, and convenient concoction. By mid- to late-twentieth century, pizza had taken the city by storm, with one pizzeria after another coming on the scene and developing a loyal following.

Lombardi's stayed in the family until 1984, when it ceased operations. But no pizza quite compared for those who favored this version. After a brief absence, Lombardi's resurfaced a block away. Today, at least ten pizzerias claim to be the best in the city, among them the granddaddy of them all, Lombardi's.

OTHER ITALIAN FARE

Many foods that we think of as Italian did not originate there. When Italians came to this country, they adapted their familiar style of cooking to locally available ingredients. These culinary experiments generally took place in the home, without much fanfare, so the creators of such "Italian" dishes as spaghetti and meatballs or chicken parmigiana cannot be ascertained. Only when Italian-American restaurateurs publicized their creations could the honor of "first" be stated with certainty.

Pasta primavera, which sounds Italian, actually debuted fairly recently in an upscale French restaurant in New York City. Le Cirque served **the first pasta primavera** in 1977. One story is that the restaurant owner, Sirio Maccioni, just tossed together a bunch of ingredients; another is that his wife created it. Yet another version is that Le Cirque chef Jean

Vergnes either came up with the idea himself or adapted a recipe of artist Ed Giobbi. Regardless of who created it, pasta primavera is about as American as it gets, and it owes its popularity to a famous French—not Italian—New York restaurant.

Cappuccino, on the other hand, is a true Italian import. When Domenico Parisi opened Caffe Reggio in Greenwich Village in 1927, he installed an espresso machine from Italy. The big, shiny contraption was essential to make cappuccino, a combination of espresso, steamed milk, and foam topped with cinnamon. Caffe Reggio served **the first cappuccino in America**. The famed coffee house, home-away-from-home for generations of writers, bohemians, Village residents, coffee lovers, and nostalgia worshippers, remains at its original location. The same espresso machine still occupies a prominent place in the tiny bistro. (*See* Walking Tour 2 for an opportunity to stop by Caffe Reggio.)

REUBEN SANDWICH

Many years ago when I was having lunch someplace other than the New York area, a waiter announced that the special sandwich of the day was a Ruby. I asked what was in it. He described it: a grilled sandwich with corned beef, Swiss cheese, sauerkraut, and Thousand Island dressing on rye. "A Reuben!" I exclaimed. The waiter's misnomer is nothing compared with the confusing origin stories about the Reuben sandwich.

It would make sense that this deli fare came from a New York delicatessen. Indeed, Reuben's Restaurant, operated by Arnold Reuben, has been credited with making **the first Reuben sandwich** in 1914. At one time, that was the origin listed in the Random House College Dictionary. The story goes that an actress, a regular at Reuben's, came in one night and asked for a big sandwich combining a lot of ingredients. The chef piled ham, turkey, Swiss cheese, cole slaw, and dressing on rye. The actress loved it and asked Reuben to name the sandwich after her, but he called it Reuben's Special instead.

The wrong meat gives credence to the possibility that an Omaha man named Reuben Kulakofsky invented the sandwich for his poker buddies playing at a local hotel in 1925. Well, he didn't exactly; he asked a chef at the hotel to come up with a sandwich for the night. It used the ingredients that we have come to associate with a Reuben. It was a big hit that night, and soon the Reuben, named for the poker player, became a standard on the hotel menu. In 1956, a waitress there entered the Reuben in a national sandwich competition, and it won.

Oddly, the obituaries of neither Arnold Reuben nor Reuben Kulakofsky mentioned that he had created or was in any way associated with the sandwich. None of the advocates for the two Reubens was eyewitness at the birth of the sandwich, and no menu or other documentation of a Reuben sandwich appears anywhere until 1937—from a hotel in Lincoln, Nebraska.

Given these conflicting and equally plausible (or not) stories, it's hard to say for certain that the Reuben sandwich is a New York original. I think it is. Somehow, a classic deli sandwich just had to come from New York, not Omaha.

Ice Cream

Then as now, ice cream was a popular treat in the late nineteenth and early twentieth centuries. Leave it to enterprising New Yorkers to come up with novel ways to enjoy the frozen treat.

Pushcart vendors sold ice cream on the street in small glass containers. After licking the cup clean, customers returned it to the vendor, who rinsed it out for the next buyer. Yuck! Not the most sanitary practice. Plus, the cups could break, and customers sometimes walked off with them, raising the overhead of a business operating for a mere penny a serving (hence the nickname "penny lick").

Italo Marchiony, who sold ices and ice cream from a cart on Wall Street, set out to solve this problem. He created an edible container by folding a thin waffle, hot off the iron, into a cone shape. It hardened as it cooled, making a perfect holder for ice cream. Wall Street workers bought **the first ice cream cones** in 1896. They were such a hit that Marchiony had to come up with a quicker way to make the cones. In 1903, he patented a device that could produce ten cones at once.

The next year, St. Louis hosted a World's Fair to celebrate the centennial of the Louisiana Purchase. A popular concessionaire at the fair sold ice cream, and the vendor beside him sold a crisp Syrian wafer called zalabia. Italo Marchiony was the ice cream man, according to his daughter; other accounts don't name the vendor. Regardless of who was selling ice cream, when he ran out of containers, he teamed up with the neighboring concessionaire, who rolled his wafer cookie into a cone. The ice cream cone thus went from the streets of New York to the national and international stage.

Let's go back to New York at the very end of the nineteenth century. In 1899, a pushcart vendor in the Bowery (apparently not Marchiony, whose beat was farther south on Wall Street) came up with another way to sell ice cream in an edible container. He put a thin slab of the frozen treat between two wafers, creating **the first ice cream sandwich**. A contemporary newspaper account reported that business was so brisk that the vendor had no time to make change and insisted on receiving the actual price of the product, one cent.

Twenty years later, the Kohr brothers discovered that ice cream was smoother and melted slower when they added egg yolk. This, it turns out, is the recipe for frozen custard. The Kohrs introduced **the first frozen custard** in 1919 on the Coney Island boardwalk. On the first weekend, the Kohrs sold more than 18,000 cones for a nickel each—the same as the price of nearby Nathan's hot dogs. (*See* Hot Dog in this section.)

The quality of ice cream goes up as the fat content increases and the amount of air churned into it decreases. In 1960, Reuben and Rose Mattus created an ice cream in their Bronx plant with a higher fat content and less air than had ever been used before. This was **the first superpremium ice cream** (that's a recognized category in the ice cream industry). The couple called it Häagen-Dazs. It was richer than other ice creams available at the time, both in taste and cost—a whopping seventy-five cents a pint.

Has reading this made you hungry for ice cream? Go enjoy some, and thank enterprising New Yorkers for their contributions.

AMERICA'S FAVORITE COOKIE

Whether you twist it apart, dunk it in milk, or simply bite into the cookie sandwich, chances are you have enjoyed Oreos. So many people do that the Oreo has been dubbed "America's favorite cookie."

The National Biscuit Company produced **the first Oreos** in its Manhattan bakery in the spring of 1912. The Oreo was one of three new cookies that the company, now known as Nabisco, introduced simultaneously, describing them as a trio of high-class biscuits. The other two cookies—Mother Goose and Veronese—went the way of the buttonhook. But the Oreo has had real staying power.

Few people know that the Oreo was a knock-off, not the original cookie with a cream filling between two chocolate wafers. Sunshine Biscuits began producing and selling the nearly identical Hydrox cookie a few years earlier. But it never challenged the Oreo as America's favorite.

Nothing can last more than a century without a few tweaks. The diameter of the Oreo has changed slightly, as has the design on the wafer. Packaging and price also have changed. The name of the cookie has had a few different words after Oreo over the years, including biscuit, sandwich, and creme sandwich. New flavors and fillings have resulted in variations of the basic Oreo. Nabisco has twice replaced the fat in the filling, first swapping out lard for partially hydrogenated vegetable oil and then replacing that with healthier non-hydrogenated oil. None of these changes affected consumers' hunger for Oreos. Americans alone gobble up a good 12 billion Oreos a year. The brand is also made and sold overseas.

Nabisco moved out of its Manhattan plant in 1958. The building still stands on Ninth Avenue between 15th and 16th Streets. The cavernous former bakery has become home to Chelsea Market, a food mall and tourist destination. At this location, the streets are marked not with the typical white-on-green street signs but with white-on-black signs in honor of the Oreo. And the official name of 15th Street between Ninth and Tenth Avenues is Oreo Way.

Donuts and Cronuts

The humble donut and its recent offspring, the cronut, owe their popularity to a succession of foreigners who made their home in New York City. The original settlers here, the Dutch, introduced the fat-fried lump of dough to the New World. But donuts weren't a big seller until 1920, when Adolph Levitt, a Russian émigré with a New York City bakery, invented **the first donut machine.**

Levitt created more than a fast way to make donuts; he created a spectacle. Patrons came not just to buy donuts but to watch their production. As a 1931 edition of *The New Yorker* dramatically observed, the donuts "float around in a glass-enclosed machine, walk dreamily up a moving ramp, and then tumble down into a basket." Forget about donuts dreaming! Before long it was Levitt who was dreaming, that is, living the American dream. He raked in $25 million from the sale of donut machines.

Almost a century after the invention of the donut machine, Dominique Ansel Bakery in the Soho neighborhood of Manhattan captured the city's sweet tooth when it sold **the first cronut** in 2013. A cronut is a cream-filled, fried pastry, a sort of cross between a croissant and a donut. Whereas Levitt's goal was to make more donuts, Parisian émigré Dominique Ansel took the opposite approach; he limited the supply of his new creation. A line formed for hot cronuts every morning before the bakery opened, and the day's offering sold out in a couple of hours despite the limit of two to a customer. Chef Ansel knew how to keep customers coming back: he produced a different flavor every month. Almost immediately, the cronut was mimicked around the world.

One of the strangest episodes in cronut history occurred on July 22, 2016. A typical crowd had lined up in front of Dominique Ansel Bakery to get their morning treats. Many did not seem to notice the dead man on a nearby bench. Or maybe they saw him but were afraid they'd lose their chance to buy cronuts if the police came. No worries. The police, understanding the priorities of the cronut-crazed, rerouted the line while they dealt with the deceased, a neighborhood resident.

SWEETENERS IN PACKETS

On the tables of many restaurants, you're likely to find containers of colored packets with sugar and artificial sweeteners. That's a late twentieth-century phenomenon, but you probably knew that, certainly about artificial sweeteners. Did you know that the packets themselves, as well as the first sugar substitute in a packet, were the brainchild of a Brooklyn manufacturer?

That New Yorker was Benjamin Eisenstadt, whose Cumberland Packing Corporation opened shortly after the end of World War II. The company's main product was tea bags. One day when Eisenstadt and his wife were eating in a restaurant, she complained about the unsanitary sugar bowl on the table. That simple comment was an inspiration. Why not use his tea-bagging plant, thought Eisenstadt, to put sugar into packets? Thus **the first sweetener in a packet** was created.

About a decade later, artificially sweetened products were becoming popular. By this time, Benjamin Eisenstadt's son Marvin had joined Cumberland Packing. Father and son put their heads together and came up with an idea to put a zero-calorie sweetener in a single-serving container like the sugar packet. They made the new packet pink and called it Sweet'N Low, **the first artificial sweetener in a packet**. For the first six years, only restaurants could buy the product. Sweet'N Low hit the grocery shelves in 1963. And the rest, as they say, is history.

BREWERIES

Beer making and drinking are fine old American traditions—so old, in fact, that they predate the founding of the United States. Beer was a staple in Colonial America and as far back as pre-colonial days, when native inhabitants of the New World made beer from corn. Barrels and barrels of beer crossed the Atlantic in the holds of ships carrying European explorers west. But the supply couldn't last forever, and as early as 1587 English colonists in Virginia brewed beer for their personal consumption. **The first brewery in the New World** appeared in 1612 in an accidental settlement in present-day New York City.

Two Dutch traders, Adrian Block and Hans Christiansen, crossed the Atlantic between 1611 and 1614—they made several trips, but the exact dates are a bit iffy—to trade with the inhabitants of the area that Henry Hudson had explored a few years earlier. Block and Christiansen came on separate ships, each with a small crew. They hadn't intended to stay for long, but when Block's ship burned, they set up temporary quarters for the winter at the southern end of Manhattan. One thing they established wasn't so temporary. The Block & Christiansen Brewery started fueling the seamen in 1612 and kept them in beer for the next twenty years.

This next story is where the dates get really iffy. Supposedly, in 1614 the tavern was the birthplace of **the first male of European descent born** in America. As unlikely as it might seem today, it is plausible that the brewery, a relatively sturdy structure in a primitive landscape, could be where a woman would give birth. The child's name was Jean (sometimes spelled Jan) Vigne, and his parents were early settlers from Europe. The story is full of holes, however. The Vignes crossed the ocean in 1624, and reputable sources list the infant's birth year as 1624 or 1625. What is known for certain is that when Jean Vigne grew up, he went back and forth between the New Amsterdam colony (that is, New York City) and Holland several times before settling on this side of the Atlantic. He was a farmer, and around 1670 he became **the first American-born brewer**. How ironic that the boy born in a brewery wound up operating one!

Apparently, the brewery where Jean Vigne took his first breath was more of a community gathering spot than a money-making venture. The West India Company, sponsors of the Dutch colony, built **the first commercial brewery in America** in 1632. That was the same year that the Block & Christiansen Brewery folded.

Before long, the Dutch settlers had their choice of watering holes. By 1660, New Amsterdam had twenty-six breweries and taverns. Beer-making had become one of the young settlement's most successful industries.

COCKTAIL RECIPE BOOK

One of the most colorful New Yorkers in the second half of the nineteenth century was a bartender named Jerry Thomas. Standing behind his bar—he owned several New York City drinking establishments between 1851 and his death in 1885—he would awe customers as he juggled liquor bottles and poured flaming cocktails from one mixing container to another. Thomas often took his show on the road, tending bar in cities across the country and in Europe. Along the way, his knowledge of cocktails grew so extensive that he became known as "The Professor."

Wanting to share his knowledge with other barkeeps, Thomas wrote a book on how to mix drinks. When the *Bartenders Guide* was published in 1862, it was **the first cocktail recipe book** ever written. "The father of American mixology," as Thomas is sometimes called, updated the guide several times as he added more cocktails to his repertoire.

Anyone wanting to know Thomas' not-so-secret recipes can easily buy the original edition of the *Bartenders Guide*. In 2016, it was reprinted and made available as a hardcover, paperback, and ebook. The prices range from $5 to $17. That's a steal, considering that the actual original edition has fetched thousands of dollars at auction.

COCKTAILS

It seems that everyone wants credit for inventing cocktails. That goes for some that might—or might not—have originated in New York, including the Tom Collins, Bloody Mary, and martini.

Take the martini, for example. A bartender named Martini di Arma di Taggia, who worked at the Knickerbocker Hotel in New York City in the early 1900s, is sometimes cited as the creator of this eponymous drink. But long before that, in the 1880s, the cocktail was in the bartender's guide from the Occidental Hotel in San Francisco, where "Professor" Jerry Thomas (*see* Cocktail Recipe Book in this section) had tended bar on one of his sojourns. And even before that, during the Gold Rush days, a saloon owner supposedly created the martini for a miner in the town of Martinez, California, who wanted to celebrate a lucky strike. Another origin story maintains that the martini was invented in San Francisco for miners on their way to Martinez. Yet another possibility: the drink got its name from one of its ingredients, Martini and Rossi vermouth.

One of the few unquestionable New York originals in the cocktail category is an obvious one: the Manhattan. But controversy does cloud the creation story. Possibly, **the first Manhattan** was mixed at the Manhattan Club in the 1870s. A popular tale is that Jennie Jerome, who was known the world over as Lady Randolph Churchill, was hosting a party at the Manhattan Club when a guest mixed a drink that would forever afterward be called the Manhattan. This story has been called into question because Lady Churchill was in Europe at the time, pregnant with the future leader of England. Another possibility is that the Manhattan was invented by a different New Yorker whose last name was Black; nothing else seems to be known about him. Whichever tale is true, the island of Manhattan seems the logical birthplace of the cocktail by the same name.

Another drink owes its popularity to the ladies of the TV show *Sex and the City,* which ran from 1998 to 2004. Although the drink may have had its roots, with similar but different ingredients, in San Francisco, Miami Beach, or Provincetown, **the first Cosmopolitan** was made in 1987 by Toby Cecchini, bartender at The Odeon restaurant in New York. The Odeon was a hot spot, but the cosmo took off because it was the cocktail of choice for the characters in the television show. Hey, if you couldn't be Carrie Bradshaw, you could at least drink like her.

FIRST RESTAURANT

Eating out regularly is a phenomenon that began in the late twentieth century. Throughout most of history, nearly all meals were consumed at home, whether that was a family domicile or a boardinghouse, where residents ate whatever the proprietor had prepared. Similarly, travelers took their meals at the inn or hotel where they were staying, and they had no choice in what they ate, which tended to be heavy and bland; providing lodging rather than gourmet fare was the business of these establishments. If people wanted to go out to socialize where refreshments were available, they might stop by a tavern to enjoy an alcoholic beverage, perhaps with the so-so single-option food of the day, or go to a café for coffee or tea and sweets. Everywhere, food tended to be gobbled down quickly, as eating was not the genteel experience associated with the word *dining.* This was true not just in New York or in America but in Europe as well.

This approach to eating began to change in 1765, when a man named Boulanger opened a shop in Paris that served a single dish, a hearty soup. He called his soup a restorative, which in French is *restaurant.* Soon other Parisian food-sellers copied his idea, and the word *restaurant* became a place to eat the house specialty. After a while, French restaurants began to offer more than one dish, and they listed the choices on something called a menu.

In 1828 a Boston hotel, the Tremont House, decided to do as the French did. The Tremont House offered a menu with the choices of the day and sat patrons at individual tables rather than at a communal board. But the Boston venue is not considered the first American restaurant, because it was a hotel dining room rather than a freestanding eating establishment.

In New York City, the Delmonico brothers were enjoying good business in their café, where they sold coffee, wine, pastries, and sweets. They bought the land next door and expanded into a restaurant in the French style. In 1837, this Delmonico's became **the first restaurant in America**.

Delmonico's was the epitome of fine dining. It was the home of the Delmonico steak and possibly the creator of eggs Benedict (*see* that story in this section). The ritzy restaurant changed locations several times, following its clientele as the elite moved farther north in Manhattan. Today, Delmonico's is back at its original site, although in a different building, where it offers a bit of elegance to Financial District movers and shakers. (*See* Walking Tour 1 for the location of Delmonico's.)

Singles Bar

Until fairly recently, bars were the province of men. American women who wanted an evening of drinking and socializing attended cocktail parties in private homes.

In 1965, a young New Yorker named Alan Stillman decided to create a bar that women as well as men would frequent. He chose his home turf, the Upper East Side, which was teeming with singles like himself, people who wanted to meet other young adults of the opposite sex. He borrowed $5,000 and redecorated a neighborhood bar with a softer, homier, brighter touch. The menu included sweet drinks that would appeal to women. And the women came! What was the name of this new bar? TGI Fridays. That's right, the family-friendly suburban chain began as **the first singles bar** in the nation. (I understand that some younger readers may not know the term "singles bar." It was a place where young adults of your parents' or grandparents' generation might have gone to meet potential partners in the days before cell phones and dating apps.)

As at other bars and cocktail parties, drinking and chatting were the objectives at TGI Fridays in the early days. Eating was secondary, and food consisted of nibbles and noshes, not meals. As the food menu expanded over time, the chefs added some novel creations. One of them was scooped out potato skins topped with cheddar cheese, bacon, and sour cream, which Fridays added to the menu in 1974. Although many people think Fridays introduced loaded potato skins to America, a Chicago restaurant, R.J. Grunts, actually offered them several years earlier. The Chicago skins were not a big seller, but at Fridays they became a signature item.

Government and Law

New York City may be the financial capital of the country, but it was also once the actual capital, as in the seat of the federal government. When the United States of America was brand new, New York was the first capital of the nation.

Previously, representatives of the colonies had come to New York to create a joint response to British action that they viewed as unjust and unlawful. This meeting was a sort of test case for the concept that separate states can act in a peaceful, united fashion for the good of the entire federation.

Later, New York introduced legislation that became models for other cities. New York City passed the first health codes and comprehensive zoning regulations in the nation. Courtrooms here introduced innovative practices, such as recording trials and holding sessions at night. The

Equitable Building, erected in 1915. It was so massive that it blocked light from getting to surrounding buildings. That led to passage the next year of the nation's first comprehensive zoning laws.

first legal aid society in the nation provided a lawyer for people who could not afford one.

As the first capital, New York was where the first president of the United States took the oath of office. More than 230 years later, another president, a New York native, was impeached twice for violating that oath—something we hope will never happen again.

STAMP ACT CONGRESS

"No taxation without representation!" That was the rallying cry among Americans when they lived in the thirteen colonies, before the United States existed. The colonists were protesting the Stamp Act, which the British Parliament passed in March 1765. The Stamp Act imposed a tax on all printed paper: newspapers, magazines, even playing cards. The colonists' objection centered on the principle that because they had no representatives in the British Parliament, that legislative body had no legal right to tax them.

After many local protests, delegates from nine of the thirteen colonies met in New York at City Hall for almost three weeks, starting on October 7, 1765, as the Stamp Act Congress. It was **the first peaceful, organized, mass resistance** in what would become the United States of America. The Stamp Act Congress produced the Declaration of Rights and Grievances, which contained thirteen resolutions. The document began with acknowledgment of the colonists' allegiance to the British king and Parliament and stated that Americans were entitled to the same rights as other British subjects. That included the right to not be taxed unless they had a voice in the government. To drive the point home, the colonists subsequently boycotted British goods.

Mainly because of economic pressures, Parliament repealed the Stamp Act the next year. At the same time, it passed the Declaratory Act, reaffirming its right to impose taxes in the colonies. Not exactly a triumphant victory for young America.

But it was a win in another way. The Stamp Act Congress demonstrated that the colonies could come together peacefully and take action for their common good. This is the basis of the federal government of independent but united states.

Fast forward to 1789. After a quick remodel job, the building where the Stamp Act Congress had met, City Hall, became Federal Hall. **The first U.S. Congress** met here and wrote the Bill of Rights, a fitting follow-up to an earlier congress concerned with the right for representation in decisions regarding taxes.

First Capital of the United States

If you went to elementary school in this country, you probably learned but may have forgotten that New York City was **the first capital of the United States**. **The first Congress** under the Constitution met in a building that had been City Hall but was renamed Federal Hall. Several weeks later, on April 30, 1789, George Washington stood on the balcony of that building and took the oath as **the first president of the United States**.

Architect and civil engineer Pierre L'Enfant redesigned New York's City Hall to make it appropriate for the new federal government. L'Enfant would soon create the master plan for the permanent capital of the United States, Washington, D.C.

Between New York and Washington came Philadelphia, which was the capital of the United States between 1790 and 1800. Philadelphia claims to be the first capital because that was where the first Continental Congress met in 1774 and where Congresses convened under the Articles of Confederation before the Constitution established the U.S. Congress as we know it today. Other cities that take credit as the one-time capital, however briefly, are Baltimore and Annapolis, Maryland; Lancaster and York, Pennsylvania; and Princeton and Trenton, New Jersey. Although these cities (like New York) were scenes of important events leading up to the establishment of the United States government, the first capital under the Constitution—in other words, the first capital of the United States as it officially came to be—was New York.

The building across from the New York Stock Exchange that is usually called Federal Hall is not the one where Washington became president and early sessions of Congress met. That building was already old when it was converted to the Capitol, and it came down in 1812. The current Federal Hall (more correctly, Federal Hall National Memorial) was erected on the same site in 1842; it was built as the U.S. Custom

House. Twenty years later, it became a federal Sub-Treasury, part of the system that the Federal Reserve ultimately replaced. It's worth a visit just to see the bank vaults and the thick columns on the lower level that at one time supported a large chunk of the nation's money supply. In case you don't know which building it is, look for John Quincy Adams Ward's huge statue of George Washington on the front steps, in the approximate location where he stood to take the oath of office. (*See* the building on Walking Tour 1.)

FIRST RECORDED MURDER TRIAL

The 1800 trial of Levi Weeks for the murder of Gulielma (a.k.a. Elma) Sands was the sort of fodder that makes tabloids prosper. The case involved sexual impropriety, a prominent family, a dream team for the defense, and a relatively long trial with an almost instantaneous verdict. It also was **the first recorded murder trial in the United States**.

Sands and Weeks were boarders at a New York City rooming house. Living under the same roof made it easy to sneak around, and their illicit affair was an open secret to their housemates. The couple decided to make it legal by eloping.

On the evening of December 22, 1799, they both went out. He returned a few hours later; she never came back. In early January, her body was discovered in a well not too far away. Weeks, the brother of a leading architect, was charged with her murder.

Among Weeks' attorneys were two top lawyers: the unlikely pairing of Alexander Hamilton and Aaron Burr. (Sands' body, by the way, had been found in a well owned by Burr's Manhattan Company.) The prosecutor was a future mayor of New York City, Cadwallader D. Colden. Also present during the trial was a court clerk, William Coleman, who recorded the proceedings in shorthand.

At a time when criminal trials usually were one-day events, this trial stretched well into the wee hours on two consecutive days. Most of the evidence was circumstantial. The dream team called witnesses who supported their client, raised doubts about the victim's mental state (could her death have been a suicide?), and dramatically attacked a key prosecution witness. The presiding judge, John Lansing, gave instructions to the jury that came close to telling them that there was insufficient proof to find Weeks guilty. After deliberating only five minutes, the jury rendered a not-guilty verdict.

That was on April 1, 1800. On April 12, a complete report of the trial by court clerk William Coleman was published. As quick as that was, two other people who had been in the courtroom had already published their versions, which were less extensive and more interpretive. In the preface to his 100-page report, which has been published by the Library of Congress (http://lcweb2.loc.gov/service/gdc/scd0001/2005/20051214001re /20051214001re.pdf), Coleman noted: "Five other note-books besides my own, have been examined and the whole have been carefully collated, and if there is any merit in the performance it lies in its correctness. The testimony of the principal witnesses is given in their own words . . ."

Alexander Hamilton apparently was impressed with Coleman's skill. Hamilton soon founded the *New York Evening Post* and appointed Coleman its first editor, a position he held for almost thirty years. Initially a serious, respected newspaper, today the *Post* (no longer called *Evening Post*, as it comes out in the morning) is a tabloid-style paper—the sort that thrives on salacious stories such as the Weeks trial.

SANITARY (HEALTH) CODE

Only one word can describe New York City in the mid-1800s: filthy. To get rid of their household garbage, residents simply threw it into the streets, where it might remain for days or even weeks. Indoor plumbing was almost unheard of, and privies were seldom disinfected. Animals roamed the streets, leaving their mark. Slaughterhouses and manufacturing businesses—which often were in or near residential areas so workers could get there easily in the absence of good public transportation—produced waste that flowed into the streets and remained there because the city lacked good drainage systems. Although New York was already an industrial city, farms dotted the areas more remote from the populated sectors. Manure on farms, as well as from horses stabled near residences, piled up. Serious, deadly illnesses such as cholera spread like wildfire.

To be fair, all big cities suffered from these unsanitary conditions. But New York was different, because city leaders decided to do something about it. In February 1866, New York City passed **the first sanitary code in the nation** and set up comprehensive methods to enforce it.

The sanitary code created the Metropolitan Board of Health. The board comprised a president, four police commissioners, a health officer, and four other sanitary commissioners, at least three of them physicians. They went to work immediately. In the first year alone, they ordered the removal of 160,000 tons of manure. The same year, 6,400 privies were disinfected and 4,000 yards cleaned. The board urged institutions and private citizens to clean up their property, and the presence of police commissioners on the board served a useful enforcement function. Threatened with a cholera epidemic, the board hired sanitary inspectors, who disinfected homes where the disease was present, removed soiled bedding and clothing, and temporarily relocated healthy household members. Although more than a thousand New Yorkers died in the 1866 cholera outbreak, the death toll was only one tenth that of the 1849 epidemic.

Other cities were impressed with these results. The New York model became an inspiration for sanitary or health codes elsewhere.

LEGAL AID SOCIETY

Leaving one's homeland for another country, especially one with a different language, takes a lot of guts. It's easier when locals willingly offer a helping hand. In 1876, New York's German Society did just that, forming an organization to help defend German immigrants who needed an attorney but could not afford one. It was **the first formal legal aid society** in America.

This legal aid society, which once had a long German name, started small, handling only civil cases. In the initial year, a single attorney helped 212 German immigrants. The caseload more than tripled within a year, and more attorneys joined him. Most of the early cases involved wage or rent disputes or attempts to defraud immigrants with little understanding of American ways.

By 1890, the group had dropped its German affiliation and was representing indigent New Yorkers of any national background. Twenty years later, The Legal Aid Society, as it was now officially called, also was handling many criminal cases. Almost 34,000 people a year sought help from Legal Aid at that time.

About 900 lawyers in The Legal Aid Society of New York now handle some 300,000 cases a year. Municipalities throughout the country also have legal aid societies to help their poorer residents navigate the complex judicial system and get the fair treatment everyone deserves.

Night Court

The Sixth Amendment of the U.S. Constitution guarantees a speedy trial, and New York City has taken its obligation seriously. In 1907, New York held **the first night court in the nation** at the Jefferson Market courthouse in Greenwich Village. Night court was then and still is for arraignment, not for jury trials. In night court, men and women arrested late in the day for minor crimes appear before a judge to hear the charges, potentially avoiding a night in jail.

For eleven years, the Jefferson Market courthouse was the home of night court. After the first three years, it heard only cases involving women, mainly on charges of prostitution and shoplifting. Subsequently, night court moved downtown to the criminal court building at 100 Centre Street. Manhattanites may be familiar with the building from serving on jury duty. After 5 PM and until 1 AM, about seventy to ninety cases are heard in night court; no jurors are needed.

One of the most bizarre things about New York's night court is that it became a tourist attraction. It's a no-cost alternative to a Broadway show or a five-course dinner at a fancy restaurant. But you don't have to be cash-strapped to sit in the gallery at night court. Back when it met at the Jefferson Market courthouse, John D. Rockefeller was said to enjoy the diversion.

Although the courts have left the Jefferson Market building, the Victorian Gothic edifice, complete with turrets and tower, still stands. Built in 1877, the courthouse was the design work of Frederick Clarke Withers and Calvert Vaux (co-designer of Central Park). After the courts moved out, the building fell into disrepair and was threatened with demolition. Community activists fought to save the building, a Village icon. In the mid-1960s, architect Giorgio Cavaglieri remodeled the former courthouse into the Jefferson Market branch of the New York Public Library (*see* it on Walking Tour 2). If you happen to go to the reference room in the lower level, you'll be in the former holding area for prisoners.

Zoning Regulations

By the early twentieth century, skyscrapers were taking over Manhattan. There seemed to be no limit to how big a building could get—until the Equitable Building went too far.

When the Equitable Building was completed in 1915, it filled every inch of the Financial District plot and rose forty-two stories straight up. It contained far more office space than any other structure. Big may have seemed great to the developers, but not to the neighboring buildings. The behemoth cast a huge shadow and deprived nearby offices of natural light and air, two necessities in the days before good indoor lighting and air conditioning. (*See* the Equitable Building on Walking Tour 1.)

It was too late to do anything about the Equitable Building, but the city knew it had to act fast to prevent copycats. In 1916, New York City passed **the first comprehensive zoning regulations in the country**. The new set of laws limited how tall a building could rise straight up from its base. It was okay to go high, but at a certain point the façade could no longer be flush with the base; it had to be set back. The higher the building went, the more setbacks were needed.

This zoning code created a distinctive New York style of architecture. Some refer to it as "stacked boxes," with the biggest box at the base topped by progressively smaller boxes. A more common name for this post-1916 New York skyscraper style is tiered or "wedding cake architecture."

After experimenting with this style for about a decade, some architects got more creative. Narrow towers rose on top of the setbacks. Think of the Chrysler Building and the Empire State Building. You don't even realize the lower floors have progressive setbacks; you know these buildings only by their tops. In addition to allowing light and air to penetrate the surrounding space, the revolutionary zoning regulations of 1916 resulted in New York City's magnificent skyline.

The 1916 zoning code also addressed another problem. In the nineteenth century, before good public transportation, people needed to live close to work. In the "modern" early twentieth century, that was no longer necessary or desirable. The zoning code established separate residential and business districts, as well as areas where use was unrestricted. Other cities soon zoned similar use restrictions. When the zoning laws of Euclid, Ohio, were challenged in 1926, the Supreme Court found that such land use restrictions are indeed constitutional.

Twice Impeached President

The Founding Fathers had the foresight to create a constitutional mechanism for impeaching and removing a president from office for "treason, bribery, or other high crimes and misdemeanors." The House of Representatives decides whether to impeach the president; if they vote to, the Senate conducts a trial. Impeachment has rarely been deemed necessary. Andrew Johnson was impeached in 1868, Bill Clinton in 1998. Knowing that Congress was going to vote on impeachment, Richard Nixon resigned in 1974. Donald Trump, a New Yorker for most of his life, was **the first president to be impeached twice** and **the first president whose impeachment trial occurred after he left office**. Each of the four impeachment trials in the history of the United States ended in acquittal.

Two charges were brought against Trump in his first impeachment: abuse of power and obstruction of Congress. The charges related to his alleged attempt to coerce the Ukrainian government to investigate business dealings of the son of a Trump political rival, Joe Biden, and the subsequent hampering of the congressional probe. The House of Representatives voted to impeach Trump on December 18, 2019, and the Senate trial began the next month.

Later that year, Joe Biden triumphed over Trump in his reelection bid. Trump had been suggesting election fraud both before and after tally of the votes, and he urged his supporters to protest what he claimed was a stolen election. On January 6, 2021—the day that Congress was certifying the election results and formally declaring Biden the winner—Trump rallied supporters who had gathered in Washington, telling them to march to the Capitol and fight. Never before in the history of this country had a mob stormed the Capitol, but it happened that day, with deadly results. Violently breaking into the building, the mob disrupted proceedings and caused elected officials and their staff to flee for safety. A week later, the House impeached Trump for inciting the insurrection. The trial took place during the early weeks of the Biden presidency, making Trump's second impeachment trial the only one to take place when the accused was no longer in office. More senators voted for indictment than in the first Trump impeachment trial, but not the two-thirds majority needed to convict.

Inventions

New Yorkers are a creative, inventive lot. Their inventions are as diverse as the city itself. New York originals have ranged from the tiny (the safety pin) to the huge (municipal incinerators). Other inventions have helped people stay neat and clean (dry cleaning, toilet paper),

Elisha Otis demonstrating the elevator safety brake in 1854.

remain cool (air conditioning), enjoy music (long-playing record), keep informed (news ticker), get easily from one place to another in a vertical city (elevators and escalators), and be safe (home security system, firefighters' tools). Some items described in this section were not totally new but were modifications of existing products, such as baby carriages and cardboard.

New York inventions haven't always been immediate success stories. Many have gone through multiple permutations, some the work of the original creator, as in the case of air conditioning, others the successive changes of different inventors, as in the case of baby carriages. Some inventors, like the developer of the safety pin and the first modern sewing machine, have been creative geniuses but lousy businessmen. The key to business success for inventors is having a patent on their unique creation, so you'll see the word *patent* often in this section.

One thing can be said about nearly every New York invention described here. Life was never the same afterward, not just in New York or in the United States, but throughout the world.

FIRST BLACK PERSON TO RECEIVE A U.S. PATENT

On March 3, 1821, a Manhattan tailor named Thomas L. Jennings received a patent for a method to "dry scour" clothes, especially woolens, and have them keep their shape. This was **the first patent for dry cleaning**. We don't know much about Jennings' invention, because the patent documents were among almost 10,000 destroyed in a fire in 1836.

Obtaining a patent for a new invention is a great accomplishment for anyone, but it was a pioneering achievement for Jennings, as he was **the first Black person to receive a U.S. patent**, at least to our knowledge. It's possible that other Blacks had come up with patent-worthy innovations before him. But if they were slaves—as were most Blacks living in America up to that point—the laws of the land at the time dictated that they and anything they produced were the property of their master. Jennings was a free man, not a slave, so he was able to apply for a patent. His wife, however, was born in slavery, and one of the first things he did with the profits from his invention was obtain her freedom.

53

Jennings went on to become a leader in the abolition and civil rights movements. He was a founding member of the Abyssinian Baptist Church, as well as several equal rights and legal aid organizations. He also helped support *Freedom's Journal*, the first African American newspaper (*see* Newspaper by and for African Americans in the Media section).

Jennings' daughter Elizabeth learned from the example he set. You might say she was a Rosa Parks a century before THE Rosa Parks. Coming home from church one Sunday in 1854, Elizabeth Jennings boarded and refused to leave a whites-only streetcar. Her father hired an attorney to argue for her right to ride. The lawyer: Chester A. Arthur, who won the case and later became president of the United States.

Baby Carriages

Something that most parents of young children today consider a necessity—a baby carriage or stroller—started out as an amusement for privileged little Brits. Although an Englishman invented the baby carriage, several New Yorkers introduced improvements that made it more practical. One of these New York models became a big hit overseas.

It began in 1733, when an English architect named William Kent invented a baby carriage for the children of a duke. The duke wanted a way to transport his youngsters and amuse them at the same time. Essentially, Kent's carriage was a basket mounted on wheels and pulled by a goat or small pony. The baby carriage quickly became popular in British high society.

A hundred years later, a New York toymaker named Benjamin Potter Crandall introduced **the first baby carriages made in America**. His son Jesse Armour Crandall, who was as much an inventor as a toymaker, patented improvements, including a brake, a parasol to shade the child, and a folding model. But most Americans in the 1830s expressed little interest in baby carriages, considering them a luxury for the well-to-do.

In 1848, another New Yorker, Charles Burton, came up with a revolutionary new concept: **the first push stroller**. Previous models were pulled from the front. Burton put a handle on his carriage so that parents could stand behind it and push. The child's seat straddled three wheels, two large ones in back and a smaller one in front—a design seen in many present-day models.

Once again, the American reception was lukewarm. Undeterred, Burton took his design to England, where the baby carriage had been invented more than a century earlier. The Queen of England thought it was a great idea. What was good enough for the queen was good enough for her subjects. Soon the carriage, which Burton called a perambulator and locals shortened to pram, filled the parks of England.

PINS AND NEEDLES

New Yorker inventor and real estate speculator Walter Hunt was absent-mindedly twisting a wire as he tried to come up with a way to pay off a debt. He looked down at his wire doodle and saw the answer. He had twisted the wire into **the first safety pin** ever created. In his application for a patent, which he received in 1849, Hunt described the pin as a single piece of wire coiled into a spring at one end. The spring forced the point of the wire into a clasp at the other end.

More interested in paying his debt and feeding his family than in making money off his invention, Hunt immediately sold the patent for the safety pin. He went on inventing, just as he had done before. In his sixty-two years, more than half of them spent in New York City, he invented such diverse tools as a foot-operated alarm bell for streetcars, a knife sharpener with a protective edge, a fountain pen, and an ice plow for boats. Alas, Hunt was more of an idea man than a business man. He often sold his patents because he needed money.

Hunt didn't try to patent his greatest invention, besides the safety pin, until it was too late: **the first modern sewing machine**, which used a needle with an eye at the point and created a lockstitch. Hunt invented this revolutionary sewing machine in 1834. He decided not to patent it because he feared it would take business away from people who worked hard to support their families by sewing clothes and other goods by hand.

Other inventors were not so altruistic. In 1846 Elias Howe of Massachusetts earned a patent for a machine similar to Hunt's, and Howe went down in history as the creator of the sewing machine. In the next decade, Isaac Singer's name became associated with sewing machines. It seemed that everyone wanted credit for inventing the device, even, at long last, Walter Hunt. In 1853 he applied for a patent for his 1834 machine. Although the U.S. Patent Office recognized that Hunt was the true inventor, he was denied the patent because he had not applied before Howe. As a result, trivia buffs and tailors know Howe as the sewing machine wizard. Who remembers the name of the prolific New York inventor who preceded him?

Elevators and Escalators

So many stories to tell about elevators and escalators! After all, New York has long prided itself on its tall buildings, and these devices are ways to get up to the top and back down.

When E. V. Haughwout's five-floor china and glassware emporium opened on Broadway and Broome Street in 1857, it featured **the first passenger elevator in the world**. It was the creation of a man whose name is closely associated with elevators: Elisha Otis.

Elevators were nothing new. They were a convenient way to hoist large and heavy objects but were considered unfit to transport people, because passengers likely would plunge to their death if the ropes or pulleys broke. Otis found a way to stop the elevator in its mad descent, creating **the first elevator safety brake**. He dramatically demonstrated his invention at the Crystal Palace Exposition in 1854 (*see* World's Fair in the Museums and Exhibitions section). Before a crowd of spectators, Otis mounted a platform near the top of Latting Observatory, at 315 feet the tallest structure in New York City at the time. He signaled to an assistant to cut the connected cable. The crowd gasped as he started to descend—then immediately stopped thanks to his elevator safety brake. (*See* the scene of this event on Walking Tour 4.)

Although the Haughwout Building had the first passenger elevator, **the first shaft for a passenger elevator** was included in plans for Cooper Union, the free institute of higher education founded by industrialist and inventor Peter Cooper less than a mile to the north. When he commissioned the building in 1853, Cooper assumed that elevators would be *de rigueur* by the time construction was completed, and he had the architects include a round elevator shaft. He guessed correctly about the desire for elevators but was wrong about their shape. Otis elevators always have been rectangular. But Otis personally made a special one to fit the Cooper Union shaft. (*See* Cooper Union on Walking Tour 2.)

The first hotel with a passenger elevator was the posh Fifth Avenue Hotel, which opened in 1859, the same year that Cooper Union was completed. The traveling clientele referred to the steam-operated contraption as a vertical railway. (*See* the site of the Fifth Avenue Hotel on Walking Tour 3.)

The first office building with passenger elevators was the eight-story Equitable Building on Lower Broadway (not to be confused with its successor by the same name on the same site, the bulky skyscraper that led to the nation's first zoning law [*see* Zoning Regulations in Government and Law and Walking Tour 1]). When the original Equitable Building started renting space in 1870, the challenge was to find tenants willing to take a chance on the top floors. It would be a long climb up if the elevators were out of service and a fast and potentially fatal trip down if the mechanism failed.

In 1884, a new type of residence began accepting tenants far north of New York's general population. The Dakota, the first luxury apartment building (*see* Apartment Buildings in Residences and Residential Areas), was meant to appeal to the well-to-do. The wealthy inhabitants experimenting with this alternative to a private mansion were accustomed to servants and delivery people using separate staircases from their own. The Dakota, therefore, was **the first residential building with a service elevator**. Across the park, Andrew Carnegie's mansion later became **the first private home with multiple electric elevators** (*see* Carnegie Mansion in the Residences and Residential Areas section).

Before long, the elevator spawned a cousin. Its patent-holder, Jesse Reno, called it an inclined elevator or an endless conveyor elevator. We know it by a different name. This contraption, **the first escalator**, made a brief appearance in 1896 at Coney Island in Brooklyn.

Macy's at Herald Square was **the first building in the world with modern escalators**. At the store's opening in 1902, "modern" meant two things in regard to escalators: made of wood, and horizontal or flat steps. Macy's installed a new fleet of wooden escalators in the 1920s. They were later upgraded, and most have been replaced. But at this writing, a few wooden escalators remain on higher floors on the Broadway side of the building. (*See* Macy's on Walking Tour 3.)

TOILET PAPER

Throughout history, people have found a way to clean themselves after elimination, but the choice of materials often was less hygienic than an unclean bottom: sand, dirt, leaves, corncobs, rags, printed paper. A New Yorker named Joseph Gayetty found a solution, introducing **the first commercial toilet paper** in 1857. He marketed it as Medicated Paper for the Water-Closet and sold it in packs of 500 scented sheets. The papers were moistened with aloe and watermarked with his name. Advertisements called it "the greatest necessity of the age" and extolled its virtues compared with other paper used for the same purpose: "Individuals would not put printers [sic] ink in their mouths [...] yet they have no hesitation in [...] applying that ink to the tenderest part of the body."

Gayetty claimed that his medicated paper could prevent or cure hemorrhoids. The medical establishment pounced on this assertion, declaring it false. Their debunking of the product contributed to its lack of commercial success. But other entrepreneurs saw a good idea and made improvements, including selling it in rolls rather than flat sheets. The names of some of these manufacturers, such as Scott and Northern (not New York companies), still appear in the toilet paper aisles—but not Gayetty.

CARDBOARD

Cardboard wasn't invented in New York, but two enhancements originated in this city. In 1871, a New Yorker named Albert Jones was looking for a better way to ship delicate glass objects like bottles. He pleated some cardboard and noticed that the folds cushioned the bottles better than several layers of smooth packing material. Jones bonded a single layer of smooth cardboard to the crimped material, thus creating **the first corrugated cardboard**. Subsequently, sandwiching the pleated material between two sheets of smooth paper resulted in the corrugated cardboard most commonly seen today.

A few years later, a mistake in a Manhattan paper bag factory led to **the first precut foldable cardboard boxes**. One day a ruler that was supposed to crease the paper bags accidentally cut through a stack of them. It was a "Eureka!" moment for factory owner Robert Gair. He tinkered with the machinery, realizing that if he put a sharp cutting blade a little higher than the dull creasing blade, he could cut and crease the bags in one step and greatly improve productivity. From there, it was a simple matter to replace the paper for bags with cardboard for boxes. Gair patented the machine that created foldable cardboard boxes in 1879. With business booming, he moved his operation in 1888 to the Dumbo section of Brooklyn. The Gair name can still be found in this once industrial, now trendy area.

By the turn of the century, both of these modified cardboard products, corrugated cardboard and precut foldable boxes, had become standard. Thanks to the ingenuity of two New Yorkers.

MUNICIPAL INCINERATORS

Whether it's called garbage, trash, waste, disposables, or whatever, it's not glamorous, and it cannot be ignored. Waste has always been a problem in New York. Consider that in 1880 there were at least 150,000 horses in the city—many of them literally the horsepower that moved public transportation—and each animal produced more than twenty pounds of manure a day. Add to that the human equivalent, uneaten food, industrial waste—it was a big stinky mess!

In the late nineteenth century, New York became an innovator in waste disposal. In 1885, **the first garbage incinerator in America** began operating on Governors Island, a military outpost since early American days that is located in New York Harbor between Lower Manhattan and Brooklyn. A few years before the incinerator started burning New York City's garbage, military families began to move to Governors Island. Apparently, they were not disturbed by the presence of the incinerator, probably because the population was sparse and the incinerator small. The stack rose taller than other buildings on the island, but the plant had a capacity of just a metric ton a day.

A decade later, other municipal incinerators appeared in Staten Island and Queens, also sparsely populated areas at the time. Soon other

American cities saw what New York was doing and built their own waste management facilities. Because they burned only food waste, these incinerators (including those in New York) operated at low temperatures, which led to foul odors. As a result, sixty percent of the 180 municipal incinerators in the country closed by 1908.

That year, Staten Island became home to **the first high-temperature, mixed-refuse municipal incinerator in America**. Compared with the Governors Island facility, this one was a biggie; it had a capacity of fifty-five metric tons per day. The extremely high temperature, in excess of 675 degrees Centigrade, kept odors to a minimum. The Staten Island plant quickly became the model that other cities copied. By the end of World War I, more than 200 high-temperature municipal incinerators were disposing of America's waste.

How times change! The impetus for the first incinerator was the need to rid the streets of garbage. A century later, the cry was for clean air. Incinerators are major air polluters. The last incinerator in New York City closed in 1994. New York, like municipalities everywhere, continues to look for efficient, safe, clean, and inexpensive ways to dispose of its dirtiest detritus.

Air Conditioning

Air conditioning was invented not to keep people comfortable in hot, humid weather but to solve an industrial problem. Humidity was hampering production in a Brooklyn printing plant. To realize the extent of the problem, you need to understand the four-color printing process. Each color of ink is put into the press separately. Once on the paper, the ink must dry thoroughly before the next color is applied. Ink takes longer to dry when the humidity is high. In addition, the paper can wrinkle when it absorbs moisture from the air. This also throws off the four-color printing process, which requires precise alignment as one color after another goes through the press.

A young engineer named Willis Carrier found a solution. He invented a system in which air passed through water-cooled coils, maintaining a constant humidity of fifty-five percent. In 1902, Carrier installed this mechanism, which he patented as an Apparatus for

Treating Air, in the Sackett & Wilhelms Lithographing and Printing Company. The Brooklyn printing plant became **the first building with air conditioning.**

Over the next several decades, Carrier kept modifying his system as he installed it in other factories and public buildings. After trying out variations of his apparatus in a few Los Angeles and Texas movie theaters, he added a centrifugal chiller for the Rivoli Theater in Times Square, making this **the first movie theater with modern air conditioning.** Since this 1925 breakthrough, crowds have flocked to the movies in hot, sticky weather to enjoy a few hours of comfort.

Air conditioning slowly made its way into stores, offices, and other places where people gathered. Home air conditioning remained a luxury for a long time. In 1965, only ten percent of American homes had air conditioning. But by the end of the twentieth century, home air conditioning was the rule rather than the exception.

Incidentally, an engineer named Stuart Cramer coined the term "air conditioning" in 1906. Cramer developed systems for humidity control in cotton mills in the South similar to Carrier's system.

NEWS TICKER

If you happened to be in Times Square on November 6, 1928, you would have seen an amazing sight. Giant letters scrolled around the fourth floor of the Times Tower, spelling out the breaking news on this Election Day: HERBERT HOOVER DEFEATS AL SMITH. That was the initial headline on **the first electronic news ticker in the world.**

Officially called the Motograph News Bulletin or Motogram but often dubbed "the zipper," the news ticker was a marvel of electrical engineering. The brainchild of Frank C. Reilly, it contained almost 15,000 light bulbs, more than 39,000 metal brushes, and 88,000 soldered connections. An operator worked the gizmo similarly to the way an old-fashioned typesetter created a printed page, placing the words letter by letter into a frame and adding spaces where needed. As the frame traveled along a track, each letter brushed multiple contacts. With every contact, a light quickly flashed on the outdoor sign. Reilly estimated that the sign flashed 261,925,664 times an hour.

In 1997, the zipper underwent a major upgrade. About 230,000 light-emitting diodes (LEDs) replaced the incandescent bulbs. The new amber-colored lighting used one-tenth the electricity and lasted thirty times as long as the original bulbs.

The building once known as the Times Tower—named for its original occupant, the *New York Times* newspaper—has changed hands repeatedly. These days, the building is known as One Times Square, and advertising is its main function. The oddly shaped building is usually covered from top to bottom with electronic and print ads. One day a year, nobody pays much attention to the ads, because all eyes are glued to the top, waiting for the ball to drop on New Year's Eve. (*See* the building on Walking Tour 4.)

The Motograph zipper was the forerunner of another type of electronic news ticker. Turn on a television, especially on a day with breaking news (or any time on CNN), and you'll see words scrolling across the bottom of the screen. The small-scale news crawl is the next generation of the giant-sized ticker that originated in Times Square.

FIREFIGHTERS' TOOLS

The city's fire department (FDNY) has been dubbed "New York's Bravest." "Most inventive" would be another appropriate nickname, as several New York firefighters have created tools for forcible entry, an essential part of their job. The inventors' equipment has been used by firefighters everywhere.

The supposed inspiration for these firefighters' implements was a claw tool that bank robbers had left behind after they set fire to the scene of the crime. Reasoning that a device that could break into a bank would be useful for forcible entry at a fire, clever New York firefighters (names unknown) modified the tool in the early 1920s, putting a claw on one end and a fork on the other. This claw tool did the job, but it was heavy and difficult—even dangerous—to use.

Within a decade or so, FDNY Captain John Kelly shortened the claw tool nearly a foot to about 25 inches. He replaced the fork with a chisel and the claw with an adze, creating **the first Kelly tool**. Made of welded steel, it weighed about 12 pounds. Firefighters usually carried both a claw and a Kelly tool—quite a heavy burden.

Two decades later, FDNY Chief Hugh Halligan figured out how to combine the utility of these tools into a single implement. He patented and introduced **the first Halligan bar** in 1948. This instrument was made from a single piece of high-carbon steel. Initially about 30 inches long and weighing 8½ pounds, the Halligan bar had three features. At one end was a fork for breaking latches and locks and shutting off gas valves. At the other end of the shaft were two gizmos: a pick for breaching locked doors and an adze for prying, which also provided extra leverage. The Halligan bar has proven useful for many other purposes, such as clearing window frames, tearing down interior walls, and lifting manhole covers.

Fire departments around the country bought the Halligan bar, but the FDNY did not, claiming it would be a conflict of interest to purchase equipment from one of its own. The tool was so good that some New York firefighters paid for it with their own money. When Halligan's patent expired and other companies started to make knock-offs or modify the original, FDNY made a purchase. The one they settled on, the Pro-Bar, continues a long tradition, for it is a modified Halligan bar designed by a pair of cousins who had worked for the FDNY.

LONG-PLAYING RECORD

On the rare occasions when I sort through my accumulated junk, I come upon a stack of long-playing (LP) records that have moved with me every time I've changed residences. The stack has gotten smaller over the years. It really should be nonexistent because I no longer have a turntable to play the records. But for one reason or another, I just can't part with these mementos. I didn't realize until recently that I have New York to thank for them. Columbia Records, based in the city, introduced **the first long-playing record** on June 21, 1948. The product was nearly a decade in development.

In the 1930s, the standard record was a shellac disc playing at a speed of seventy-eight revolutions per minute: the 78. The sound was contained in grooves cut into the disc, eighty to 100 grooves per inch. A ten-inch 78 could hold only three to four minutes of music on each side. To make a longer playing, better sounding record, Columbia engineer Peter Goldmark and his colleagues replaced the shellac with vinyl, a harder substance. They were able to cut microgrooves in the vinyl, 225 grooves per inch. The Columbia engineers increased the diameter of the disc to twelve inches and slowed the playing speed to 33⅓ revolutions per minute. Voila! The LP was born. It could hold about twenty-three minutes per side, enabling a record to have not just a single song or two but an entire album of popular music or a complete symphony.

The vinyl LP ruled until the 1980s, when the compact disc (CD) became popular. In the ever-changing recorded music world, digital downloads on devices like MP3 players were appealing to music lovers by the turn of the century. They were soon overshadowed by streaming. The Recording Industry Association of America reported that in the first half of 2020, streaming services such as Spotify and Pandora accounted for eighty-five percent of the revenue pie. At six percent, digital downloads brought in slightly less revenue than physical products. In the latter category, vinyl sales were making a comeback, exceeding CD revenue for the first time since the 1980s.

Home Security System

Necessity, they say, is the mother of invention. Marie Van Brittan Brown felt it was necessary to have more security in her home in the high-crime neighborhood of Jamaica, Queens. She had the ideas; her husband Albert, an electronics technician, had the know-how. Together, they put together a plan and applied for a patent in August 1966 for **the first closed-circuit television (CCTV) home security system**. They received the patent three years later.

Their system consisted of multiple elements. A camera on the inside of the front door moved over several peepholes positioned to detect people of different heights. The images were projected on a television monitor in an interior room. Upon seeing the images, the occupant could communicate with the person on the outside through a two-way microphone and push a button to either unlock the door or send an alarm to the police.

The Browns' invention was novel for two reasons. First, the Browns were African American, a relative rarity among patent applicants. Second, home security systems were not a thing yet. Before long, though, apartment managers hoping to attract residents with amenities, small businesses concerned about break-ins, and later, homeowners trying to catch package thieves were installing such security systems. Ring!

LGBTQ

Most firsts involving lesbian, gay, bisexual, transvestite, and queer (LGBTQ) people occurred in the mid-twentieth century. It was a time when other groups, specifically Blacks and women, were also speaking up for their rights. At least one first in the LGBTQ community, though, occurred very early in that century, when New York City police raided a gay bathhouse. In the 1960s and 1970s, LGBTQ achievements involved an overlapping cast of characters and events. For example, the owner of the first gay bookstore offered his shop to planners of the first pride march, which honored the birth of the gay rights movement a year

The Stonewall Inn, 2016. In June 1969, it was the site of the Stonewall Rebellion, considered to be the birth of the gay rights movement.

earlier. The mother of a collegian who tried to get Columbia University to create a gay student lounge went on to organize the first support group for parents of gays and lesbians. First-of-their-kind accomplishments affecting the LGBTQ community continued later in the twentieth century, with an employer offering domestic partner benefits.

As I wrote this section, I faced a challenge with nomenclature. The most accepted, inclusive term today is LGBTQ, and I have tried to use this wherever it makes sense. However, when the rights movement began, "gay" was the common term, so I have usually used that word when it is historically correct. "Gay" often referred to both male and female homosexuals, but sometimes the terminology was expanded to "gay and lesbian." Specification of the other terms in the LGBTQ designation did not come until later. I apologize to anyone I have unintentionally offended by using terminology that you feel is incorrect or too limiting (or, conversely, too broad).

BATHHOUSE RAID

In the late nineteenth and early twentieth centuries, few dwellings in poor neighborhoods had private baths. When people wanted to bathe, they'd go to a public bathhouse. (*See* Public Baths in the Social Welfare section.) Other types of bathhouses catered to religious needs or cultural practices. For example, married Jewish women went to the ritual bath, or *mikvah*. Russian and Turkish baths offered vigorous scrubbing and camaraderie in the traditions of those countries. Some Turkish baths also were popular among gay men seeking casual sex.

In February 1903, New York City police began to keep a close eye on the Turkish baths in the basement of the Ariston Hotel at 55th Street and Broadway in Manhattan. Acting on their suspicions, they entered on February 21, conducting **the first known raid on a gay bathhouse**. At least fourteen men were arrested. Most were brought to trial for sodomy and sentenced to prison.

Despite the threat of police raids, bathhouses continued to attract a gay clientele. By mid-century, bathhouses were common in gay communities throughout America.

Then came the AIDS epidemic and with it fear of sex with strangers. Many gay men stopped visiting bathhouses. In 1985, the New York

City Health Department ordered gay bathhouses closed, although a few establishments ignored the order. Bathhouses still exist across the country but are not nearly as popular as they once were.

GAY STUDENT ACTIVITIES

In 1966, a sophomore at Columbia University approached the school about creating an organization for gay students. He had the support of the university chaplain, who offered space in Earl Hall, where the chaplaincy office was located. The next year the university granted a charter to the group. It was originally called the Student Homophile League and was **the first official group in America for LGBTQ college students**. A few years later the group became known as Gay People at Columbia-Barnard; today it is the Columbia Queer Alliance.

The university's original charter banned the group from offering social activities. Gay People at Columbia-Barnard sought to change that. Starting in 1970, Earl Hall became the scene of popular dances on the first Friday of the month. The events were open to the public and were **the first dances for gays and lesbians at any school**. In the 1980s, more than a thousand people attended the dances, which offered a safe way for gays and lesbians to socialize in the midst of the AIDS crisis.

The dances were great, but gay students wanted a place they could hang out more often. In 1971, a student named Morty Manford asked Columbia for a gay lounge. When the university denied the request, students took over an unused utility closet in the basement of the Furnald Hall dormitory. Twenty-five years later, in 1996, the university finally recognized the lounge, which was named for Stephen Donaldson. That was the pseudonym of the student (real name, Robert Martin) who had approached the administration years earlier about creating a campus group for gays. In 2017—fifty years after formation of the first LGBTQ group on a college campus—the lounge literally came out of the closet, moving to a bright, above-ground location in another Columbia building.

GAY BOOKSTORE

On November 18, 1967, just a few weeks after he turned twenty-seven, Craig Rodwell opened the Oscar Wilde Memorial Bookshop, **the first**

bookstore in America devoted to books by and about gays and lesbians. (*See* the site on Walking Tour 2.) It was a bold move, for several reasons. For starters, Rodwell knew nothing about running a bookstore. He refused to sell pornography, because he wanted the store to promote a positive image of gays. There were so few books and periodicals at the time that he had to spread them out to fill the shelves. That almost didn't matter to the store owner. He envisioned his shop as a gathering place for homosexuals. Indeed it was, being one site where organizers planned the first gay pride parade (*see* Gay Pride in the Parades section).

Rodwell moved the bookstore a few blocks away, to the heart of the gay community on Christopher Street, in 1973. That store remained open until March 2009, when weak sales during the economic recession forced the Oscar Wilde Memorial Bookshop to close.

Birth of the Gay Rights Movement

Until the 1960s or thereabouts, most people who identified as LGBTQ tried to keep a low profile. Gatherings usually were quiet, local events. That changed in the summer of 1969. What became known as the Stonewall Rebellion is widely considered **the first major event in the modern gay rights movement**.

The Stonewall Inn was (and still is) a well-known gay bar on Christopher Street in Greenwich Village. Police frequently raided gay bars, so patrons were not surprised when the NYPD stormed Stonewall in the wee hours of Saturday, June 28, 1969. What was surprising was the reaction of the patrons and the growing crowd just outside the bar. Instead of cooperating with the police and dispersing as they usually did, the crowd resisted and even attacked police who tried to arrest some bar-goers and unruly protesters.

For several nights, demonstrators congregated outside the Stonewall Inn, spilling into the park across the way and onto nearby streets. The LGBTQ community was making a bold statement: We have rights too! At one point, the police fled into the bar for protection against the angry crowd.

Emboldened by the New York City experience, LGBTQ enclaves across the country began to organize. The Stonewall Rebellion had given birth to a new civil rights movement.

The next year, the Christopher Street Liberation Day March marked the first anniversary of the Stonewall Rebellion. The march subsequently became the annual Pride Parade, which is held not just in New York but around the world. (*See* Gay Pride in the Parades section.)

Thirty years after the uprising, the area around the Stonewall Inn was listed on the National Register of Historic Places. It has received other honors by the city, state, and federal governments. On June 24, 2016, President Barak Obama bestowed national monument status on the Stonewall Inn and Christopher Park, where the protesting crowd had gathered. (*See* these sites on Walking Tour 2.)

SUPPORT GROUPS

One duo caught a lot of eyes during the 1972 Christopher Street Liberation Day March, the forerunner of the gay pride parade (*see* Gay Pride in the Parades section). The duo comprised a middle-aged woman and her college-aged son. She was Jeanne Manford, and her son was Morty Manford, who a year earlier had asked administrators at Columbia University for space for a gay student lounge (*see* Gay Student Activities in this section). Many young people approached Mrs. Manford during the march and asked her to talk to their parents, perhaps hoping that someday their mothers and fathers would be so supportive that they too would walk side by side during a public event for gays.

Although being there for her son came naturally to the elementary school teacher, Jeanne Manford realized that other parents might need help accepting their children for who they were. On March 26, 1973, she held the initial meeting of **the first support group for parents of gay people**. About twenty people attended. The group grew, sprouted up across the country, and eventually became known as Parents, Families, and Friends of Lesbians and Gays. In 2014, it officially changed its name to PFLAG. The organization now has hundreds of chapters in the United States and has expanded its mission to educating the public, assuring safe schools for LGBTQ students, and advocating for LGBTQ rights and equality.

About a year after Manford held her first support group meeting, Dr. Fritz Klein, a bisexual psychiatrist, put an ad in the *Village Voice*, a popular weekly newspaper (*see* Weekly Alternative Newspaper in the Media section), seeking people interested in getting together to talk about bisexuality. The weekly discussions quickly turned into **the first support group for bisexuals**, which Klein called the Bisexual Forum. Fifteen to twenty people attended each week. Klein ran the New York group from 1974 to 1982, when he moved to San Diego and organized a similar Bisexual Forum there.

Domestic Partner Benefits

Should companies offer their employees' domestic partners—people who live together in a committed relationship but are not married—the same benefits they offer employees' spouses? For many years, every employer answered this question the same way: Absolutely not!

In 1982, the *Village Voice*, a weekly alternative newspaper in New York City (*see* Weekly Alternative Newspaper in the Media section), became **the first company in the nation to offer domestic partner benefits** to its gay and lesbian employees. This groundbreaking achievement resulted from contract negotiations with the employees' union (oddly, the United Auto Workers, which would seem to have little in common with newspaper staff).

Although other alternative newspapers looked up to and tried to emulate the *Voice* in its approach to journalism, few companies of any sort chose to follow its lead in extending benefits to domestic partners. By 1990, only about twenty companies in the United States offered "perks" to their employees' domestic partners that were similar to benefits for spouses.

The trend changed in the 1990s, with more and more employers adding domestic partner benefits, whether for same-sex or opposite-sex couples or both. By early in the twenty-first century, companies that did not recognize domestic partnerships by offering corporate benefits risked losing workers to the many firms that did have such perks. Then, as cries for universal health care coverage in the United States grew strong, the possibility of major changes to the employer-based health care insurance system put a big question mark over the entire issue of domestic partner benefits. Stay tuned!

Media

NEW YORK IS OFTEN CONSIDERED THE MEDIA CAPITAL OF THE UNITED States, although Los Angeles (with its Hollywood studios) and Silicon Valley (with its digital media enterprises) might disagree. Without a doubt, however, New York City led the nation with traditional media. Over the years, more than 100 newspapers have been published in this city. Many had short runs, but other papers celebrated their centennial

Jacob Riis's "Lodgers in a Crowded Bayard Street Tenement," 1889. His photography captured the deplorable conditions of tenement life and was a major advance in photojournalism.

anniversaries and beyond. As a newspaper town, New York has been an innovator in this type of media, introducing new forms of journalism (such as the penny press and the alternative newspaper), adding new features (like photographs and comic strips), and reaching untapped audiences (including Black and working-class readers).

New York City was also a pioneer in electronic media in the first half of the twentieth century. The city had experimental stations that tried out various types of programming, including public radio and televised sports. New York radio and television stations aired the first commercials. This was in an era when *media* implied something to be heard or seen, rather than something to foster connections (à la social media).

NEWSPAPER BY AND FOR AFRICAN AMERICANS

Before radio and television, long before the internet, people stayed informed through newspapers. There was no shortage of newspapers in early America, but until 1827 none of them was produced by and specifically addressed issues of interest to Black Americans.

On March 16, 1827, the inaugural issue of *Freedom's Journal*, **the first African American newspaper**, rolled off the presses. The editors were Samuel Cornish and John Russwurm, both free-born men of mixed Black ancestry. They produced a weekly four-page, four-column paper filled with local, national, and foreign news, as well as educational and opinion pieces.

Cornish and Russwurm started the paper mainly to give expression to viewpoints about issues affecting their people that might be different from opinions expressed in other newspapers. The editors saw the paper as an educating, uplifting, and unifying force among Black communities. Although published in New York, *Freedom's Journal* was distributed and read far beyond the city's borders, even in Canada and the Caribbean.

Just six months after beginning *Freedom's Journal*, Cornish left the publication. He had a falling-out with Russwurm, who was using the paper to promote African colonization, that is, the return of free Black Americans to their ancestral homeland overseas. Like Cornish, many subscribers to the newspaper opposed the idea of African colonization, and the paper's readership dropped. After only two years, the last issue of *Freedom's Journal* appeared. Russwurm then acted on his beliefs and moved to Liberia, where he edited the first Black newspaper there and became governor of a colony for free Blacks.

Although *Freedom's Journal* was short lived, it set a precedent. By the start of the Civil War, more than forty newspapers in the United States were owned and operated by Black Americans.

PENNY PRESS

Newspapers in the early nineteenth century were read mainly by the well-to-do, who could afford the subscription cost of six cents an issue and were interested in serious reports that jibed with their political leanings. In 1833, publisher Benjamin Day came up with a novel idea for a newspaper. His *New York Sun* featured stories meant to appeal to the common man at a price that also appealed, just one cent a copy. The *Sun* was **the first successful penny paper**, and it revolutionized the newspaper industry.

The *Sun* ran reports from police blotters and featured scandalous stories. The public loved these tales and eagerly handed over a penny a day to newsboys hawking the paper on street corners. That was another *Sun* innovation, because until then distribution was limited to subscription sales. To help offset costs, the *Sun* took advertising (which often looked exactly like the news reporting). The new content and distribution immediately proved successful. Circulation reached 5,000 within six months and then doubled within the year. Another year later, circulation had doubled yet again.

The *Sun* was an early publisher of fake news (a mantra much later of the Donald Trump presidency). The most famous report, serialized in 1835, was the Great Moon Hoax. Supposedly, a respected astronomer had discovered life on the moon—water bodies, vegetation, unusual animals, mythical beings like unicorns, and half-human winged creatures. The story captured the public's imagination and helped drive circulation higher. Other papers, some as far away as Europe, picked up the story. But some publications debunked it, including a new penny paper that was the *Sun*'s rival, the *New York Herald*.

In its own way, the *Herald* was as innovative as the *Sun*. At a time when Americans were hungry for news from abroad, the founding publisher of the *Herald*, James Gordon Bennett, sent reporters to sea to get stories from ships coming from Europe. Then he went even closer to the source. In 1838, the *Herald* became **the first American newspaper with foreign correspondents**. (For an interesting story about Bennett's son, who eventually took over the *Herald*, *see* Transatlantic Yacht Race in the Sports section.)

The New York penny press was very popular in the 1830s, with more than thirty newspapers hitting the streets. Only the *Sun* and *Herald* had long runs, however. The idea that ordinary people wanted to read titillating stories in an inexpensive daily caught on in other East Coast cities, including Boston, Philadelphia, and Baltimore.

PHOTOJOURNALISM

While photography was still in its infancy, a few New Yorkers who were good with a camera recognized that it had the potential to change the way people saw and understood the world. One of the most famous nineteenth-century photographers was Mathew Brady. Praised for his studio portraits of presidents and other leaders, Brady organized a team of photographers to go to battlefields during the Civil War and capture the realities of warfare. These images, reproduced in the New York-based magazine *Harper's Weekly*, were **the first photographs of an American war**, in all of its horror and honor. (The Romanian photographer Carol Szathmari had created similar pictures of the Crimean War a decade earlier.)

Brady self-financed his Civil War photography project, which cost him a small fortune, almost $100,000. He never recovered financially, and he was nearly destitute when he died in 1896. Later—too late for Brady—the Library of Congress acquired more than 1,500 of the Brady Studio's Civil War negatives.

Printing techniques caused challenges for the publication of early photographs. The presses of the mid-nineteenth century could not print actual photographs such as the Civil War scenes; the photos had to be converted to sketches or engravings. Photojournalism took a major leap forward on March 4, 1880, with **the first publication of an actual photograph in a newspaper**, the *Daily Graphic*. This New York paper was **the first illustrated daily newspaper**. Published between 1873 and 1889, the *Daily Graphic* included photographs, cartoons, drawings, and, for several years, a daily weather map.

A newspaper beat was how another famous photojournalist, Jacob Riis, got his start. Capturing on camera the deplorable conditions of tenement life on New York's Lower East Side, Riis often worked at night and was probably **the first photographer to use flash powder to shoot dark scenes**. His photos were startling, sad, and accurate pictures illustrating the need for social reform—something that many New Yorkers had heard about but had never been able to visualize until they saw Riis' photographs. His photos appeared in newspapers and magazines starting around 1888. A large collection of Riis' photos formed the heart of his famous book *How the Other Half Lives*, which was published in 1890.

NEWSPAPER COMIC STRIPS

Starting in the mid-1800s, some magazines regularly featured cartoons and caricatures. Think of the British humor magazine *Punch* and Thomas Nast's political cartoons, often about New York City's Boss Tweed, in *Harper's Weekly*. But illustrated humor was uncommon in newspapers until 1896. To understand how single-panel cartoons grew into newspaper comic strips, you need to follow the bouncing ball from one rival New York newspaper to another and back and forth again.

It began in February 1896. Joseph Pulitzer, publisher of the *New York World*, tested the yellow in his new color press with a single-panel cartoon by Richard F. Outcault. The star of the cartoon was a tot in a bright yellow nightshirt who lived in the slums of New York. The Yellow Kid, as this cartoon character became known, wore the same shirt in subsequent issues. Well, not exactly the same, because different snarky messages appeared on the shirt.

Readers loved the Yellow Kid, so much that William Randolph Hearst, owner of the rival *New York Journal*, had to have the character for his paper. In October, less than a year after the Yellow Kid was born, Hearst lured Outcault to the *Journal* with a better deal: more money and the opportunity to showcase his talent and tell a story in a series of connected panels. This was **the first newspaper comic strip**.

Did I mention that Pulitzer and Hearst were rivals? Not to be outdone by his arch-enemy, Pulitzer offered Outcault even more money. Hearst retaliated by outpricing Pulitzer yet again. Finally, Pulitzer decided to stop the game. He hired another cartoonist, George Luks, to draw his version of the Yellow Kid for the *World*.

The Yellow Kid inspired a new term for the kind of newspapers where the comic strip appeared. Both the *World* and the *Journal* would do anything to sell papers, and what sold best was scandal, sensationalism, even stories that stretched the truth. The style of these newspapers became known as yellow journalism.

After more than ten years at the *Journal*, Outcault defected to another competing newspaper, the *New York Herald*. He created a new comic strip for that paper in 1902. This comic had a more upscale boy who was always getting into mischief. The boy's name was Buster Brown; he had a sidekick named Mary Jane and a dog named Tige. The Brown Shoe Company licensed the characters and created a marketing slogan about Buster Brown and his little dog Tige who lived in a shoe. Although Outcault's comic strip disappeared long ago, Mary Jane and Buster Brown shoes for children survived into the twenty-first century.

WEEKLY ALTERNATIVE NEWSPAPER

In 1955, three men who called Greenwich Village home—Norman Mailer, Dan Wolf, and Ed Fancher—decided to publish a different kind of newspaper. It would come out weekly and have a local slant so far as news was concerned. It would provide thorough coverage of the New York arts and culture scenes. Without an ideological slant or political affiliation, it could dig deep into its stories and take an irreverent tone. Financially, it would depend on advertising revenue, including classified ads, rather than readers' purchases. So began the *Village Voice*, **the first weekly alternative newspaper in America**.

It was tough going at first. Although the founders intended the *Voice* to be a profit-making venture, the paper operated in the red for about a decade. But readers loved the *Voice* and made it one of the highest-circulating newspapers in the country. As Louis Menand wrote in a 2009 issue of *The New Yorker*, "The *Voice* was the medium through which a mainstream middle-class readership stayed in touch with its inner bohemian. It was the ponytail on the man in the gray flannel suit."

Other cities across America followed the *Voice*'s lead, creating papers that emphasized their local interests, highlighted their cultural assets, did investigative reporting, and aired viewpoints that might not be accepted elsewhere—all for the newsstand price of, well, nothing. The Association of Alternative Newsmedia, an organization for publications like the *Voice*, now has about 100 member papers in North America.

In the new millennium, many newspapers struggled to stay alive, and the *Voice* was no exception. Staff left after ownership changes and again as the final print edition came out in September 2017. A year later, the granddaddy of all alt-weeklies announced that its online operation was also coming to an end. But did it? Check out www.villagevoice.com, and you may be surprised.

PUBLIC RADIO BROADCAST

Opera is standard fare on public radio stations, so it is not surprising that **the first public radio broadcast** was an opera. Two, actually: *Cavalleria Rusticana* and *Pagliacci*, which often are performed together. The broadcast came live from New York City's Metropolitan Opera House on January 13, 1910. Mind you, radio was almost unknown at the time. Federally funded National Public Radio, which many people consider synonymous with opera-airing stations, was not created until 1969. But the 1910 broadcast from the Metropolitan Opera is universally recognized as the first public radio broadcast, that is, the first that the public could hear if they were within earshot of a radio receiver.

Lee De Forest, inventor of an electrical amplification device similar to a radio tube, had set up transmitting equipment in the Opera House, where the legendary Enrico Caruso was among the performers. De Forest also had positioned receivers in various locations, including his own radio laboratory, several Times Square hotels, and ships in New York Harbor. The broadcast was to be considered an experiment, what we might call proof of concept.

De Forest was wise to forewarn listeners that the broadcast might not be perfect. To avoid interference from radiotelegraph operators, he had asked them not to transmit during the broadcast. At least one operator, however, forgot or simply ignored the request, and the static of Morse code periodically drowned out the singing voices. But the experiment was a success in that people on a ship more than twelve miles away could hear the transmission—music, Morse code, and all.

RADIO COMMERCIAL

In the Roaring Twenties, technological advances and labor-saving devices created leisure time that Americans had never enjoyed before. Radio was one way to fill those leisure hours. The first real (not experimental) radio broadcast was in Pittsburgh on November 2, 1920—Election Day. If you were lucky enough to be near a radio, you didn't need to wait for the next edition of the newspaper to learn that Warren G. Harding had won the presidential race by a landslide.

From then, radio purchases and programming took off like wildfire. Within a few years, almost every home in America had a radio, and about 600 radio stations were on the air across the country.

Trust New Yorkers to monetize a popular pastime. Less than two years after the initial Pittsburgh broadcast, on August 28, 1922, a New York radio station, WEAF (later WNBC), ran **the first radio commercial**. It was for a new apartment complex in Jackson Heights, Queens, and it lasted a full ten minutes. Can you imagine listeners today staying tuned to a commercial for ten minutes? But the novelty of the radio and the allure of the multibuilding Hawthorne Court apartments, with just two units per floor and a private interior courtyard, kept listeners glued to their sets.

The ad, which cost $50 for the ten minutes, must have been effective, because the developer of Hawthorne Court bought more air time. Other companies quickly followed. Not only was radio a great unifying force among Americans; it also was going to be a good way to reach customers. The young radio industry embraced a new revenue source: advertising.

Televised Sports

Are you or do you know a football widow? Have you ever stayed up late watching the NCAA finals? Did you see Michael Phelps win his record-breaking number of Olympic medals? If you can answer "yes" to any of these questions, you probably cannot imagine a world without televised sports.

The broadcast sports pioneer was NBC's experimental television station in New York City, W2XBS. It made history in 1939 when it aired a variety of professional and college ball games. At the time, only about 400 to 500 homes in New York had television sets. But the World's Fair was taking place in Queens, and the RCA Pavilion there proudly displayed the capability of this new-fangled invention called television.

As an experimental station, W2XBS began slowly. It aired **the first college baseball game on television** in May 1939, between Columbia and Princeton universities. With only one camera on Columbia's Baker Field, the broadcast was a flop. A few months later, on August 26, 1939, the station used two cameras to broadcast **the first professional baseball game on television**. Or perhaps I should say games, because the show was a double-header between the Brooklyn Dodgers and the Cincinnati Reds. The use of two cameras, one in the visitors' dugout in Ebbets Field in Brooklyn and the other in the stands behind home plate, made for better coverage. Red Barber, whose voice was familiar to Dodgers' fans as a radio announcer, filled in what the cameras missed.

On October 22 of the same year, W2XBS aired **the first televised professional football game**. Ebbets Field was the scene once again, and this time the Brooklyn Dodgers football team (not to be confused with the baseball team by the same name) hosted the Philadelphia Eagles. It was a two-camera broadcast, with one camera in box seats on the 40-yard line and the other in mezzanine seating. From time to time the sun went behind clouds and the picture became so dark that the broadcast became sound only—essentially radio rather than television.

That fall, the experimental television station also went back to college. **The first televised college football game** was between Fordham University and Wayne State University and was played on Randall's Island in the East River. Fordham and the University of Pittsburgh played **the first**

televised college basketball game on February 28, 1940, at Madison Square Garden. It was immediately followed by a game between New York University and Georgetown University.

Incidentally, home turf was not necessarily an advantage for most of these games. The New York City teams may not have been big winners, but they helped paved the way for televised sports.

Fast forward a few years, to September 1947. The World Series that year was an all-NYC event, between the Yankees and the Dodgers. More than 73,000 fans poured into Yankee Stadium on opening day, September 30. Millions more listened to the game on the radio. And in New York, Philadelphia, Albany, and Washington, thousands filled bars to watch **the first televised World Series**. It was a history-making event for another reason too. Jackie Robinson, **the first Black major-league baseball player**, was in the Dodgers' camp. (*See* Jackie Robinson in the Sports section for more about his first-of-their-kind achievements.) The Yankees won the first game and continued to take the series.

TELEVISION COMMERCIALS

Almost one quarter of a typical hour-long TV show isn't the show itself but commercial time. Advertisers spend thousands of dollars—millions during big-audience events like the Super Bowl—for a brief chance to entice television viewers.

That's a big difference from **the first TV commercial**, a ten-second ad for Bulova, the Queens-based watch company. It cost Bulova a mere $9. The commercial aired on July 1, 1941, just before a baseball game at Ebbets Field, home turf of the Brooklyn Dodgers, who were playing against Philadelphia. By today's standards, the commercial was quite simple. A still graphic of a watch centered on a map of the United States (in black and white, of course, in those early days of television) and five spoken words: "America runs on Bulova time!"

After that first commercial, many companies took to television to promote their products. Because advertisers targeted people with money to spend, more than a decade passed before the appearance of **the first commercial on television aimed at children**. The toy was Mr. Potato Head, which had been invented by a New Yorker named George Lerner (*see* Mr. Potato Head in the Toys, Games, and Other Diversions section). The commercial aired on April 30, 1952, the day before the toy went on sale. Within a year, more than a million Mr. Potato Head kits were in little tykes' hands. Ah, the power of television!

Museums and Exhibitions

NEW YORK IS A MUSEUM TOWN. DEPENDING ON HOW YOU DEFINE "museum," the city has between sixty and one hundred of these cultural institutions. Some, like the Metropolitan Museum of Art, are large and world famous. Many more are small and have yet to be discovered by a wide audience. Some New York museums are the first of their kind in America. These include a children's museum, Jewish museum, museums

The Crystal Palace, home of the first world's fair in America, 1853.

for particular genres (modern art, posters), and museums on subjects not usually thought of as meriting a cultural institution (sex; food; and radio, television, and movies).

In addition to permanent museums, New York also has hosted temporary exhibitions, essentially short-lived displays of museum-quality art, technological achievements, or the best of the best. The city was the first American location for some of these extravaganzas, including a world's fair, cat show, and car show. Temporary exhibitions in New York have introduced Americans to modern art and showcased other art forms, including minimalism.

When it comes to museums and temporary cultural exhibitions, New York City truly has something for everyone.

WORLD'S FAIR

The first world's fair, in London in 1851, showcased the accomplishments of European nations, especially England's prowess in the Industrial Age. Not to be outdone, the United States decided to host a world's fair soon afterward. The goal: to demonstrate that this young nation had as much to boast about as the great countries of Europe with their hundreds of years of history and culture. New York City was the site of **the first world's fair in America**, which ran from July 1853 to November 1854.

The United States didn't steal just the idea of a world's fair from England; it also stole its design. London's exposition was in a magnificent glass and iron structure dubbed the Crystal Palace. New York had its own version of the Crystal Palace, a huge glass and iron building in the shape of a Greek cross, with an enormous dome in the center. The structure alone was a big attraction. So were the paintings, sculptures, and myriad exhibits demonstrating the official name of the fair, Exhibition of the Industry of All Nations. The fair also offered occasional sideshows, as it were, the most dramatic being Elisha Otis's initial demonstration of the elevator safety brake (*see* Elevators and Escalators in the Inventions section).

After the fair closed, visitors continued to come to the Crystal Palace, which was in the present Bryant Park behind the New York Public

Library (*see* the site on Walking Tour 4). The exhibition space was still attracting crowds four years later when fire broke out. The Crystal Palace, which had been thought to be fireproof, clearly wasn't. The building burned to nothing in just twenty minutes.

The United States has hosted quite a few world's fairs since the first one. Some of the most memorable are the 1876 Centennial Exhibition in Philadelphia (celebrating the hundredth birthday of this country), the 1893 World's Columbian Exposition in Chicago (which introduced the Ferris wheel and had the nickname in the second half of the title of the best-selling book *The Devil in the White City*), the 1904 fair in St. Louis (popularized in the Judy Garland movie *Meet Me in St. Louis*), and the 1962 Century 21 Exposition in Seattle (which brought the Space Needle to that city). New York was the scene of important world's fairs in Queens in 1939-40 (where television was demonstrated; [*see* Televised Sports in the Media section]) and in 1964-65. The last world's fair in the United States was in New Orleans in 1984.

CATS AND CARS

Sorry, cat fanciers. The dog show came first. And the Brits beat the Americans on both counts.

I'm referring to the large-scale shows where dogs or cats are judged by accepted standards for their breed.

The first formal dog show took place in England in 1859. The initial dog show in America was in Chicago fifteen years later. The popularity of dog exhibitions led to similar shows for cats. London was the scene of the first cat show, in 1871. **The first cat show in America** was in New York in 1895.

The American cat display took place in Stanford White's magnificent Madison Square Garden. (*See* the site on Walking Tour 3.) A full square block, this huge edifice, unlike the current arena of the same name, actually was at Madison Square, at East 26th Street. The Garden was the scene of many large exhibitions, sporting events, and musical and theatrical performances—and one of the most talked-about murders in New York City history. More on that later.

Five years after the initial cat show, in 1900, Madison Square Garden was the venue for **the first automobile show**. Some 48,000 visitors came to see the finest in a new industry. On display at this exhibition were 160 vehicles, including some of a type still considered cutting-edge more than a hundred years later: electric cars.

Both the cat and car shows predated the famous murder at Madison Square Garden. The architect of this showplace, Stanford White, was quite a philanderer. One of his paramours was a teenage actress and model named Evelyn Nesbit. By the time she married Harry Thaw in 1905, Nesbit and the much older White were no longer an item. But that didn't temper Thaw's hatred of the architect. On June 25, 1906, White was enjoying a performance at Madison Square Garden when Harry Thaw fatally shot him. He died on the spot in one of his architectural masterpieces. Thaw's trial, sometimes dubbed "the trial of the century" (as was the O. J. Simpson trial at the end of the same century), kept the tabloids busy for years.

Children's Museum

Look but don't touch! That's a warning children hear all the time. Adults hear it too, usually worded more politely, in places with priceless and delicate objects such as museums. Sometimes those are the very places where the urge to touch is greatest. Especially for little hands.

To satisfy that urge and give children a different way of learning, a new type of museum opened in the Bedford Park neighborhood of Crown Heights, Brooklyn, in 1899. The Brooklyn Children's Museum was **the first museum in the world designed specifically for children**. Emphasizing hands-on experiences, the museum offered participatory exhibits where youngsters could interact with the displays. Early exhibitions featured natural history specimens and models of birds, insects, shells, and minerals.

The original home of the museum was a stately Victorian mansion. The Brooklyn Children's Museum now is in a larger facility in the same general location. In a city of museums, it is New York's first LEED-certified green museum. The permanent collection comprises about

30,000 cultural and natural science objects. Interactive exhibits designed to appeal to youngsters remain the draw.

The benefits of a children's museum caught on slowly. One opened in Boston in 1913 and another in Detroit four years later. These days, more than 300 children's museums can be found throughout the world. And it all began in Brooklyn.

JEWISH MUSEUM

When a group is victim of attacks bordering on genocide, symbolic objects and cultural artifacts are as much at risk of annihilation as are the people. Perhaps the desire to preserve religious objects and art, given a history of anti-Semitism and waves of pogroms, helped spur the creation of Jewish museums in a few European cities in the late nineteenth century. So the concept of a Jewish museum was not new in 1904 when Mayer Sulzberger, a Philadelphia judge, donated twenty-five ceremonial art objects to the Jewish Theological Seminary in New York. This was the beginning of **the first Jewish museum in America**.

The collection grew, and so did the Jewish Museum's home. In 1944, the widow of a prominent Jewish philanthropist, Felix Warburg, donated her Upper East Side mansion to house the Jewish Museum. The home was on Fifth Avenue, where several other museums (including the Metropolitan Museum of Art) were already located and where others would soon appear, some—like the Jewish Museum—in former mansions. The Warburg mansion has undergone several expansions and now holds some 30,000 objects of global Jewish significance, ranging from ancient artifacts to contemporary pieces. The Jewish Museum also hosts special exhibitions, such as the minimalism shows described later in this section (*see* Minimalism, below).

The New York institution was once the only Jewish museum in America. Now there are upwards of seventy. Some concentrate on the Holocaust. Some collections are small enough to be housed in synagogues. Without question, though, New York led the way for Jewish museums throughout America.

MODERN ART

Imagine a large group of people seeing modern art for the first time—people who were accustomed to classical art, to realism, to something you can look at and immediately recognize.

That actually happened when the International Exhibition of Modern Art opened in New York City on February 17, 1913. Commonly called the Armory Show because it took place in the cavernous 69th Regiment Armory, this was **the first exhibition of modern art in America**. (*See* the Armory on Walking Tour 3.)

A group of young artists called the Association of American Painters and Sculptors organized the show. Their main goal was to introduce Americans to contemporary European art and artists, although the show was broader than that. It comprised more than 1,200 works by some 300 artists from Europe and the United States, including some familiar painters in more traditional styles. The works that sent shock waves through the American art world were by avant-garde Europeans little known in this country, including Picasso, Matisse, and Duchamp. The single most talked-about item was Marcel Duchamp's painting in the Cubist genre, *Nude Descending a Staircase*. You either loved it, or you hated it.

Perhaps fear of missing out caused New Yorkers to flock to the Armory. During the month the exhibition was there, about 87,000 people went to see it. Then the exhibition traveled to Chicago and Boston, attracting large crowds and much controversy. The age-old question "What is art?" took on new significance as Americans had their initial experiences with modern art.

Before long, several wealthy New Yorkers decided that the type of works displayed at the Armory Show were indeed art. These movers and shakers assembled private collections, which they subsequently turned into museums. A. E. Gallatin moved his collection to the Gallery of Living Art at New York University in December 1927. Two years later, the Museum of Modern Art (MOMA) opened with the backing of Abby Aldrich Rockefeller and two friends. (*See* MOMA on Walking Tour 4.) Both of these institutions claim to be **the first modern art museum in America**. We won't quibble about which should be called the first; it's enough to say that the first modern art museum in America was in

New York City. These museums showcased the work of Americans as well as Europeans. **The first museum dedicated strictly to living American artists** was the Whitney Museum of American Art, which Gertrude Vanderbilt Whitney began in 1931 with hundreds of works from her private collection. (*See* the original building on Walking Tour 2.) She had previously offered her collection to the Metropolitan Museum of Art, which declined it. Your loss, Met!

MINIMALISM
Bold geometric forms. Usually three-dimensional. An object without an emotional message, revealing nothing about the artist and conjuring nothing but itself. Made from manufactured or industrial materials, like fiberglass, plastic, tiles, even fluorescent light tubes. These are the hallmarks of minimalism, a genre that emerged in the early 1960s. Like most other art movements of the mid-twentieth century, minimalism flourished in New York City.

In the spring of 1966, the Jewish Museum on Fifth Avenue (*see* Jewish Museum in this section) held **the first group exhibition of minimalism,** called Primary Structures. Artists with works in the show included Carl Andre, Dan Flavin, Donald Judd, Sol LeWitt, Walter De Maria, and Robert Morris. The earliest pieces in the exhibition were *Free Ride* by Tony Smith and *Peach Wheels* by Tim Scott, both completed in 1962.

This groundbreaking exhibition had a second life, so to speak, in 2014, when the Jewish Museum mounted a new exhibition called Other Primary Structures. The original Primary Structures show included works only by American and British sculptors. The reprise featured works also created in the 1960s but by artists from other countries, demonstrating the global reach of the minimalist movement. A highlight of the 2014 show was a ten-foot-tall scale model of the 1966 exhibition, complete with miniature versions of the art works.

TV, RADIO, AND MOVIES
People often don't realize that something is worth saving for history's sake until it's too late. That was the case in the early days of broadcast radio and television. Programming was ephemeral, heard or seen only

once. A few private collectors and the major networks had small archives, but these were for personal use only.

Then CBS founder William S. Paley realized that radio and television stations were throwing away their past. In 1975, Paley created the Museum of Broadcasting, **the first museum of radio and television in the world**. The museum opened the next year in a Midtown Manhattan office building, and its initial collection of 718 broadcasts became available to the public.

The institution has grown by leaps and bounds since then and has had several name changes. In 1991, it became the Museum of Television & Radio. In 2007, it was renamed the Paley Center for Media, in memory of its founder. Between these name changes, a branch opened in Los Angeles. In both cities, visitors can attend public programs and enjoy the 160,000 TV and radio programs and ads in the Paley Center's collection. (*See* the Paley Center on Walking Tour 4.)

New York City also has **the first movie museum in the United States**. The city once had a thriving film industry. In the 1920s, a large studio complex in Astoria, Queens, produced hundreds of silent films and early talkies. The studio later created military training films for World War II. Since 1988, one building in this complex has been home to the Museum of the Moving Image. Its public programming overlaps somewhat with the Paley Center's, because moving images are part and parcel of television as well as movies. The collection of the Museum of the Moving Image totals more than 130,000 items, from costumes to movie theater furnishings to video games. Like the Paley Center, the Museum of the Moving Image also offers public screenings, exhibits, and other programs.

Nobody should ever get bored in New York; there's so much to see and do. But if boredom does strike and you can't decide whether to go somewhere or be a couch potato, head over to the Paley Center or the Museum of the Moving Image. There you can enjoy passive entertainment in a unique New York cultural institution.

LIFE'S PLEASURES

If you find museums too high-brow, in your opinion offering only lofty works of art and esoteric displays of science, you haven't explored New

York's smaller, twenty-first-century museums. Some deal in mundane matters, like food or sex.

That's right, sex. Opened in 2002, the Museum of Sex is **the first museum in the United States devoted to human sexuality**. (Several European cities already had sex museums, and a few other American cities do now.) With a permanent collection of more than 20,000 objects, the New York Museum of Sex attracts both the general public and academics. (*See* it on Walking Tour 3.)

A more recent addition to the cultural scene is the Museum of Food and Drink (MOFAD). Raking in more than $100,000 from Kickstarter (at the time the most ever for a museum from this crowd-funding source), MOFAD began in 2013 with a mobile exhibit called BOOM!, which was about cereal and featured a puffing gun. In 2015, MOFAD found a permanent home in Brooklyn. MOFAD boasts that it is "a new kind of museum that brings the world of food to life with exhibits you can taste, touch, and smell." It is **the first general museum about food and drink** with a brick-and-mortar location. (Some food companies maintain museums about their own history and products, but that's not the same.)

POSTERS

Posters adorn many kids' bedrooms and college dorms. Adults enjoy posters, too, for the way they combine words and pictures to communicate a message and to reflect a moment in society. Whether the purpose is propaganda, advertising, or self-expression, posters may be considered a form of commercial art for the masses.

In June 2019, Poster House opened in Manhattan, **the first museum in the United States dedicated exclusively to posters**. The museum showcases posters from around the world from the late 1800s, when posters first emerged as a popular art form, to the present. The inaugural exhibitions featured the art nouveau posters of European artist Alphonse Mucha and the contemporary work, about a century after Mucha, of the German design group Cyan. After these exhibitions left, the museum mounted shows of posters from the 2017 Women's March, the Japan Red Cross Society, and movies in Ghana. Quite a range!

Poster House is not the first museum in the world dedicated to this art form. That would be the Poster Museum in Warsaw, which opened in 1968. Other cities with poster museums include Prague and Shanghai.

Music

SOME CITIES SPECIALIZE IN A PARTICULAR STYLE OF MUSIC. NEW YORK has always thrived on diversity in music, as well as in many other areas. From minstrel shows to musical comedy, from classical to jazz to rock to hip hop, New York has created or introduced Americans to a variety of musical genres and compositions. Performances have appealed to diverse groups, from the so-called high-brow audiences listening to new

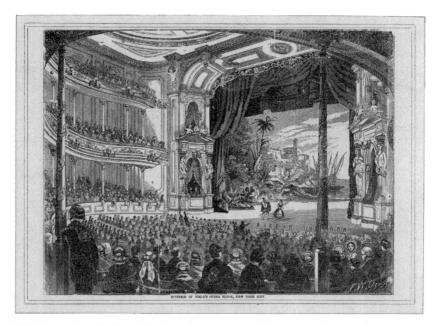

Niblo's Garden, the huge theater where some contenders for first musical comedy, an original American theatrical form, debuted.

symphonies and operas to the common folk laughing at the first musical comedies. New Yorkers haven't just listened to music; they've also sung and danced.

Musical innovations and introductions in New York are as old as colonial times (the first performance of Handel's *Messiah* in America) and as recent as the present century (the first venue in the world specifically designed for jazz). Between those periods, in the nineteenth and twentieth centuries, New Yorkers enjoyed revues and musical comedies; the first rock concert in a stadium; the first rock musical; the Lindy, bebop, and other forms of jazz; early hip hop; and punk. Who knows what will be the next new big thing in New York—that is, American—music?

HANDEL'S *MESSIAH*

Without written documentation, such as a program, we can't know for certain when many musical works were first performed. But we do know the when and the where of **the first performance in America of Handel's *Messiah***. Or rather parts of the oratorio. If we can believe the advertisement. Spoiler alert: we can't.

The date listed in the advertisement in a New York newspaper was Tuesday, January 9, 1770. The time was 6:00 and the place "Mr. Burns's Room." The "Concert of Church Music," as the event was described, was "for the benefit of Mr. Tuckey."

Mr. Tuckey was William Tuckey, a composer of hymns who had worked for four years as clerk at Trinity Church in Manhattan. In this role, he was responsible for leading the singing of psalms and teaching the choir. After he lost the clerk's position (he apparently was fired, but no details are available), he had trouble making a go of it.

Impoverished and owing money to a number of people, Mr. Tuckey came up with an idea: a fund-raising concert. He enticed music-lovers by including selections from a piece never before heard in the colonies (remember, this story takes place before America became the United States). He arranged for performers and secured a venue, a drinking establishment run by a guy named Burns. After Tuckey took out the ad in the newspaper, he heard that some of the people he hoped would attend had other plans for the evening. As a result, he postponed his concert for a week. So much for believing advertisements!

There's no record of how much money the concert brought in, at eight shillings a ticket, or whether it got William Tuckey out of the hole. We do know, however, that he died in September 1781 and was interred at Christ Church Burial Ground in Philadelphia.

MASTER JUBA

Although they would be considered politically incorrect today, minstrel shows were a popular form of entertainment in the mid- to late-1800s. Men in blackface sang, danced, and told jokes in stereotyped imitation of slaves on southern plantations. The performers were always white men, usually Irish—until 1838, when **the first Black man performed in a minstrel show**. His birth name was William Henry Lane, but he was known by his stage name, Master Juba.

Born a free man in Rhode Island, Master Juba honed his craft in Manhattan's notorious Five Points neighborhood, an impoverished Irish enclave. After observing the local dances, he added the steps and rhythms of Irish jigs, reels, and clog dancing to traditional African American body drumming, foot stamping, and shuffling. Master Juba's unique style is often viewed as **the first tap dancing** in America.

In 1842, the English novelist Charles Dickens made a trip to the United States and went slumming in Five Points. In his book *American Notes*, he described Master Juba's performance at Almack's Dance Hall, where he regularly entertained: "Single shuffle, double shuffle, cut and cross-cut; snapping his fingers, rolling his eyes, turning in his knees, presenting the backs of his legs in front, spinning about on his toes and heels like nothing but the man's fingers on the tambourine; dancing with two left legs, two right legs, two wooden legs, two wire legs, two spring legs—all sorts of legs and no legs—what is this to him? And in what walk of life, or dance of life, does man ever get such stimulating applause as thunders about him, when, having danced his partner off her feet, and himself too, he finishes by leaping gloriously on the bar-counter, and calling for something to drink."

Such energetic performing took its toll. Master Juba died in 1852, when he was only twenty-seven years old. He was living in Europe at the time, where his performances drew enthusiastic praise.

Musical Comedy

Experts generally agree that the musical comedy originated in America. They disagree, however, about what was the first show in this genre. Whatever it was, it opened on Broadway; in other words, **the first musical comedy** was staged in New York.

The main reason for the dispute about the first is the lack of a clear definition of *musical comedy*. This type of entertainment didn't spring up out of nowhere; it was part of a continuum. Predecessors included comic opera, minstrel shows, vaudeville, burlesque, follies, and musical revues. Early entries in the musical comedy category incorporated elements of these genres to varying degrees. The creators referred to their works by various names, but they usually did not call them musical comedy.

The earliest contender for musical comedy was *The Black Crook*, which opened on Broadway in 1866. Playwright Charles M. Barras based his drama on older works, including Faust, and incorporated fairies and black magic (hence the name of the play). William Wheatley, manager of Niblo's Garden, the theater that had booked the melodrama, intended to enliven the show with songs. Shortly before opening day, a tragedy turned serendipitous for the production. The elegant Academy of Music suffered a disastrous fire, leaving a French ballet troupe stuck in New York without a place to perform. Wheatley recruited them and produced a show with a plot, singing, and dancing. The extravaganza was a big hit with audiences, which included patrons of serious theater and opera as well as lovers of burlesque. *The Black Crook* opened on September 12, 1866, and ran for sixteen months—an unheard-of accomplishment in those days.

Some contend that *The Black Crook* was an accidental creation, not an intentional innovation in a new genre. Could the real first musical comedy have been *Evangeline, or the Belle of Acadia*? Creators Edward E. Rice and J. Cheever Goodwin produced an original score for what they variously called an American burlesque, American opéra bouffe, or American extravaganza; they emphasized American, because the show was based on Longfellow's poem "Evangeline." The show opened in Niblo's Garden in 1874.

Or was the first musical comedy *The Mulligan Guard Ball?* Written by Ned Harrigan and performed by him and Tony Hart, the show opened in New York in 1879. Harrigan and Hart had previously created comedy acts about lower-class New Yorkers. They used the same characters in this show, the first in a series of full-length musical farces.

The same year that *The Mulligan Guard Ball* debuted, *The Brook* by Nate Salsbury also came to the New York stage. Some experts maintain that this was the first musical comedy. But it was a touring production that had already played in several other cities, so we will ignore it.

CLASSICAL MUSIC

The large classical music organizations in New York City—the New York Philharmonic and the Metropolitan Opera—were not the first of their kind in the United States. But they did premiere many symphonies and operas in this country and even in the world. The lists are too extensive to name but a few examples.

The New York Philharmonic began in 1842 as the Philharmonic Society of New York. The next year, it gave **the first American performances of Beethoven symphonies** No. 3 (*Eroica*) and No. 7. The following year, the Philharmonic premiered Beethoven No. 8, and it introduced Beethoven No. 9 (the choral symphony) to America in 1846. Later, the Philharmonic gave **the first world performances of other classical works**, including Tchaikovsky's Piano Concerto No. 2 (1881) and Dvorak's Symphony No. 9 in E Minor, better known as *From the New World* (1893). The orchestra does not limit itself to the traditional repertoire. Philharmonic audiences have enjoyed **the first world performances of contemporary works**, including compositions by the American composers Leonard Bernstein (1960s and later) and jazz great Wynton Marsalis (1999 and later [*see* Jazz in this section]).

The Metropolitan Opera is younger than the Philharmonic, beginning its life in 1883. Within the first decade, the Met, as it is affectionately known, thrilled American audiences with **the first U.S. performances of several Wagner operas**, including *Die Meistersinger, Tristan und Isolde,*

Siegfried, and *Das Rheingold.* The Met has staged many world premieres, beginning in 1910 with **the first performances ever of some European operas,** Puccini's *La fanciulla del West* and Humperdinck's *Königskinder.*

Enjoyment of opera can be compromised for those not well versed in the language in which it is sung, such as Italian or German. To increase audience appreciation, in 1983 the Canadian Opera Company introduced supertitles, that is, translations that are usually projected above the stage. Later that same year, the New York City Opera became **the first opera company in the United States to use supertitles.**

JAZZ

Jazz had its roots in African and European music. In the United States, these musical traditions combined with American styles, resulting in a new genre. New Orleans is usually considered the birthplace of jazz. So why does a book about New York City firsts merit an entry on jazz? For several reasons.

Both local Black residents and white people looking for a night on the town filled the jazz clubs of Harlem in the 1920s and 1930s. Unlike most clubs, the huge Savoy welcomed revelers of both races. Clubgoers came not just to listen to music, but also to dance. **The first Lindy Hop** was danced sometime in the mid-1920s, but it was not yet called that. During a dance marathon in 1928, the energetic hoofer George "Shorty" Snowden named it in honor of Charles Lindbergh's solo hop across the Atlantic.

One form of jazz—bebop—developed in New York in the 1940s. Minton's Playhouse in Harlem was **the first club to feature bebop.** Well-known performers at this famed club included saxophonist Charlie Parker, trumpeter Dizzy Gillespie, pianist Thelonious Monk, and drummer Max Roach.

Clubs and outdoor festivals used to be the only places people could hear jazz. On rare occasions, jazz musicians performed in concert halls that usually offered classical music. Then in 2004, Jazz at Lincoln Center, **the first venue in the world specifically designed for jazz,** came on the scene. The New York jazz center has several performance spaces, from the intimate Dizzy's Club to the Rose Theater, which seats more than 1,000 people.

The mastermind behind Jazz at Lincoln Center was its first managing and artistic director, Wynton Marsalis. Two decades before the Lincoln Center venue opened, Marsalis became **the first person to win Grammy awards for both classical music and jazz**, a feat he achieved in five consecutive years (1983-1987). In 1997, his oratorio *Blood on the Fields* was **the first jazz work to win a Pulitzer Prize**. Previously, the Pulitzer board had awarded the prize only for classical music, and it had denied a special citation to another New York jazz great, Duke Ellington. After Marsalis's win, Ellington posthumously received a Pulitzer special citation, as did New York jazz masters George Gershwin, Thelonious Monk, and John Coltrane.

New York is a jazz-lovers paradise, with Lincoln Center, clubs throughout the city, and outdoor festivals in the summer. Many a jazz fan discovered the genre by attending a free outdoor program, such as the Charlie Parker Jazz Festival. The various options for jazz fit any budget and assure a future in New York City for this uniquely American form of music.

Stadium Concert

If you were born in the late twentieth century or afterward, you may be surprised to learn that pop and rock concerts have not always taken place in stadiums. That venue seemed ridiculous. Who would fill all those seats? What about acoustics?

A hot, shaggy-haired quartet from England gave it a try on August 15, 1965. The Beatles played **the first rock concert in a stadium**, Shea Stadium in Queens, to be exact.

It was the height of Beatlemania. Young fans scooped up the tickets, grabbing all 55,600 seats in the stadium where the New York Mets baseball team played. Many in attendance could barely see the Fab Four on the stage, which was set up at second base. Nobody could hear, not even the band-mates, because the screams of the audience drowned out the music. The new 100-watt amplifiers were no match for the enthusiastic crowd.

Not only did this concert have record-setting attendance; it also set a world record for gross revenue: $304,000. The Beatles netted $160,000. They then toured the United States, raking in more.

A year later, The Beatles returned to Shea Stadium. Beatle fever was already dying down by then, and maybe some fans who attended the first concert decided not to fork out money for a show they couldn't hear. A lot of seats were empty for the repeat performance, 11,000 of them. The gross revenue was less than in 1965, but The Beatles' cut was bigger, and they left this concert $189,000 richer.

Now that I have told the story of what is usually called the first rock concert in a stadium, I feel obliged to acknowledge another event nine years earlier. On October 11, 1956, Elvis Presley performed at the Cotton Bowl in Dallas. I don't know why this is not considered the first stadium concert. Perhaps it is because the concert was part of the Texas state fair that year. Elvis's audience was much smaller than The Beatles', only about 27,000, which left two thirds of the Bowl's seats empty. Like at The Beatles' concert, the screaming crowds drowned out the music. But Elvis was not discouraged. He launched a world tour the next year, playing in several stadiums.

An interesting footnote. Shea Stadium is no more. Guess who performed there just before the stadium was demolished in 2008? Paul McCartney, one of the two surviving Beatles. The event was a Billy Joel concert, and McCartney joined him at the end of the program, closing with The Beatles' great "Let It Be."

Rock Musical

Theater-goers had never seen anything like it. Oh, maybe they'd seen some aspects of it before, but not all of the daring features rolled into one. It was topical. It was irreverent. It was open about sex and drugs. It had a nude scene. And it had music, but not typical show tunes. This was rock! I'm referring to *Hair*, **the first rock musical**.

Hair debuted on October 17, 1967. It wasn't just opening day for the show; it was opening day for the theater where *Hair* premiered, Joseph Papp's Public Theater in Greenwich Village. (*See* the building on Walking Tour 2.)

After a six-week run at the Public and considerable tinkering, *Hair* moved to Broadway. Although common today for a play to test the waters off-Broadway before opening on The Great White Way, it was unusual in those days. On Broadway, the show really took off, with 1,750 performances. It was nominated for the Best Musical Tony and spawned many touring productions. The Broadway cast album of *Hair* earned top-of-the-charts status.

Hair introduced a new genre in musical theater. Within a few years, theaters were rocking with *Bye Bye Birdie*, *Oh! Calcutta!*, and *Jesus Christ Superstar*. More recent hit rock musicals include *Rent*. It's a genre that's here to stay.

In the summer of 2008, *Hair* made a brief comeback in another Papp venue, the open-air Delacorte Theater in Central Park. Walking home from the show, I found myself surrounded by multigenerational families: grandparents (who were perhaps contemporaries of the original cast members), middle-aged parents, and school-aged children. Regardless of age, everyone was singing songs from the show. I had the sense that the once-controversial *Hair* was now considered as mainstream as a Rodgers and Hammerstein musical. No more shock value, although I did hear one little boy ask, "Were they really naked?"

Hip Hop

Hip hop is associated with urban youth culture, so it seems logical that it was created by an urban youth. That young man was Clive Campbell, better known as DJ Kool Herc. (Herc was short for Hercules, a nickname of the big guy.) Just eighteen years old, he was already an accomplished disc jockey. On August 11, 1973, he served as DJ at his younger sister's back-to-school party in the rec room of their Bronx apartment building. This turned out to be **the first hip hop event**.

DJ Kool Herc did something special at this party, and it was a big hit. At previous DJ gigs, he had noticed that party-goers danced mainly during the break portion of a record, when vocalists were silent and the beat of the music was dominant. To create more time for dancing, Herc put the same record on two turntables and kept switching between them, repeating the break section over and over. Sometimes he or a friend talked over the beat; this was the start of the MC role in hip hop and the style known as rap.

Although DJ Kool Herc is considered the father of hip hop, that term didn't come into popular usage for several years. Meanwhile, the new music genre continued to gain popularity and to evolve. It changed so much that Herc's style is now dubbed old-school hip hop.

It's fitting that the city that gave birth to hip hop is home to a museum about that genre. The Hip Hop Hall of Fame Museum is opening in stages in Harlem in the early 2020s. Part of its mission is to empower youth and encourage social responsibility.

PUNK ROCK

Although the legendary New York club CBGB closed in 2006, it maintains a website (at least it did through 2021). The headline on the About Us page reads "CBGB is the undisputed birthplace of punk." British punk fans might disagree. But without a doubt, in 1975 CBGB was **the first venue in America to feature punk rock**. The Ramones, Patti Smith, Iggy Pop, and other stars of the punk world all performed there.

Punk spoke to the disgruntled youth of the mid-1970s. The music was raucous, energetic, and aggressive. The instrumentation was fast but simple, the vocals often obscene and practically shouted. Black leather, metal spikes and studs, and body piercings were standard attire of punksters. Punk was as much performance art as music.

This form of punk rock was a short-lived craze, lasting about five years. As a result, a common question in the music and culture scene was: "Is punk dead?" Not necessarily. Both exaggerated forms like hardcore and toned-down descendants like pop punk followed.

Parades

New York loves parades, and it always has. The parade frenzy began in colonial times, with Irishmen marching on St. Patrick's Day. Today there is at least one parade in New York almost every weekend from late spring through early fall. People complain about the way parades mess up traffic, but nevertheless they come out in droves to enjoy the festivities.

Special features of the city—tall buildings along narrow streets, creating a canyon effect and, at one time, the abundance of a certain type

Ticker-tape parade for presidential candidate Richard M. Nixon, November 2, 1960. His opponent, John F. Kennedy, had a ticker-tape parade the month before. Kennedy won the election.

of scrap paper—launched a new way to fete parade honorees: ticker-tape parades along the "Canyon of Heroes." Most New York parades, though, don't honor individuals; they celebrate an entire group. Workers, the LGBTQ community, and people of various national backgrounds all enjoyed their first American parades in New York City—and still turn out annually for their special day.

Some well-known parades didn't make this section because they are specific to New York and, in general, qualify more as costumed community gatherings than organized parades. They include the Easter Parade along Fifth Avenue, the Coney Island Mermaid Parade in early summer, and the Greenwich Village Halloween Parade. And don't forget Macy's Thanksgiving Day Parade, a true parade with floats and balloons. Other cities (Philadelphia and Detroit, for example) claim to have had the first, but the big, famous Thanksgiving Day parade is in New York.

ST. PATRICK'S DAY

You may be surprised to learn that the St. Patrick's Day parade did not originate in Ireland. It is an American tradition. More correctly, it should be called a colonial American tradition, because **the first St. Patrick's Day parade** predated the official start of the United States. It took place on March 17, 1762, in New York City. The marchers were Irish soldiers serving in the British army in colonial New York, as well as some Irishmen who had settled there. They realized that being on American soil, they could do something that was forbidden in their homeland. They could proudly wear green and enjoy Irish music as they marched to pipes and drums in honor of the patron saint of Ireland.

In the nineteenth century, as more and more Irish immigrants arrived in New York, St. Patrick's Day festivities grew bigger and bolder. Starting around 1850, the "Irish" 69th Regiment has been the group leading the parade. (*See* the Armory, the 69th Regiment's home base since 1904, on Walking Tour 3.)

Celebrations spread to other cities with large Irish populations, but the New York parade remains the biggest in the nation. Various Irish societies, school bands, Celtic dancers, and bagpipes galore—a good 200,000 participants—march in the parade, which stretches for almost two miles and attracts millions of spectators. As the saying goes, everyone is Irish on St. Patrick's Day.

Two other cities lay claim to the first St. Patrick's Day celebration. In 1737, a group of well-to-do Irishmen living in Boston got together for dinner on March 17 to mark the day. But that wasn't a parade. A Spanish document studied in 2017 suggests that St. Augustine, Florida, was the actual leader, holding a St. Patrick's Day celebration in 1600 and a parade the next year. Since the revelation of this document, St. Augustine has boasted of being the first to mark the occasion. To my knowledge, this claim has not been independently verified.

St. Patrick's Day was a rather staid, religious observance in Ireland until recently. The first parade there was in the twentieth century, in Dublin. Late in the century, the celebration became a multiday affair, but the parade itself is smaller than New York's.

LABOR DAY

How ironic that the city with **the first Labor Day parade** now holds its parade almost a week after the official Labor Day! That's just one of several ironies associated with this holiday in New York.

Labor Day was the brainchild of union organizers in the late nineteenth century. They wanted to celebrate workers and give them a holiday all their own. The organizers designated Tuesday, September 5, 1882, as Labor Day and planned a parade of workers followed by a picnic, concert, and speeches to entertain marchers and their families. About 10,000 workers showed up. The parade began at City Hall and went north to 42nd Street.

New York repeated the event to honor workers the next year. The celebrations here were so successful that other cities soon held their own Labor Day events. Five years after the initial observance in New York City, five states made Labor Day an official holiday. New York was among those states, but ironically it was not the first; Oregon was. In 1894, Congress declared Labor Day a national holiday, to be celebrated on the first Monday in September.

In modern times, Labor Day has taken on a different meaning; it is the unofficial end of summer. Like other Americans, many New Yorkers go out of town to take advantage of a three-day weekend, flock to local beaches, and go shopping for back-to-school necessities. New Yorkers are so busy with their final summer flings that they don't have time for a parade. As a result, the Labor Day parade in New York ironically is no longer on Labor Day; it occurs on the following Saturday.

Final irony: New York does have an annual parade on Labor Day, but it is not to honor American workers. About two million parade-lovers enjoy the colorful, costumed West Indian Day Carnival in Brooklyn. (*See* National Cultural Heritage in this section for more about this and other ethnic parades in New York City.)

TICKER-TAPE PARADE

Nobody had planned to throw things from the windows onto the procession below. It just happened spontaneously. But after that first time, it happened intentionally again and again, at more than 200 parades in New York City since **the first ticker-tape parade** on October 28, 1886.

That initial event was a celebration for the unveiling of the Statue of Liberty. Thousands of workers watched the parade along Broadway from their high-rise Financial District offices. Somebody (no one knows who) picked up a piece of ticker tape, the inch-wide paper ribbon with up-to-the-minute stock prices, and tossed it out the window. The streamer must have looked nice as it floated down, leading somebody else to fling out another strip of ticker tape. Soon ticker tape was filling the sky and littering the ground. A new tradition was born.

The tradition has changed out of necessity, as ticker tape is a thing of the past. Now the parade route gets showered with confetti and shredded paper. A spinoff of this change is that "ticker-tape parades" can be held in any city with tall buildings along the route.

Since 1919, the mayor of New York has decided when a ticker-tape parade will occur here. Some mayors were more enthusiastic than others, authorizing 130 ticker-tape parades in the twenty years beginning 1945. Since 1994, nearly all ticker-tape parades have been for sports heroes.

Speaking of heroes, the mile-long parade route, from the lower tip of Manhattan north to City Hall, has been dubbed the Canyon of Heroes. The skyscrapers along the narrow path create a canyon-like effect; "heroes" refers to the parade honorees. If you want to know who they were, just look down at the sidewalk. Black granite markers along Broadway indicate the date of the ticker-tape parade and whom it honored. (*See* the markers on Walking Tour 1.)

Recipients of ticker-tape parades have included military heroes, foreign dignitaries, sports champions, pioneers in aviation and space exploration, and ordinary people doing extraordinary things, like firefighters. A few firsts:

- The first presidential honoree: the centennial of George Washington's inauguration; April 29, 1889 (ticker-tape parade no. 2)
- The first military hero: Admiral George Dewey, Spanish-American War hero; September 30, 1899 (parade no. 3)
- The first foreign heads of state: Albert and Elizabeth, king and queen of Belgium; October 3, 1919 (parade no. 7)
- The first sports heroes: U.S. Olympic athletes returning from the Paris Games; August 6, 1924 (parade no. 14)

GAY PRIDE

Is there any better way to keep the memory of an historic event alive than to celebrate its anniversary? That was the original impetus for **the first gay pride parade**.

The event being commemorated was the Stonewall Rebellion, which had sparked the gay rights movement a year earlier (*see* Birth of the Gay Rights Movement in the LGBTQ section). Craig Rodwell, owner of the first bookstore devoted to literature by and about gays (*see* Gay Bookstore in the LGBTQ section), helped organize the Christopher Street Liberation Day March on June 28, 1970. The Stonewall Inn was on Christopher Street; hence the name of the march.

The organizers were surprised at the size of the crowd for the first gay pride parade, on the one-year anniversary of the Stonewall Rebellion. Thousands of people walked several miles from Greenwich Village to Central Park, where they held a "gay-in"—an amazing turnout during a period when members of the LGBTQ community tended to keep a low profile.

Since the 1970 march, the event has undergone some changes. It is now called the Pride Parade, and it ends rather than begins in Greenwich

Village. The number of participants makes the original turnout look minuscule. The Pride Parade is the climax of a month-long celebration of all things LGBTQ. Pride Parades occur throughout the country and beyond its borders. The first New York march certainly set the stage for something big.

NATIONAL CULTURAL HERITAGE

Almost every weekend from late spring through early fall, New York City hosts a parade. Many of these events celebrate particular nations that have contributed to the great melting pot called the United States of America. People with roots in that nationality come from all over the country, and even the world, to join the festivities. Some New York parades are firsts of their kind that have spawned similar events in American cities with large ethnic populations; others are the one and only celebration for transplants in America, at least for now.

The granddaddy of them all is older than the United States. **The first St. Patrick's Day parade** took place on March 17, 1762. Irishmen, mainly soldiers in the British army, marched through the streets of New York to honor the patron saint of Ireland. (*See* St. Patrick's Day in this section.)

By the early 1900s, New York had more Italian than Irish immigrants. Two religious events that feature festive processions came to this country with the Italians and remain popular, each festival now extending more than ten days. Southern Italian immigrants celebrated **the first Giglio feast** in Williamsburg, Brooklyn, in 1903. During this festival, men hoist huge flower-covered wooden towers and carry them through the streets. In 1926, Neapolitans who had settled in Manhattan reenacted a tradition of their homeland, holding **the first Feast of San Gennaro**. The highlight is a procession in which a statute of the patron saint of Naples is carried through the streets of Little Italy (although some people say the real highlight is the endless Italian food).

A major, multiday event each Labor Day weekend honors not one nation but several. **The first West Indian Day Carnival and parade** occurred in Harlem in 1947. Carnival has since moved to Brooklyn. Revelers celebrate and dance in colorful costumes of Caribbean lands, including Trinidad, Jamaica, and Haiti.

That is not the only special event for Caribbean Islands. Puerto Ricans hold their own festivities on the second Sunday in June. **The first Puerto Rican Day parade** was in 1958, and it has become a huge event. Immigrants from a nearby island hosted **the first Dominican Day parade** in 1982. South Americans also have an opportunity to celebrate in New York. **The first Brazilian Day parade** was in 1984. The two latter events occur every August.

Other parades honor cultures in the Middle East. **The first Salute to Israel parade** (now called Celebrate Israel) was in 1965, less than twenty years after the founding of that nation. This event takes place the week before the Puerto Rican Day parade. One of the newer annual ethnic festivities celebrates an ancient group. **The first Persian Parade** occurred in 2003. Both parades are in Manhattan.

The long list of yearly parades celebrating different nations and their cultural heritage proves that everyone, at least in New York City, loves a parade. It also demonstrates that people from across the globe are welcome in New York.

Parks and Playgrounds

NEW YORK MAY BE ASSOCIATED WITH SKYSCRAPERS AND HIGH-POWERED financial dealings, but the city is also a park-lover's paradise. This is such a fast-paced, intense place that areas to relax and let off steam are not a luxury; they are a necessity. The New York City Department of Parks and Recreation (a.k.a., the Parks Department) oversees thousands of parks, playgrounds, and other recreational spots. A few of them were the first of their kind. That includes the city's premier park, Central Park, and one of its newest, the High Line. New York boasts the first municipal playground and the first pocket park in the country. A city park also was home to the first starlings in America.

New Yorkers enjoying Central Park on a snowy day, 2016.

I repeat, New York is a park-lover's paradise. Whether you like intimate pocket parks or huge city parks, whether you want to people-watch
from a park bench or get a bird's-eye view of city streets, whether you
enjoy bird-watching or releasing your inner child on a swing, you'll find
what you're looking for in a New York City park.

CENTRAL PARK

Like thousands of New Yorkers, I cannot imagine living here without
Central Park. New Yorkers aren't the only ones who love the park. Central
Park is one of the top tourist destinations in the city. I could go on and on
about the virtues of the park, but for the purposes of this book I will simply state that Central Park was **the first planned public park in America**.

The idea for a park came about in the middle of the nineteenth century. New York was already a thriving metropolis but it, like the United
States overall, lacked the cultural offerings and refinement of the great
European cities. Leading thinkers proposed creating a public park to rival
those across the Pond. The park would serve as an escape from the dirt
and stresses of city life and be a place for the wealthy to enjoy leisurely
strolls and carriage rides.

The land chosen for the park was more or less in the geographic center of the island of Manhattan but far north of New York's main residential area at the time. This tract seemed ideal for a park because large rock
outcroppings and swampy areas made it unsuitable for residential or commercial development in the days before modern building techniques. A
competition offered designers the opportunity to present their visions for
converting this wasteland into a park. The winners were two men partner-
ing together for the first time, Frederick Law Olmsted and Calvert Vaux.

Central Park was an incredible feat of imagination and engineering.
Within a few months after construction began in 1858, the first area,
the Lake, opened for ice skating. Work on the park continued for fifteen
years. Some 20,000 workers contributed manpower to build Central Park,
following the design plan of Olmsted and Vaux. Their plan included three
types of landscapes: pastoral meadows and ponds, a formal area where the
upper crust could "see and be seen," and picturesque woodlands. All of it
was man-made. Workers drained the swamps, then refilled the lowlands

to make lakes and ponds. The brawny crew chopped away at rocks and blasted apart large outcroppings with the only detonating material available: gunpowder. The area was devoid of vegetation, so gardeners planted grass, shrubs, and trees. Workers built separate pathways to keep pedestrians, horseback riders, and people in carriages from interfering with each other's enjoyment.

One of the most remarkable things about Central Park is that it remains close to the way Olmsted and Vaux envisioned it more than 150 years ago. A big difference is the addition of playground equipment, starting in the 1920s, to accommodate contemporary ideas about the best form of recreation for youngsters. (Olmsted and Vaux designated certain areas as playgrounds, but they were just open fields where children could run.) Adult activities have changed too, with joggers and inline skaters replacing horseback riders. But the basic landscape of the park has stood the test of time and continues to delight New Yorkers and tourists alike. (*See* it for yourself on Walking Tour 4.)

STARLINGS

Blame it on Shakespeare. Or rather, a lover of Shakespeare and of birds.

Toward the end of the nineteenth century, a New Yorker named Eugene Schieffelin, decided that America should have all the birds mentioned in Shakespeare. Today that idea would not likely get off the ground; we know that introduction of nonnative species can have disastrous effects on the native population. But back then it seemed like a way to honor the bard and unite the two great English-speaking nations.

In 1890, Schieffelin imported European starlings and released sixty to a hundred birds (accounts vary as to the exact number) in Central Park. These were **the first starlings in North America**. Today, about 200 million starlings make their homes on the continent.

Starlings thrive in a city environment provided they have access to water and open fields where they can forage for insects, seeds, and fruit. They need trees or buildings with cavities where they can nest. In other words, an urban park is an ideal habitat for starlings.

Although starlings can be aggressive, especially by taking over nesting spots of other birds, they don't seem to have caused great harm to native avian species—yet. But they were responsible for the deaths of sixty-two people in 1960, when a large flock flew into a plane taking off from Boston.

Incidentally, Shakespeare mentioned starlings only once, in *Henry IV, Part I*. In Act I, Scene 3, Hotspur claims he'll teach a starling to speak. Indeed, starlings are good vocal mimics and can learn to speak, although they're more likely to imitate other birds.

Playgrounds

Childhood in New York in the late nineteenth century wasn't easy, especially for immigrant families. Most lived in dark, airless, three-room apartments, which parents and their many children and maybe a few other relatives might have shared with some unrelated folks. The home often served double-duty as a workplace, as many tenement dwellers eked out a living in home-based sweatshops, usually doing piecework for the garment industry. The whole family got involved in this work, children too. They didn't have much time to play, and it almost didn't matter because there was no good place to play in their homes or in the dirty, crowded streets of the city.

At the turn of the century, a few social reformers vowed to do something to improve children's lives and give them the chance to be kids. In 1898, Charles B. Stover and Lillian D. Wald formed the Outdoor Recreation League, which provided equipment for playgrounds in poorer New York neighborhoods. In 1902, the city took over the nine playgrounds, including one in Seward Park on the Lower East Side. The next year, the city outfitted Seward Park with permanent equipment and created **the first municipal playground** in the United States.

Thousands of children flocked to the new playground. They enjoyed running on the soft cinder surfaces, playing on the slide and in the sandbox, and getting their hands dirty in the children's farm garden. Within a year, park-goers (including adults) were enjoying a pavilion with a gym and the first public bathhouse in a New York City park. (*See* Public Baths in the Social Welfare section for more on public bathhouses.)

The Seward Park playground was so successful that it became the model for other municipal playgrounds. By 1915, New York City had seventy such playgrounds.

POCKET PARKS

Walking through crowded, bustling Midtown Manhattan, you'll often stumble upon little pocket parks nestled between towering skyscrapers. Most of these parks have plants and seating of some kind; some have art works or waterfalls that drown out city noise. These pocket parks invite harried workers to chill, if only for a few minutes, before returning to the office rat-race.

Pocket parks do not dot Midtown and other places with mammoth buildings because developers wanted to provide a touch of greenery and a place to relax. Rather, the developers took advantage of a 1961 zoning law that allows buildings to rise higher if they offer open, public spaces at or near ground level. Sometimes developers simply set back their extra-tall buildings from the sidewalk and call it public space. Others furnish an interior space with a few places to sit. The most considerate developers, in my opinion (not everyone agrees), create pocket parks.

Although pocket parks are most common in areas packed with tall buildings, that's not where they began. **The first pocket park in the nation** was in Harlem. It opened in May 1965 on a vacant lot and bears the name of one of the driving forces behind its creation, Harlem minister and community activist Rev. Linnette C. Williamson. Two other pocket parks opened on the same block, West 128th Street, later that year.

In 1967, William S. Paley, head honcho of CBS, created a charming waterfall-enhanced park in Midtown and named it for his father. That's when the pocket park concept really took off. Today, New York City has more than 500 privately owned pocket parks and many others managed by the Parks Department. Across the country, municipalities that are not nearly as crowded and hectic as New York have added pocket parks to their landscape. It just makes sense.

HIGH LINE

Since the late twentieth century, the rail-to-trail movement, preservationists, and advocates for green spaces have found creative ways to repurpose two types of eyesores. The first ugly sight is on ground level: a strip of land beside an abandoned railroad track, canal, or other generally straight pathway. The second eyesore is above the street: a rooftop or an abandoned elevated train track or road. One solution to eliminate both types of unsightly sites is to turn them into parks. Linear parks have blossomed on or beside unused surface tracks, and elevated parks have sprung up above city streets. The Promenade Plantée in Paris was the first green space to combine these ideas, that is, it was the first elevated linear park in the world.

The Paris park was the inspiration for New York's High Line, **the first elevated linear park in the United States**. Built on and above industrial railroad tracks on the West Side of Manhattan, the High Line opened in sections. The first part of the park, the southernmost section, opened on June 9, 2009. The next half-mile became usable two years later, and the final section debuted in 2014. This last part extends above the Hudson Yards railroad tracks, whereas the other sections rise over city streets on a former elevated track.

The railroad tracks that became the High Line had been unused for more than twenty-five years, but they were not devoid of life. A self-seeded landscape had sprouted spontaneously. These plantings suggested the greenery for the High Line park. Creative seating, art installations, and of course the cityscape add diversity to a stroll along the 1.45-mile High Line.

The High Line rapidly became one of the must-see attractions in New York. The constant stream of visitors helped revitalize neighborhoods that the park passes through, including the Meatpacking District and Chelsea. High-end restaurants, shops, and even a museum offer diversion before or after a walk on the High Line. Fancy new apartment buildings have risen beside once-cheap tenements. A new community, Hudson Yards, has developed at the northern end of the elevated park, rising high in the sky with the benefit of air rights from the train tracks below. (*See* Air Rights in the Buildings and Bridges section.)

Religion

SOME COLONIES IN PRE-REVOLUTIONARY WAR AMERICA BEGAN AS RELIgious havens, but not New York. Even in those days, though, religious firsts occurred here. The young city saw the arrival of the first Jews in America and the establishment of the first Methodist church on this side of the Atlantic.

Over the years, individual New Yorkers have had pioneering religious accomplishments. One resident established the first Episcopal seminary. Both the first American saint and the first American cardinal were New York-ers. Various people began Christmas traditions in New York City that have become synonymous with the way America celebrates the holiday. A New York rabbi started a new branch of Judaism, and another established the fastest growing Orthodox

Chabad Jews performing a religious ritual in New York's Union Square, 2009.

Jewish sect. Foreign and native-born Muslim and Hindu leaders brought their beliefs to the city and its people, and the religions spread across the country.

With successive waves of immigration, the religious make-up of New York has changed. Whereas most early New York City residents were Protestant, today Catholicism is the dominant religion, accounting for about thirty percent of the residents. Jews represent seven percent of the city's population, versus one and a half percent nationwide. Since the mid-1900s, the Muslim and Hindu populations of the city, while still small, have been growing.

In religion as in so many other ways, New York City is a great melting pot. Thanks to its diversity, size, and generally tolerant attitude, New York has experienced firsts in many different religions.

METHODIST CHURCH

Skyscrapers overshadow some historic old structures in the Financial District, where the settlement of New York began in colonial times. Some of these historic buildings are not nearly as old as their roots. The present Trinity Church, for example, dates from 1846, but the congregation began on the same site before the Revolutionary War. That's also true for John Street Methodist Church. The church building nestled among skyscrapers was erected in 1841, but the congregation formed much earlier. It was **the first Methodist congregation in America**.

Many settlers in colonial America crossed the Atlantic in search of religious freedom, but not the founder of this Methodist church. Philip Embury, a Methodist lay preacher, emigrated from Ireland with several extended family members in 1760. He had no intention of taking to the pulpit again; he just wanted to farm and raise his family. But in 1766, six years after they came to the New World, a cousin caught others in their group playing cards, and she pleaded with Embury to start preaching again to save them from such sins. He relented, initially holding services in his home. As the congregation grew, it rented a place to worship, changing locations several times when it needed more space. In 1768, the Methodists bought two adjacent lots on John Street and erected their first building, which they called Wesley Chapel.

From the beginning, the church was inclusive and a strong proponent of social justice. One of the early members was a slave named Peter Williams. When he feared that he would be sold on the auction block, parishioners at Wesley Chapel bought him and granted him freedom. He prospered as a free man and remained active in the church. But bothered that Black and white members had to sit separately, Williams and a Black deacon of the church formed an all-Black Methodist congregation, the African Methodist Episcopal Zion Church, in 1796. It was the second such church in America; the first Black Methodist congregation began in Philadelphia two years earlier.

In 1817, the first John Street church came down to make way for a larger chapel. The present building replaced it when John Street was widened. The foundation of the current chapel has stones from Embury's church and structural elements from the second building.

John Street United Methodist Church remains an active congregation. The building also houses a museum that recalls life in Philip Embury's time and features relics from that era. Lovers of colonial American history will enjoy a visit. (*See* it on Walking Tour 1.)

EPISCOPAL SEMINARY

Back when America was a British colony, the only "right" church was the Church of England, or the Anglican church. Other denominations existed, but the elite colonists as well as the British-in-residence worshipped at the Anglican church. In New York City, Trinity was the Anglican church, and it set down its roots on Wall Street in the late seventeenth century. A few years later, Queen Anne gave Trinity Church a huge tract of land stretching all the way north to the village of Greenwich (later called Greenwich Village). Although most of the land has been sold off over time, Trinity for many years held more real estate in Manhattan than any other entity.

Travel, even short distances, was difficult in early American days. Trinity took advantage of its extensive landholdings and created parish churches to accommodate congregants who lived farther north. In 1766, St. Paul's Chapel rose less than one-third mile away. That was the church where George Washington prayed. In 1821, construction began on a church so remote—although it's only about two and a half miles north of Trinity—that the easiest access was by water, up the Hudson River. Located in the midst of farmland, the church was called St. Luke in the Fields. Its first warden was Clement Clarke Moore, whose father was bishop of the Episcopal diocese in New York.

Huh? Weren't we talking about Anglicans? How did Episcopalians enter the picture? Quite simply, they are more or less one and the same. After the Revolutionary War, Americans shunned things British and did not want to worship at something called the Church of England. They started to refer to their churches not as Anglican but as Episcopal.

Back to Clement Clarke Moore. His mother came from a wealthy old New York family with a large estate, called Chelsea. A Greek and Hebrew scholar, Moore followed in his father's footsteps, studying and teaching religion. If his name sounds familiar, it's probably because he wrote "A Visit from St. Nicholas," known more commonly by its opening words, "'Twas the night before Christmas." (*See* Christmas in this section for more about Moore's poem.)

Are you wondering where the "first" is in this story? In 1819—several years before the laying of the cornerstone of St. Luke in the Fields—Clement Clarke Moore donated a large portion of the Chelsea estate, which he had inherited, for an Episcopal seminary. The General Theological Seminary, erected in 1827 on a site that had been an apple orchard in the Chelsea estate, was **the first Episcopal seminary**. There are now eleven such institutions in the United States.

All of the religious institutions mentioned in this story—Trinity Church, St. Paul's Chapel, St. Luke in the Fields, and the General Theological Seminary—still exist. That's amazing, considering how old they are. Each is worth a visit, especially for history buffs and, of course, Episcopalians.

First American Cardinal

In the hierarchy of the Catholic church, the only priest higher than a cardinal is the Pope. The Pope decides who will be given the title of cardinal. Historically, cardinals were clergy in Rome, although other priests have been elevated to cardinal in more recent times.

The first American cardinal was John McCloskey. At various times, he had ties to three of the present five boroughs of New York. Born in Brooklyn, this son of Irish immigrants became a priest in 1834. He served as pastor of St. Joseph's Church in Greenwich Village and was the first president of St. John's College (Fordham) in the Bronx. In 1847, he moved upstate to serve as the first bishop of a newly created diocese in Albany, where he established numerous schools and orphanages.

In 1864, after the death of Archbishop John Hughes, McCloskey became the archbishop of New York. He oversaw the rebuilding of St. Patrick's (Old) Cathedral in Manhattan, which had been destroyed in a fire. Pope Pius IX elevated him to cardinal in 1875. Since then, fifty-six other Americans have been named cardinal.

FIRST AMERICAN SAINT

Exactly who was the first American saint is a question of semantics. Was it the first person born in America who was named a saint? Or was it the first time a Pope recognized an American as a saint? Whichever definition you choose, the first American saint was a woman who lived in New York City.

The first American-born saint had an unlikely beginning; she was raised Episcopalian, not Catholic. Elizabeth Ann Seton, nee Bayley, was born in New York City to a prominent family and was raised there during the British occupation in the Revolutionary War period. She married a wealthy businessman and was active in New York society. Then her husband lost first his fortune, then his health, and finally his life. They were in Italy at the time, and it was there that the widow became acquainted with Catholicism. Upon her return to New York in 1805, Seton converted to Catholicism—at a time when the city had only one Catholic church and Episcopalians were considered the cream of society. She moved with her children to Maryland in 1808, where she opened a school for girls and founded the first religious order for women in America, the Sisters of Charity of St. Joseph's.

Pope Paul VI canonized Elizabeth Ann Seton in 1975, making her the first American-born saint. A shrine in her honor is in the former James B. Watson house at the southern tip of Manhattan, next to where she once lived. Originally the home of a wealthy merchant, the Federal-style house is the only remaining building in the area from the late eighteenth/early nineteenth centuries. (*See* the shrine on Walking Tour 1.)

About thirty years before Elizabeth Ann Seton became a saint, Pope Pius XII canonized a different woman. In 1946, Frances Cabrini was **the first American named a saint**. Born in Italy in 1850, she became an American citizen in 1909. She had hoped to be a missionary to China, but on the advice of Pope Leo XIII to go "not to the East, but to the West," Cabrini instead relocated to New York City in 1889 to help the thousands of Italian immigrants who were living in poor conditions. Focusing her efforts on children, Mother Cabrini set up orphanages and schools, first in New York and then throughout the western hemisphere. A shrine to her is in northern Manhattan, overlooking the Hudson River at a site that she found especially peaceful.

CHRISTMAS

Of course, Christmas is a lot older than the United States. But many symbols and traditions of Christmas as it is celebrated in America are creations of New Yorkers.

In colonial days, some religious communities, such as the Puritans, banned Christmas celebrations because they were too rowdy and paganistic. After the Revolutionary War, many Americans shunned English traditions, including Christmas festivities. It wasn't until the early nineteenth century when Washington Irving, a New Yorker, wrote popular stories about warm-hearted English Christmases that Americans began to long for the holiday. Irving also wrote about St. Nicholas and the presents he brought to children, leading Americans to turn Christmas into a child-centered, family affair. Some maintain that Washington Irving almost single-handedly created the American Christmas.

A fellow New Yorker from the same period, Clement Clarke Moore, wrote a poem for his children that gave form to St. Nick. (*See* Episcopal Seminary in this section for more about Moore.) **The first printing of Moore's poem "A Visit from St. Nicholas"** (a.k.a. "'Twas the night before Christmas") was in 1823; it was published anonymously. Forty years later, New York cartoonist Thomas Nast started drawing pictures of Santa Claus—St. Nick by another name—for *Harper's Weekly*. Now nobody would have trouble picturing the jolly fat man.

Macy's claims to have had **the first department store Santa**, introduced in 1862. Previously, in 1841, Philadelphia delicatessen owner J. W. Parkinson enticed children to his shop (not a department store) with a man dressed like Santa. James Edgar of Brockton, Massachusetts, maintained that the Santa in his department store in 1890 was the first, because Macy's character didn't look like the Thomas Nast figure. The first department store Santa may be disputed, but **the first store with a Black Santa Claus** is certain. It was Blumstein's department store in Harlem, and the year was 1943. Only nine years earlier, Blumstein's had been the target of a boycott for refusing to hire African American sales staff, even though most of its customers were Black.

A decorated, lit tree is as symbolic of Christmas as is Santa. Initially, the illumination came from candles. In 1882, Edward H. Johnson, a colleague of Thomas Edison, decided to use this new-fangled thing called electricity to illuminate the Christmas tree in his Manhattan home. He strung together eighty small, colorful light bulbs and placed them around the tree. As if that wasn't enough, he rotated the tree using electricity, wowing everyone who came by to see **the first electric Christmas tree lights**. The use of electric lights on Christmas trees was slow to catch on, however, because they were expensive and had to be put together by a knowledgeable electrician, such as the inventor Johnson.

A Christmas tree for the home was a luxury that many of New York's poorest in the early twentieth century could ill afford. In 1912, a seventy-foot pine cut down in the Adirondack Mountains was put up in Madison Square Park and decorated with lights. This was **the first outdoor community Christmas tree in the United States**. Thousands of New Yorkers gathered around the tree and enjoyed holiday music. The Star of Hope, a five-pointed star on a pole half as tall as the original tree, marks the site today (*see* it on Walking Tour 3).

Did I mention holiday music? Several of the best-selling songs of the Yule season are creations of New Yorkers. The top of the charts—not just for seasonal songs but for the best-selling single of all time among all genres—is "White Christmas," written by Irving Berlin and recorded in 1941 by Bing Crosby. In 2019, Mariah Carey's "All I Want for Christmas Is You" became the biggest hit. Both Berlin and Carey lived in New York City. Being Jewish, Berlin did not celebrate Christmas. In fact, it was a sad day for him, because his infant son had died years earlier on December 25.

FIRST JEWS

Historians believe that Jews might have sailed with Christopher Columbus on his famous 1492 voyage, and some suspect that the man who "discovered" America was himself Jewish. Whether Jews came to this part of the globe with Columbus or they arrived later during the colonial period, without a doubt they were among the early settlers here.

How Jews originally came to present-day New York City is a convoluted, multinational story of anti-Semitism, resettlement, piracy, and forced acceptance. The saga began around Columbus' time, during the Inquisition, when Jews from Spain and Portugal sought refuge in the Netherlands. Fast forward to 1630, when the Dutch gained control of the northern part of Brazil from the Portuguese. Quite a few Dutch, including about 600 Jews, decided to try life in the New World and settled in Recife. When the Portuguese regained control of Brazil in 1654, the Dutch settlers thought it wise to return to Europe. Sixteen ships set sail, but the one carrying twenty-three Jews did not get very far. It was captured first by Spanish pirates and then by a French privateer, who agreed to take the displaced persons to the nearest Dutch port—for an outlandish price. That port was New Amsterdam, as New York City was known in those days. The Dutch colonial governor, Peter Stuyvesant, was less than welcoming. But when he got orders from the Netherlands to accept the Jews, he had no choice but to let them stay. And that is how **the first group of Jews arrived in America.**

When the sea-weary group fleeing Brazil embarked on North American soil, they were greeted by a Jewish man, Jacob Bar Simson. He had come from Amsterdam just a few weeks earlier, making him **the first Jew in America.**

The displaced Dutch Jews arrived a week before Rosh Hashanah (the Jewish New Year) and observed the holy days in New Amsterdam.

That year, 1654, marks the founding of **the first Jewish congregation in North America**, Congregation Shearith Israel. The Jews met in homes for prayers initially and then in the loft of a mill. As odd as that may seem, it wasn't the first time that kind of space was used for religious purposes. The earliest settlers, members of the Dutch Reformed Church, had also worshipped in a mill loft. In 1728, Congregation Shearith Israel acquired land at the site and built **the first synagogue in America** in 1730. Shearith Israel—the only Jewish congregation in New York until 1825—is still going strong, now on the Upper West Side.

Although Shearith Israel built the first synagogue in America, it cannot claim to be the oldest because the original building no longer exists. The title of oldest synagogue in America goes to Touro Synagogue in Newport, Rhode Island. The Newport congregation began in 1658 with another group of Jews of Portuguese and Spanish origin who had fled to the Netherlands and resettled in Brazil; they then spent several years in Barbados before arriving in the American colonies. The Touro Synagogue building dates from 1763.

RECONSTRUCTIONIST JUDAISM

In the nineteenth century, European and American Jews introduced changes that led to the Conservative and Reform movements, departures from the Orthodox Judaism that had been the norm since ancient times. Orthodox, Conservative, and Reform are the three main branches of Judaism today. In the twentieth century, a New York City rabbi, Mordecai Kaplan, started a fourth branch: Reconstructionism.

Recognizing that Judaism had evolved over the course of its long history, Kaplan sought ways to meld the ancient traditions with the challenges of modern life. In 1922, he founded the Society for the Advancement of Judaism, **the first Reconstructionist congregation**. Today there are about 100 Reconstructionist congregations, mostly in the United States.

An example of the changes that Kaplan introduced was the treatment of young women. According to Jewish tradition, a girl becomes a woman at twelve years of age, a year before a boy is considered a man. To mark his entry into adulthood, a thirteen-year-old boy participates in a ceremony called a bar mitzvah, in which he stands before the congregation and reads from the Torah. No such ceremony existed to celebrate a girl coming of age—until March 18, 1922. On that date, Rabbi Kaplan's twelve-year-old daughter Judith stood at the front of her father's newly formed synagogue in **the first bat mitzvah** anywhere in the world. These days, bat mitzvahs (similar to bar mitzvahs but for girls) are common in Reform, Conservative, and Reconstructionist congregations.

CHABAD (LUBAVITCH) JUDAISM

Small-town visitors may think they've stumbled upon one of those film shoots that New York is famous for. A highly decorated van blaring upbeat music pulls up, and several bearded young men in black suits and broad-brimmed black hats emerge. They approach a stranger, usually a Caucasian man, and ask "Are you Jewish?" If the answer is affirmative, they invite the random Jew-on-the-street to join them in reciting a prayer or performing some other brief religious ritual.

What these visitors have seen is a mitzvah tank, a mobile outreach center of the Chabad (Lubavitch) Hasidic Jewish community. The Orthodox sect has been in the United States since 1940, when Rebbe (rabbi) Yosef Yitzchak Schneerson arrived from Europe and established **the first Chabad community in the United States** in the Crown Heights section of Brooklyn. His daughter and son-in-law, Rebbe Menachem Mendel Schneerson, followed the next year, and the Chabad movement started to grow by leaps and bounds. Today, Chabad is the largest and fastest growing Jewish organization in the world, with institutions in about 100 countries.

The Schneersons felt that the way to keep Judaism alive was to educate young assimilated Jews in the traditions of their forefathers. On the very day he arrived in America, the elder Schneerson established a school. Menachem Mendel assumed responsibility for educating American Jewish children and adults when he joined his father-in-law on this side of the ocean. When his father-in-law died in 1950, Menachem Mendel Schneerson became leader of the Chabad community. Shortly after his death in 1994, the U.S. Congress awarded the Rebbe, as he was affectionately known, a gold medal "in recognition of his outstanding and enduring contributions toward world education, morality, and acts of charity."

Islam

Muslims were among the first people to come to the New World. In all probability, some practitioners of Islam sailed with Columbus. Without question, many slaves brought from Africa during the colonial period were Muslim, although they could not practice their religion openly. The resurgence of interest in Islam among Black Americans during the second half of the twentieth century was in part related to the religious traditions of their slave ancestors.

Even before Islam started to appeal to African Americans, however, it was capturing the attention of a few native-born white people. One of them was Alexander Russell Webb. Born in New York and raised as a Presbyterian, he explored other world religions before adopting Islam. In 1888, Webb became **the first American to convert to Islam**. Five years later, he founded *The Moslem World*, **the first Islamic newspaper in the United States**, and organized a mosque from the publication's New York City offices. The paper was short-lived, but Webb continued to produce other Islamic publications. He corresponded for many years with an Indian Muslim leader, Mirza Ghulam Ahmad.

A follower of Ahmad, Mufti Muhammad Sadiq, came from India in 1920 to establish **the first Ahmadiyya Muslim mission in America**. He set it up in New York initially but within six months moved the headquarters to Chicago because of its central location.

In 1924, Sheikh Daoud Ahmed Faisal founded the Islamic Mission of America, also known as the State Street Mosque; the home base was Brooklyn. In 1962, a group of Black congregants broke from the State Street Mosque to create **the first Darul Islam group in the United States**. It emphasized strict adherence to the Koran and often took militant positions regarding racism.

This was a period when Black Muslim splinter groups were forming. In the 1930s, when Black people began to embrace Islam, Wallace Fard Muhammad founded the Nation of Islam in Detroit. In 1964, Clarence Smith, who went by Clarence 13X and later Allah the Father, broke from the Nation of Islam and took his message to young men on the streets of Harlem. Creator of **the first group of the Five Percent Nation**, sometimes called the Nation of Gods and Earths, Allah the Father believed that only five percent of all people know the truth and choose to enlighten the world. All Black men, according to this movement, have God within them. A younger generation has embraced the philosophy and symbolism of the Five Percent Nation, including hip hop and rap artists such as Busta Rhymes, Lord Jamar, and the Wu-Tang Clan.

Today, New York City is home to many Muslims, an estimated twenty-two percent of the nation's total Muslim population. In 2015, about three percent of New Yorkers were Muslim; the number has been increasing. Most live in the outer boroughs, especially Brooklyn and Queens. Brooklyn alone has about a hundred mosques. Worshippers come from many different ethnic backgrounds: African American, Yemeni, Moroccan, Bangladeshi, and Haitian, to name a few.

Hinduism

Hinduism is an ancient religion widespread in India and some other Asian and African countries. The philosophical foundation is Vedanta, which emphasizes the equality and harmony of all religions. Hindu religious teachers are known as swamis.

In 1893, Swami Vivekananda from India spoke at the World's Parliament of Religions in Chicago and captured the interest of some Americans. The next year, he started the Vedanta Society of New York, **the first Hindu group in America**. In addition to Vedanta philosophy, the swami emphasized yoga as a way to achieve knowledge of God. The Vedanta Society has moved within the city several times and continues to attract New Yorkers who want to learn about and practice this form of Hinduism.

Another type of Hinduism, which became highly visible in the second half of the twentieth century, is the Hare Krishna movement. Swami Prabhupada brought it to the United States in 1966, when he founded the International Society for Krishna Consciousness (ISKCON) in New York City. Its members, **the first Hare Krishna group in America**, took to the streets in distinctive saffron robes, dancing and repeatedly chanting the Hare Krishna mantra. The joy of the young followers helped fuel the spread of the movement to other American cities.

According to the Hindu American Foundation, the Hindu population in the United States has been growing recently, topping three million by the end of the first decade of the twenty-first century. More than two thirds of the Hindus now living in America are of Indian origin. They are the best educated and prosperous immigrant group in the country.

Residences and Residential Areas

NEW YORK IS HOME TO MORE THAN EIGHT MILLION PEOPLE. IT'S ALWAYS been a big city, ranking among the most populous cities in the country, and even in the world, almost since its inception. With so many people needing a place to live, it stands to reason that some housing solutions were the first of their kind.

Tenth Street Studio Building, 1938. The first building designed as a home and workspace for artists, it had large windows to let in natural light. It was a favorite residence of artists and architects for almost 100 years.

Apartments are the quintessential style of New York housing. Apartment living per se took off here. Tenements, co-ops, and multistructure housing complexes are some types of apartment buildings that premiered in New York City. Housing innovations have addressed the needs of particular types of residents, such as artists, the elderly, and travelers. People at every income level, from the poor to the middle class to the extremely wealthy, have found the right places to live here.

Residents who sought green spaces populated America's first suburb and so-called garden cities in boroughs other than Manhattan. In the twenty-first century, environmental awareness led to the first residential high-rise passive house in the world. Whatever type of housing was desired, New York probably had it—or would develop it.

AMERICA'S FIRST SUBURB
In the second half of the twentieth century, people across the country fled from the cities to outlying areas where they could enjoy cleaner and greener surroundings. Living in the suburbs, they commuted to the city for work. It's a way of life that remains prevalent today.

While suburban living is associated with post–World War II America, it actually began about two centuries ago. A section of Brooklyn called Brooklyn Heights, which is located just across the East River from Lower Manhattan, was **the first suburb in America.**

The East River was critical to the development of America's first suburb. As early as colonial days, ferries traversing the river connected the village of Breukelen with Nieuw Amsterdam, the forerunners of Brooklyn and Lower Manhattan, respectively. In 1814, Robert Fulton launched steam-powered ferry service between the two areas, shrinking travel time from twenty minutes to just twelve. Now it was practical to commute from a home in Brooklyn to work in Manhattan and back to Brooklyn at the end of the day—in other words, to live in the suburbs. (*See* Steamboats in the Transportation section for more about Fulton's ventures.)

More transportation options hastened the growth of the first suburb. Other ferries began operating between Manhattan and Brooklyn, which were separate cities until 1898. The Brooklyn Bridge opened in 1883, creating a roadway to Manhattan. (*See* Bridges in the Buildings and Bridges section for more about the Brooklyn Bridge.) Rail lines, initially elevated trains and then subways, provided other modes of transportation for commuters. By the time the last ferry of that era ceased operation in 1912, a trip to Lower Manhattan from Brooklyn Heights was just a five-minute subway ride.

Some homes built for the early commuters in the 1830s and 1840s, mostly rowhouses in durable brownstone or brick and a few freestanding mansions, still grace Brooklyn Heights. Originally built for the well-to-do, many homes in the area later were divided into apartments or converted to boardinghouses. Around the time of the nationwide flight to suburbia, Brooklynites realized that they had a once-and-present suburb in their midst and started to spruce up the neighborhood. The Heights today is a well-kept, vibrant area that has all the trappings of a city—stores and restaurants, good transportation, a diverse population—with the slower pace and residential feel of a suburb. Thanks to the tender loving care of the homeowners, Brooklyn Heights projects the aura of an elegant nineteenth-century neighborhood.

The significance of the first suburb has been recognized with several formal honors. In 1965, the New York City Landmarks Preservation Commission named Brooklyn Heights an historic district, the first of its kind for the commission. It was designated a National Historic Landmark District the same year and listed on the National Register of Historic Places the following year.

TENEMENT

When you hear the word "tenement," you probably think of a crowded, decrepit building in a dirty, teeming slum. That's what the term has come to mean, but it didn't start that way. A tenement was simply a building that was home to many unrelated people; in other words, it was a type of apartment building.

The earliest tenements began as single-family residences. When the family left, usually moving to what were then the northern reaches of New York City, other people desperate for a place to live moved into the house. Often the newcomers were new not just to the building but to America. They were so happy to have made it across the ocean for a chance to start fresh that they didn't mind sharing a roof with strangers. The buildings they occupied, once home to a single family, turned into so-called tenant houses, a term that soon morphed into "tenement."

The existing housing stock could not keep pace with the flood of immigrants in the early nineteenth century. Nor could the land that residential New York City comprised at that time, which was just beginning to extend north of Houston Street. The only way to provide homes for a rapidly growing population in a space that was not expanding quickly was to build vertically. In 1824, **the first purpose-built tenement in America** opened at 65 Mott Street.

The seven-story structure towered over the two-story buildings around it. Shops were on the ground floor. Each of the other stories had two two-bedroom apartments. As many as twelve people might live in a single apartment. Privies were in the back yard. The building wasn't pretty, but it was home.

By 1865, New York City had more than 15,000 tenement apartments. They were crowded, airless, and dark. An 1879 law attempted to improve tenement conditions by requiring airshafts between buildings to let in light and air, running water in the house or yard, and a toilet for every two apartments. The most popular style of architecture resulting from the law was the dumbbell apartment building; with a front and back unit separated by a corridor, it looked like a barbell or dumbbell from a bird's-eye view. Despite the good intentions, dumbbell apartments did little to improve tenement life. A subsequent law in 1901 banned new construction of dumbbell apartments and required a window in every room and a toilet in each apartment.

Incidentally, the first tenement building on Mott Street still exists. The neighborhood has gone from grungy to ethnic to borderline chic. An apartment in the building recently rented for more than $2,000 a month. That's considerably less than other apartments in this Chinatown neighborhood, probably because the unit was on a high floor in a seven-story walk-up.

TENTH STREET STUDIO BUILDING

The Greenwich Village neighborhood of Manhattan has long appealed to artists. Over the course of almost a century, many artists shared an address: the Tenth Street Studio Building. This was **the first building designed as a home and workspace for artists.** The original structure was at 51 West 10th Street. The demand for apartment-studios was so great that an annex was built next door, at 55 West 10th Street, after fifteen years.

The idea to provide combined studio space and living quarters for artists was the brainchild of a wealthy real estate speculator named James Boorman Johnston. He purchased a large plot of land across the street from his home and hired architect Richard Morris Hunt, **the first American to study at the prestigious École des Beaux-Arts in Paris**, to design the building. Hunt knew what artists needed. He filled the working space with natural light, creating large windows in the studios and a high glass roof in the central gallery they surrounded. When the artists craved companionship with kindred souls, they could open the doors between their studios. The living space in each unit lacked these connections to assure privacy. Rent was affordable. The units were such an improvement over the boardinghouses where many artists lived and the poorly lit studios where they worked that some tenants moved in before the building was completed in 1858. Among the initial residents were John LaFarge and Frederic Church. Most of Church's colleagues who painted in the Hudson River School genre (*see* Hudson River School in the Art section) soon moved in too.

The building's architect, Richard Morris Hunt, was another initial resident. From his studio, he offered training to up-and-coming architects in what is often considered **the first architectural school in America**. One of the architects was George B. Post, who later would design the New York Stock Exchange.

Artists who want to support themselves with their talent need a way to show their work to potential buyers. The Tenth Street Studio Building served this function well. On Saturday afternoons, the public came to stroll through the studios. Twice a year, the gallery was the scene of formal exhibitions of the residents' works. That ended after 1879, however, when William Merritt Chase took over the gallery space as his own two-story studio. Although he didn't paint the large works he had intended to create in the space, his apartment-studio became a gathering place for fellow artists. When Chase moved out in 1896, sculptor A. Stirling Calder, father of sculptor and mobile creator Alexander Calder, took over the huge studio, where he did indeed create large works.

The residents of the Tenth Street Studio Building were so happy living and working there that they seldom moved out. Some went from being relatively unknown to being household names. But nothing lasts forever. In 1955, the Tenth Street Studio Building, home to some of America's greatest painters, sculptors, and architects, came down, replaced by an eleven-story apartment building where anyone, regardless of talent or occupation, could reside.

APARTMENT BUILDINGS

Most New York City residents live in apartments. That was not always the case. Before 1870, upper- and middle-class residents lived in townhouses, where a family enjoyed an entire three- or four-story building and shared walls only with the townhouses on each side. The very wealthy often had private mansions. Only poor people who could afford nothing better lived in apartments, usually in crowded tenements (*see* Tenement in this section). Early tenements are not now considered apartment buildings, however, because they lacked basic amenities, especially a private toilet, and the dark, airless units often housed more than one family in just two or three rooms.

In Paris and other European cities, apartment living had caught on with the middle class. Several prominent New Yorkers had seen this style of housing when they were in Paris, and they thought it would work well in their home town. One of these people, Rutherford Stuyvesant, hired preeminent architect Richard Morris Hunt to design an apartment building on East 18th Street. Hunt knew the French style well, for he was **the first American to study at the École des Beaux-Arts in Paris**. A little more than a decade before Stuyvesant engaged him, Hunt had created the Tenth Street Studio Building in Greenwich Village, **the first structure to combine living and working space for artists** (*see* Tenth Street Studio Building in this section). Although residential, the studio space predominated, as the name of the building implies, so the Tenth Street structure too is not considered an apartment building.

The first apartment building in America opened in 1870 at 142 East 18th Street. The Stuyvesant, as Hunt's building was called, was five stories tall, with four apartments per floor. The rooms were laid out along a long hallway. Each apartment had a bathroom with running water, behind the kitchen in the rear of the unit. Separate staircases accommodated servants; help was *de rigueur* for middle-class New Yorkers. On the top floor, the least expensive in the walk-up, were four studios for artists, for Hunt knew from experience that they would like this type of structure.

Like their French counterparts, middle-class New Yorkers loved the idea of living in their own private space under a roof shared with neighbors—the very concept of apartment living. The Stuyvesant attracted a steady stream of residents for almost ninety years, including established artists and writers as well as people who made the society pages of the local papers from time to time. More importantly, it convinced an entire nation that apartments were suitable homes for all Americans, not just the lower classes.

People at a very high level of society may demand more than an apartment building typically offers. In 1884, less than fifteen years after the Stuyvesant proved the concept of apartment living for successful people, **the first luxury apartment building** opened across from Central Park, in an area so remote (or so one story goes) that it earned the name of a distant American region: Dakota. Elegant inside and out, with spacious rooms and plentiful servants' quarters, the eight-story Dakota offered multiple elevators (including **the first service elevator in a residential building**), a private courtyard, and a residents-only restaurant. The Dakota has been home to many celebrities (one, singer-songwriter John Lennon, was tragically killed just outside the building) and remains an elite New York City address today.

Incidentally, the Pontalba Buildings in New Orleans are sometimes called the oldest apartment buildings in America. However, they were built in 1850 as separate rowhouses and not converted to apartments until the 1930s.

CO-OP APARTMENTS

Most New Yorkers who own their apartments live in co-operatives or co-ops as opposed to condominiums (the norm for apartment ownership in other cities). The earliest co-ops were in Europe. **The first residential co-op in America** was the Rembrandt, which opened in 1881 at 152 West 57th Street in Manhattan.

The Rembrandt was built to appeal to successful artists. Some apartments were duplexes with up to twelve rooms, and other units boasted tall ceilings so artists could have studios in their homes. The apartments sold for $4,000 to $5,000, and owners paid a monthly maintenance fee—as co-op dwellers do today—to cover shared services. Aware that the concept of home ownership might take some getting used to, the developers intentionally offered about half the units as rentals.

The term "co-op" was not used at the time. Rather, the Rembrandt was called a home club. That designation stressed the social aspect of like-minded neighbors sharing common expenses. The developers, the architectural firm of Hubert & Pirsson, were so convinced that the innovation would succeed that they built six similar Hubert Home Clubs within a year.

Hubert & Pirsson erected another co-op, the Chelsea, a few years later. After it went bankrupt in 1903, it reopened as the Hotel Chelsea, which became home to notable writers (Mark Twain, Thomas Wolfe, and Dylan Thomas, to name a few), artists (such as Julian Schnabel, Robert Mapplethorpe, and Jasper Johns), and musicians (including Joni Mitchell, Jimi Hendrix, and Sid Vicious).

Like the Chelsea, most of the early co-ops were on shaky financial ground around the turn of the century. That included the first co-op, the Rembrandt. In 1903, Andrew Carnegie purchased the Rembrandt—it was next to Carnegie Hall—and converted it to a rental building. The Rembrandt fell victim to the wrecking ball in 1962.

Real estate agents sometimes claim that the nine-story apartment building at 34 Gramercy Park is the first co-op. It's not, but it is the oldest still standing. Built in 1883, a few years after the Rembrandt, it has always appealed to a wealthy clientele. Actors, including James Cagney and Richard Gere, have been among its most famous resident shareholders.

Since the first co-ops, this form of apartment living has had its ups and downs. After World War I, luxury co-ops became popular with the upper class. The 1927 New York Housing Act provided tax incentives for creation of co-ops for middle-income and poorer residents. Sadly, about seventy-five percent of co-ops went bust during the Depression. Rent control laws and rising costs prompted landlords to convert their apartment buildings to co-ops in the 1940s and later. Then the stock market crash of 1987 caused a reversal, with many co-ops changing to rental units. These days, condos, which usually come with fewer restrictions and allow owners to rent or sublet their apartments, are gaining ground in New York, but co-ops still outnumber condos three to one.

Hotels

Back in the day, travel was a pastime only of the wealthy. The trip itself may have been long, dusty, and uncomfortable, but a reward often awaited the traveler at the end of the trek: a stay in a hotel that treated guests like kings. The upper crust of New York, often considering themselves a sort of royalty, also enjoyed these hotels in their home town, hosting parties and special dinners in the public rooms.

The St. Nicholas Hotel on Broadway between Broome and Spring Streets was the epitome of luxury when it opened in 1853. Elegant chandeliers graced the public rooms of the huge, white, marble building. Guest accommodations were beautifully appointed. Servants had an upper floor all to themselves. The St. Nicholas was **the first hotel with a bathroom in every suite**. A set of rooms adorned with crystal chandeliers and white satin was reserved for special guests, as the St. Nicholas was **the first hotel with a honeymoon suite.**

Similar elegance greeted visitors at the Fifth Avenue Hotel, which started to receive guests in 1859. Located at the northern end of the up-and-coming fashion district known as Ladies' Mile, the posh home-away-from-home was **the first hotel with a passenger elevator**. (*See* the site on Walking Tour 3.)

Apartment hotels became a phenomenon around the turn of the century. They were homes for temporary guests, well-to-do people who wanted to live in New York part of the year, and permanent year-round residents. Accommodations often were suites, but they generally lacked kitchens. That was not a problem, because apartment hotels had restaurants, as well as staff to take care of guests' and residents' various needs. Some of New York's most famous addresses were apartment hotels, including the Plaza, Waldorf Astoria, and Algonquin.

In the early 1930s, a luxury hotel introduced a new amenity we now take for granted when traveling. The Waldorf Astoria was **the first hotel in the world to offer room service**. The Waldorf closed for major renovation in 2017, to reopen as a mixed-use residence combining a high-end hotel and luxury condominiums. (*See* the Waldorf on Walking Tour 4.)

CARNEGIE MANSION

In the late nineteenth century, structural steel revolutionized the building industry. Now it was possible to erect tall buildings—skyscrapers—supported by a lightweight interior frame. Structural steel changed the skyline of New York and other urban business districts.

It took a man of steel, Andrew Carnegie, to expand the use of structural steel from office towers to private homes. The retirement mansion of multimillionaire Andrew Carnegie, founder of Carnegie Steel (the forerunner of U.S. Steel), was **the first private residence with a structural steel frame**.

This was one of several innovative features in Carnegie's six-story home on 91st Street and Fifth Avenue, where he lived from 1902 until his death in 1919; his widow remained there until her death twenty-seven years later. The mansion was **the first house with multiple Otis electric elevators**. One of the elevators served as Carnegie's personal transport between the first and second floors, while another elevator carried family and guests. A dumbwaiter sent food from the ground-floor kitchen to the floor above, where the Carnegies ate and entertained. Two other elevators carted messy items like fireplace ash and potted plants.

Other innovations, although not necessarily the first of their kind, included primitive air conditioning, central heating, and water filtration systems. The basement housed duplicates of these systems, just in case they went out. Electricity was the key to making these creature comforts work. Electricity was important outside the home too. The family's electric cars were kept in a private garage two blocks away. (Although electric cars might seem to be a twenty-first century phenomenon, about a third of all cars on the road in 1900 were electric.)

Anyone can visit the Carnegie mansion these days, because it has a different name: the Cooper-Hewitt, Smithsonian Design Museum. It's worth a trip just to admire the rich wood walls and magnificent staircase, part of the original structure. The garage is still standing too, and it also has a new life. It is now the Horace Mann Nursery School.

GARDEN CITIES

The Industrial Age transformed not only the way people worked but also where they lived. Instead of living and working on family farms, more and more people resided in crowded cities, and they rarely saw greenery or breathed clean air. By the late nineteenth century, some people started to question this way of life.

One such person was Ebenezer Howard. Born in London, he lived in the United States for five years as a young man before returning to England. In his 1898 book *To-morrow: A Peaceful Path to Real Reform*, he proposed a utopian city that combined the best of urban and country living. Four years later, he modified and expanded this vision in an updated edition, called *Garden Cities of To-morrow*. Howard's ideal city was a planned, privately owned and managed community surrounded by a rural belt. The city was essentially a series of concentric circles with a garden at the core. Around the garden would be a circle of civic and cultural buildings, and these structures would be ringed by parks and stores surrounded by residences and then enveloped by industry, with agricultural land on the outermost circle. In 1903, the first such garden city, Letchworth, developed north of London.

Creation of such a city obviously required wide open spaces. New York was lucky to have such areas, especially in the outer boroughs like

Queens. In 1909, **the first garden city in the United States** was built in Forest Hills Gardens, Queens, nine miles from Manhattan. To create this community, the Russell Sage Foundation purchased 142 acres of the Forest Hills area and hired architect Grosvenor Atterbury and landscape architect Frederick Law Olmsted, Jr. (son of one of the designers of Central Park). The buildings rose quickly and relatively inexpensively, because many parts were prefabricated.

The residences in Forest Hills Gardens consist of about 800 freestanding and attached houses, many in Tudor style, and eleven apartment buildings. Four parks provide plenty of green space. As in the early days, residents pay maintenance fees to cover shared expenses, and they abide by rules to keep the community looking as it had more than a century earlier.

After Forest Hills Gardens proved successful, other garden cities developed throughout the United States. In the 1920s, Queens neighborhoods including Jackson Heights and Sunnyside Gardens developed as modified garden cities. Bridge and tunnel crossings and the subway simplify the trip to Manhattan for New Yorkers who want to live amidst greenery in a quasi-suburb.

FEDERALLY FUNDED HOUSING PROJECTS

In the early twentieth century, one slum area in Lower Manhattan was worse than most others, judging by its nickname: "Lung Block." Bound by Cherry, Catherine, Market, and Hamilton Streets, the block earned its sobriquet because of the exceptionally high incidence of tuberculosis. Eight bars and five brothels were scattered among the poorly ventilated residences. Everything about this area screamed "Tear it down!" But it took a while for that to happen.

In the late 1920s, real estate developer Fred F. French began to buy lots in the area. He was already purchasing slum property farther uptown, in the 40s near the East River. There, starting in 1927, he created Tudor City, a cluster of apartment buildings, small parks, and a few businesses. Tudor City was **the first high-rise residential complex in the world**. The apartments appealed to Midtown office workers who wanted to have the amenities of suburban-style living without the commute.

By the time French had acquired most of the Lung Block, the country was in the throes of the Depression, and his plans to replicate Tudor City seemed doomed. Then in 1932, the federal government made funding available to private developers to build housing. French seized the opportunity and erected twelve thirteen-story towers surrounding courtyards. The development, called Knickerbocker Village, was **the first apartment project in the country to receive federal funding**. Like at Tudor City, the apartments were small, and the target tenants were middle-class, white-collar workers. The rent averaged $12.50 per room, about two and a half times the price of the tenement housing that Knickerbocker Village replaced.

The federal government came through three years later for New Yorkers who couldn't afford Knickerbocker Village, helping the city fund **the first low-income public housing project in the United States**. Aptly called First Houses, the eight four- and five-story apartment buildings were located on Avenue A between First and Third Streets. Some of the building materials were recycled from the tenements demolished to create First Houses.

All of these apartment complexes were built from the ground up. In 1970, a different type of housing came about with the help of the federal government. The National Endowment for the Arts joined with the J. M. Kaplan Fund and hired the then-unknown architect Richard Meier to turn the former Bell Telephone Laboratories on the industrial far west side of Greenwich Village into affordable live-work spaces for artists. Named for the intersection of two streets, Westbeth was **the first federally subsidized housing for artists in the United States**. The term "artist" could mean anything from painter to dancer to writer to actor. Among the more famous one-time residents of Westbeth were the photographer Diane Arbus, the abstract expressionist Robert De Niro, Sr. (father of the actor by the same name), the poet Muriel Rukeyser, and the actor Vin Diesel.

Over the years, residents of Westbeth found out what residents of the Tenth Street Studio Building (*see* Tenth Street Studio Building in this section) had learned decades earlier. Living among fellow artists stimulates creativity. Few residents wanted to leave the complex, leading to a years-long waitlist. The rent added to the attraction. Some of the earliest residents paid just $100 a month for their rent-controlled unit. Today a rent-stabilized complex, Westbeth's prices range from about $700 a month for a studio to about $4,000 a month for a three-bedroom unit—a steal in what has become an upscale neighborhood.

New Yorkers still live in all of these apartment complexes. Tudor City apartments are now co-ops, and the development continues to appeal to Midtown workers and, because of the small apartment size, first-time buyers and those wanting a pied-à-terre. Knickerbocker Village and First Houses are on the Lower East Side, an area that has gone from a poor one in the twentieth century to a trendy one in the twenty-first century. More than half of the present Westbeth residents were among the pioneers in this complex. Because of their advanced age, Westbeth is now considered not just an artist colony but a naturally occurring retirement community (*see* NORC below in this section).

NATURALLY OCCURRING RETIREMENT COMMUNITY (NORC)

Some people want to retire in a warm and sunny place or move near their grandchildren. Other seniors have no desire to leave their home of many years. In the early 1980s, a term to describe the result when many residents choose the latter option came into use: a naturally occurring retirement community (NORC). The precise definition of a NORC varies with the community, which could be a housing complex or a neighborhood. However a NORC is defined, it is a mixed-age residential area with an overrepresentation of older folks who have lived there a long time.

Individuals who cared for or studied residents of NORCs realized that the seniors had certain needs that weren't always being met. A variety of services, which might be provided by professionals like nurses and social workers or by community residents, could make it possible for older people to stay in their homes and thrive. A new model was necessary: a NORC Supportive Services Program (NORC-SSP). **The first NORC-SSP in the country** opened in 1986 in one building of Penn South, a fifteen-building co-operative apartment complex in the Chelsea neighborhood of Manhattan.

Even before it became home to a NORC-SSP, Penn South was a special place. Built as moderate-income co-operative housing with the support of the International Ladies Garment Workers Union, Penn South opened in 1962. President John F. Kennedy was there for the dedication; it was **the first time a president of the United States attended the dedication of a housing development**.

Twenty-three years later, a survey revealed that seventy percent of Penn South households included somebody aged sixty years or older. Residents decided to take action so the elderly could remain in their homes. The result was creation of the first NORC-SSP, called the Penn South Program for Seniors. This NORC-SSP provides on-site health and social work services, including home care and long-term care assistance. The Penn South Program for Seniors also offers educational and social programs, including trips, classes, movies, and parties. The older residents themselves, as well as their younger neighbors, help plan the services and activities in the program.

Since it debuted in 1986, the NORC-SSP model has been replicated throughout New York City and State and in many other places in the United States. Other countries also are adapting the model to help their senior citizens age in place.

Passive House

The term "passive house" is odd. What house, except perhaps for a haunted house or one in the terrifying tremors of an earthquake, isn't passive?

Actually, "passive house" refers to international energy efficiency standards for buildings. Passive houses require very little energy—about sixty to seventy percent less than similar buildings not meeting these standards—to achieve comfortable temperatures year-round. To earn the title of passive house, a building must conform to stringent criteria, including the following: (1) low energy usage per square foot, with approximately equal heating and cooling energy demands; (2) an energy-recovery ventilation system that removes stale air and pulls in fresh air to result in comfortable indoor temperatures; (3) airtightness, which depends on the building's façade and a tight exterior envelope.

Thousands of buildings that meet passive house standards have been erected around the world since the early 1990s. Most are single-family homes and other low-rise buildings. The first high-rise was a twenty-one-story office tower erected in Vienna in 2012. **The first residential high-rise passive house in the world** opened in 2017 on Roosevelt Island, in the East River halfway between Manhattan and Queens.

Called the House, the twenty-six-story residence on the Cornell Tech graduate campus has 352 apartments for students and faculty. The metal façade acts as an insulated blanket. Energy-recovery ventilation units extract heat from air pulled from the apartments through exhaust ducts and transfer the heat to incoming fresh air before it travels to the units through separate ducts. A louver system hides the heating and cooling apparatus. Triple-pane windows prevent air leaks and keep the building quiet.

As the initial residents moved into the House, the city selected its design firm, Handel Architects, to build an even larger passive house in Harlem. It is a mixed-use building, with most of the space apartments. More residential high-rise passive houses are certain to follow.

Social Welfare

In the nineteenth and early twentieth centuries, most New York City residents lived in crowded, unsanitary, immigrant communities. Social welfare organizations sprang up to meet the needs of the many people who could benefit from a helping hand. Various groups aided

Immigrants at Castle Garden, America's first official immigrant receiving center, 1868.

immigrants from the moment they stepped off the ships that brought them to America, and these and other organizations continued to help with essentials like food, lodging, English lessons, job training, and health care. Well-off citizens reached out to help the less fortunate. Examples include quite a few firsts: a home for retired sailors, public baths, "Y"s, a breadline, and settlement houses.

In a way, New York was going back to its fundamental values, for in the colonial period it was the first American city to establish a public hospital to care for the poor. During the period of mass immigration, health and social welfare were closely connected. Some innovations in health care during that time included putting nurses in schools and teaching women about family planning. School nurses and birth control clinics are two ongoing legacies from this period.

New Yorkers' caring, philanthropic bent has never ceased. In the early twenty-first century, for example, New Yorkers came up with the idea for a special day designated for charitable giving.

Who says that New York is an unfriendly place? History proves that New Yorkers have always cared for their neighbors.

BELLEVUE HOSPITAL

To many people, the term "Bellevue" conjures up images of crowded hospital corridors echoing with the screams of mentally unbalanced patients. That negative image, stemming from dramatic portrayals of goings-on in the psychiatric hospital built as part of the Bellevue campus in 1931, overshadows the positive—indeed, innovative—accomplishments at Bellevue. For starters, it was **the first public hospital** in America, founded in 1736 as a six-bed infirmary at the New York Almshouse. From that moment, Bellevue's mission was to provide health care to the poor, regardless of their ability to pay. Bellevue has always cared for the unwanted, including the mentally ill, alcoholics, and patients with fatal contagious diseases.

The initial infirmary was at the site of present-day City Hall. It was farther north than the population center of colonial New York but not far enough away from the populace in the early 1800s when the city needed a place to quarantine patients during deadly yellow fever epidemics. A new version of the old almshouse infirmary rose about two miles north, taking the name Bellevue from the rural estate it replaced.

Bellevue Hospital claims quite a few firsts that I was unable to confirm in independent sources. I have not included them in the official list of firsts in the chronological appendix or indicated them in bold here. Some of these accomplishments are worth mentioning, with the caveat that they may not have been the first but are certainly examples of medical ingenuity: a maternity ward (1799), an ambulance service (1869), a children's clinic (1874), and a cardiopulmonary laboratory (1940). In 1947, Bellevue was possibly the first general hospital to offer rehabilitation services for a nonmilitary population.

Notwithstanding the uncertainty of some of these accomplishments as the first of their kind or the negative image of Bellevue associated with its psychiatric hospital, Bellevue remains an outstanding medical facility. It has such a good reputation among the city's first responders that police officers and firefighters often ask to go to Bellevue when they suffer injuries in the line of duty.

Sailors' Snug Harbor

A life at sea, away from home for months or even years at a time, can be hard on a man's personal life. So hard that when he's old and ready to settle on dry land, the seaman might have no family and few friends to help him and to provide companionship. An early New Yorker understood this and willed property to build a place that old seadogs could call home. But it didn't end up where he had intended.

The man who left his property for a retired seaman's haven was Robert Richard Randall. His father had been a privateer before he settled in New York City in the pre–Revolutionary War period, becoming a leading citizen. When the elder Randall died, his son inherited a large farm in what is now Greenwich Village. Just a few days before the younger Randall died in 1801, he signed a will—possibly written by Alexander Hamilton—that left the land for an asylum for "aged, decrepit, and worn-out sailors." The will also established a trust to carry out this mandate, creating **the first secular philanthropy in America**.

Three decades of legal battles followed. During that time, the area surrounding Randall's farm was becoming more urban as the city population moved north from Lower Manhattan. The trustees decided to lease the Manhattan property and use the proceeds to acquire a much larger tract in rural Staten Island. There they built Sailors' Snug Harbor, **the first home for retired seamen in America**. When the initial dormitories opened in 1833, thirty-seven old tars moved in. Over the years, more buildings rose on the campus, including a music hall, church, and hospital. The health care offered the former seamen was exemplary. Sailors' Snug Harbor is often considered **the first old-age home in America**. It certainly was a model for elder care.

For more than a century, thousands of retirees lived out their last years at Sailors' Snug Harbor. Almost any seaman who had served on an ocean-going ship for at least ten years, five of them on ships carrying the U.S. flag, was eligible for residency. However, alcoholics and men of "immoral character" were denied admission.

The Staten Island site became a National Historic Landmark in 1965. By then the population of Sailors' Snug Harbor was declining as retirees took advantage of other options. With the cost of operating the huge facility rising, the trustees decided to move Sailors' Snug Harbor to North Carolina in 1976. The remaining facilities on Staten Island are now public and cultural institutions, including a botanical garden and art, maritime, and children's museums.

Public Baths

Imagine taking a bath or shower only once a month, once a year, or even less frequently. That didn't require imagination through most of history; it was reality. Immersion in a tub was a chore in the days before indoor plumbing; it necessitated carting and heating water and then disposing of it afterward. Frequent bathing was a luxury enjoyed mainly by those who could afford servants to handle the logistics, as well as a place to put a tub.

In 1849 Robert Minturn, a wealthy New York merchant, decided to do something to help the city's lower classes get clean. He founded the People's Bathing and Washing Association and built **the first public bath in America**, in the heart of the immigrant community. Although thousands of New Yorkers took advantage of it, the facility closed in a few years because the small fee was too much to allow most residents to visit frequently.

About twenty years later, the city tapped its river borders to create free floating public baths on both the Hudson and the East River. By the end of the nineteenth century, Manhattan had fifteen such facilities, Brooklyn five. These baths refreshed impoverished New Yorkers from mid-June to mid-October. They were so popular that swimmers and splashers—few people actually came to get clean—could stay for only twenty minutes. But the growing pollution of the rivers necessitated a different solution.

New York State passed a law in 1895 mandating that large cities establish indoor public baths. The first such facility in New York City opened in 1901. By 1915 Manhattan had twelve more, Brooklyn seven. The public baths generally had both showers and soaking tubs, as well as pools that children in particular enjoyed. The bathhouses were popular in the summer, especially on the hottest days, but little used during the rest of the year—proof that city dwellers appreciated the facilities more for cooling off than for cleaning up.

During the bathhouse building boom, the city was also experiencing a housing boom. A law now required a toilet in every tenement apartment. Because they had to install indoor plumbing anyhow, some developers and landlords supplied a bathtub too. By the mid-twentieth century, most apartments had tubs, making public facilities unnecessary. Only three public bathhouses were still in operation in the late 1950s. (Other bath-houses served religious needs or were popular with the gay community [*see* Bathhouse Raid in the LGBTQ section]. But these bathhouses were not primarily for getting clean.)

Before Ellis Island

Most Americans of European descent think that their ancestors came through Ellis Island. But Ellis Island operated only from 1892 to 1954. Some eight million earlier arrivals, starting in 1855, entered the United States through Castle Garden, **the first immigrant receiving center in America**. (*See* Castle Garden on Walking Tour 1.)

Located in Battery Park at the southern tip of Manhattan, the structure that became Castle Garden had been erected as a military fortification to defend New York Harbor during the War of 1812. Subsequently, it was an elaborate entertainment center. It was here that, thanks to the great showman P. T. Barnum, American audiences **first heard the singer Jenny Lind**, known as "the Swedish Nightingale," in 1850.

Five years later, a federal law meant to safeguard new arrivals to the United States led to Castle Garden becoming the nation's official immigrant receiving center. After their long and arduous journey across the Atlantic, immigrants often arrived dazed and disoriented. Many could not speak English or handle American currency, and they frequently fell victim to unscrupulous hustlers who led them to overpriced and shoddy lodgings or sold them fake train tickets. Entering their new country through the official immigration center at Castle Garden, the weary travelers now would be introduced to America by workers whose job was to protect them. The center's staff connected the newcomers to licensed boardinghouses, and those going beyond New York City received real tickets to their destination. Immigrant aid groups also helped the new arrivals with the blessing of the officials.

Although operating with federal funds, the Castle Garden landing station was run by New York State. To improve efficiency and to cut duplication of efforts by state and federal officials, the center at Castle Garden closed in 1890. A temporary processing center took over until Ellis Island was ready to welcome new arrivals.

After the immigration center left Castle Garden, the one-time fort was home to the New York Aquarium for forty-five years. Today the site is under the administration of the National Park Service. Tourists go there to get tickets for the ferry to the Statue of Liberty and Ellis Island. The National Park Service website has warned visitors about illegal ticket hustlers for the ferry boats—reminiscent of the scammers who conned new Americans more than 160 years ago.

THE "Y" FOR WOMEN

In the mid-1800s, urban life was especially challenging for the many young people who left their family farms to work in the big cities of

Europe and the United States. Having made that move themselves, a group of young men living in London organized the first Young Men's Christian Association (YMCA) in 1844. They wanted a place for prayer and Bible study to distract them from the dangers of the city. Seven years later, the first YMCA in the United States opened in Boston.

Hey! It wasn't just young men who were abandoning their God-fearing rural homes for the immoral big cities. Young women were too. England led the way to help the ladies, just as it had provided a haven for the men. The Young Women's Christian Association (YWCA) began in London in 1855. **The first YWCA in the United States** opened in New York City in 1858, when a group of upper- and middle-class ladies decided it was their Christian duty to help women coming from farms and from overseas find safe and affordable housing, inexpensive meals, job training, and social support.

Hey! Hey! It wasn't just young Christians who needed support managing life in the big city. Jewish youth did too. In 1854, the Hebrew Young Men's Literary Association in Baltimore began to serve similar functions as the YMCA, but for Jewish men. Soon YMHAs (the H for Hebrew replaces the C for Christian) and Jewish community centers were opening in cities throughout America. Many had women's affiliates. In 1902 **the first independent Young Women's Hebrew Association** appeared. In New York City, of course.

BREADLINE

Most images of breadlines come from the Depression era. **The first breadline**—the one that introduced that term into the English language—actually appeared much earlier, in late nineteenth-century New York City.

In 1876, Fleischmann's Vienna Model Bakery opened on Broadway and Tenth Street (*see* the site on Walking Tour 2). That's Fleischmann's as in the yeast in the bright yellow packaging. The New York neighborhood with Fleischmann's bakery and café was the most fashionable place in the city at the time. The aroma of freshly baked bread attracted high-end shoppers by day—and hungry down-and-outers by night.

Proprietor Charles Louis Fleischmann had a soft spot in his heart for the ragged crowd that gathered for a whiff of his tasty breads. He offered one man a loaf, then another fellow, and then another. Before long a line formed every night for the day's unsold goods, which bakery workers handed out beginning at midnight. The breadline continued even after Fleischmann's death in 1904, until the building was demolished several years later.

Fleischmann discovered a marketing advantage to giving away all the leftover baked goods to New York's neediest. He was able to promote his establishment as selling only products baked fresh each day.

Settlement House

In the late 1800s, a radical idea to improve the lives of the impoverished began to take hold. Instead of offering handouts to the less fortunate, according to this philosophy, the well-to-do should live among them and work with the community to improve their lot; in other words, members of the upper classes should settle into lower-class communities. Samuel A. Barnett, a vicar of the Church of England, promoted this philosophy and began the first settlement house, Toynbee Hall, in London in 1884. **The first settlement house in the United States** was the Neighborhood Guild, founded by Stanton Coit in New York in 1886. A few years later, the name was changed to University Settlement, an apt designation because the upper-class "settlers" were well-educated.

Other settlement houses soon appeared on New York's Lower East Side. In 1889, graduates of women's colleges started College Settlement on Rivington Street. Four years later, Lillian Wald opened Nurses' Settlement, which later became the Henry Street Settlement, and started the Visiting Nurse Service of New York. By the early 1900s, New York had almost twenty settlement houses. More than a hundred settlements took root in cities across the country.

Settlement houses offered a variety of programs, including day care and kindergarten for young children, recreational programs for older children, language classes and social services for adults, and cultural and social activities for people of all ages. Staff, volunteers, and community residents who used the services of the settlement house also worked to reform deplorable conditions in the neighborhood.

Many settlement houses, including the University and Henry Street settlements, are still going strong. The people they serve have changed with evolving neighborhood demographics, and the programs strive to meet contemporary needs. One major change is the notion of settlement; those wanting to help the struggling community no longer are obliged to live there.

SCHOOL NURSE

Do you remember visiting the school nurse when you fell on the playground or had a tummy ache? Did you ever wonder how this dispenser of tender loving care ended up in a school instead of a hospital or doctor's office?

Nurses started working in schools more than a hundred years ago. **The first school nurse**, Lina Rogers, RN, was assigned to four schools in New York's tenement district in 1902. She was associated with the Henry Street Settlement, which began about a decade earlier as Nurses' Settlement, appropriately named because the founder and most staff and volunteers were nurses (*see* Settlement House in this section). Rogers' work in the educational setting was an experiment to see whether the presence of a nurse in schools would improve the health of children and decrease absenteeism. Did it ever! Within six months, absenteeism dropped by ninety percent. Children with contagious conditions such as lice or tuberculosis were sent home, as they had been previously, but now the school nurse followed up with home visits. She taught the family about hygiene and ways to prevent illness. In addition, Nurse Rogers tended to minor injuries in the school and identified children with vision or hearing difficulties that interfered with their learning.

The experiment was such a success that New York City quickly came up with funding for more school nurses. Other cities were so impressed that they hired school nurses too.

In 1914, Lina Rogers married a school doctor, William Struthers. Although she stopped working in schools at this time, she continued to help shape the specialty by writing, under her married name, **the first textbook for school nurses**. Published in 1917, the book described duties of the school nurse, explained management of common ailments of the day such as conjunctivitis and head lice, and emphasized proper hand washing and nose blowing techniques. Google Books reproduced the text in its centennial anniversary year, stating that "this work has been selected by scholars as being culturally important, and is part of the knowledge base of civilization as we know it."

Birth Control Clinic

Some issues that arouse strong passions on opposite sides lose steam after a while. Others remain hot-button issues seemingly forever. Birth control falls into the latter category.

Margaret Sanger had plenty of reasons to be passionate about birth control. Her mother had been pregnant eighteen times, and seven of those pregnancies ended in miscarriages. With so many mouths to feed, the family could barely make ends meet. Later working as a nurse in poor immigrant communities in New York, Margaret Sanger cared for many women who were suffering from botched illegal abortions. She knew something had to be done to help women who wanted to limit their family size.

To educate women about their bodies and their reproduction options, Sanger wrote articles, published her own newspaper called *The Woman Rebel*—**the first place where the term "birth control" appeared in print**—and wrote an inexpensive book, *Family Limitation*. These activities violated Comstock laws, which banned distribution of supposedly obscene information about sex and reproduction. In a direct challenge to Comstock laws, Margaret Sanger opened **the first birth control clinic in the United States** on October 16, 1916. It was in the impoverished immigrant community of Brownsville, Brooklyn.

Women, many with babies in tow, immediately flocked to the clinic. They came not for contraceptives or abortions but simply for information about preventing pregnancy. Yet Comstock laws made it illegal to offer that information. The clinic was shut down after just ten days, and Sanger was arrested—not for the first time, or for the last time.

Although the clinic was short-lived its legacy survives. Planned Parenthood traces its beginnings to Sanger and her clinic.

For the rest of her life, Sanger continued to advocate for birth control and women's reproductive rights. She contested many inequities against women and enjoyed some victories. She lived to see the U.S. Food and Drug Administration approve the sale of oral contraceptives for birth control in 1960. But when she died in 1966, at age 86, Comstock laws were still on the books.

Giving Tuesday

Buy! Buy! Buy! Spend! Spend! Spend! That's the message at the end of the year, especially in the days immediately after Thanksgiving. At the retail outlets, the hype is all about Black Friday. For online shoppers, it's Cyber Monday.

In 2012, representatives of the United Nations Foundation and the 92nd Street Y, a New York City cultural and community organization, talked about shifting the conversation to charitable giving during the post-Thanksgiving buying binge. With help from traditional news outlets and social media, **the first Giving Tuesday** came into being just a few weeks after the notion formed. That year and every year since, Giving Tuesday is observed on the Tuesday after Thanksgiving. It is now a global movement.

The organizers of Giving Tuesday were hoping it would go viral, and they were not disappointed. In the first year, Giving Tuesday fundraisers took in about $10 million. The next year, donations tallied $28 million. In 2017, Giving Tuesday saw almost ten times that amount, in part because of a matching offer by Facebook and the Gates Foundation. In 2020, U.S. contributions totaled $2.47 billion. Although these numbers reflect more spending during a spending-crazed period, the focus is different. It's directed not on consumer goods but on contributions for the benefit of others.

Sports

New Yorkers have always loved sports. I mean always, since colonial days. During the British colonial period, the land in front of the former Dutch colony of Fort Amsterdam was dedicated to lawn bowling for the nominal community sum of one peppercorn a year. Although the area is no longer home to lawn bowling, it still bears the name. Just ask anyone riding the 4 or 5 train to Bowling Green. (*See* Bowling in Toys, Games, and Other Diversions for New York's contribution to the game.)

Like lawn bowling, sports that became popular in nineteenth-century America often were British imports. Several, including cricket, tennis, and golf, had their public U.S. debut in New York City. The first indoor

Lou Gehrig (left) and Babe Ruth, two of the New York Yankees home run kings, 1927.

ice-skating rink in the United States also was in New York. Such staid entertainment wasn't always enough for the daring. Leave it to a trio of New Yorkers to challenge each other to the first transatlantic yacht race.

The city had major roles in America's national pastime, baseball. New Yorkers wrote the rules and played the first recorded baseball game. Local teams led the way with later developments in the sport, including the use of uniforms, the making and breaking of home run records, and the erosion of racial barriers. Individual New York baseball players won honors as Hall of Famers and World Series MVPs. Football and basketball also enjoyed several milestones in New York. Whether individual or team play, indoor or outdoor, low-exertion or high-energy, sports have been a major facet of life in this city.

CRICKET

Long before the invention of America's national pastime, a different bat-and-ball sport was popular here: cricket. Like so many other things in early American days, cricket was a British import.

The first public cricket match in America, documented in two newspapers at the time, took place in New York City in 1751. The teams were named for rival cities: New York and London. The New York team won.

Almost a century later, an American cricket team played a Canadian team in what is generally acknowledged as **the first international sporting event** (not counting the ancient Olympics). The game was played in New York City in 1844, although it would have taken place on Canadian soil had everything worked out differently a few years earlier. In 1840, the St. George's Club of New York received an invitation to play a cricket match in Toronto against the local team. The New Yorkers made the difficult journey, but the Canadians were surprised when they arrived and were unprepared for a formal match. Four years later, the Americans extended an invitation to the Canadians to play in New York. This time the neighbors to the north made the grueling trip. The match, planned for two days in September 1844, became a three-day event when rain postponed play on the second day. In the end, the Canadians were victorious.

Although cricket remained a popular sport in the United States for a while, it fell into disfavor after the Civil War. By then, baseball had captured the heart of the American people. But cricket remains a popular sport elsewhere. The game is catching on in the United States as more immigrants from cricket-loving countries start teams in their new home. If that home is in New York City, players don't have to go far. Each of the five boroughs has at least one cricket field.

TRANSATLANTIC YACHT RACE

It all began with a night of drinking. Three wealthy young New Yorkers bragged that their yachts could beat the other two in a race across the Atlantic. The alcohol that the young men had consumed probably fueled the stipulation that made the challenge especially risky: a December crossing. So convinced were they of the merits of their vessels that each contestant put up $30,000 for the winner-take-all dare.

A large crowd cheered as the boats took off from New York Harbor on December 11, 1866, in **the first transatlantic yacht race**. The yachts kept pace with each other for the first eight days. Then one vessel lost six crew members as it struggled against the choppy seas. The first yacht to arrive at the destination, the seaport of Cowes, England, on the Isle of Wight, was the *Henrietta*. She completed the crossing in thirteen days and twenty-two hours, making landfall in the late afternoon of Christmas Day. The other two yachts arrived eight and ten hours later.

The winning vessel belonged to James Gordon Bennett, Jr., son of the owner of the *New York Herald* (*see* Penny Press in the Media section). Apparently the victory convinced the senior Bennett that his son had some merits, and he handed management of the *Herald* to the younger man. While overseeing the newspaper, Gordon Bennett, as he was known, continued to engage in and sponsor a variety of sporting events in addition to yachting, including tennis, polo, and balloon racing. His colorful exploits made him the talk of the town. He was the naked man seen driving his horse and carriage through the fashionable streets of the city. Once, arriving drunk to his fiancée's parents' high-society party, Gordon Bennett shocked the genteel gathering by urinating in front of the guests. Those are just a few of the social faux pas of Gordon Bennett, the playboy newspaperman with a love of competitive sports.

Tennis

Sphairistike, anyone? Now that's a mouthful! Thank goodness the name of the game in which a ball is lobbed over a net with a racket changed from that to tennis.

Tennis is actually an ancient sport. Europeans later enjoyed various versions of the game, but nobody thought to write down the rules and patent the paraphernalia until an Englishman, Major Walter Wingfield, took these steps in 1874. That's why he is called the inventor of tennis, which he called sphairistike (Greek for *playing ball*).

The game and the equipment that Wingfield patented were popular among British upper classes. British army officers brought the gear to their distant posts, including Bermuda. It was there, in the very year that Wingfield got his patent, that a vacationing New Yorker named Mary Outerbridge first saw the game. She thought it was great, especially after she tried her hand at it.

Outerbridge returned home to Staten Island with the equipment needed to play tennis. She and her brother set up a court at the Staten Island Cricket and Baseball Club, creating **the first tennis court in America**. Some sources state that play began on the court in 1874; others give the date as 1886, a few months after Mary Outerbridge died. Regardless of the timing, the honor of having America's first tennis court goes to Staten Island.

Tennis became a big hit, especially among the upper crust, but it had one major drawback: it was a fair-weather game. That changed in 1904, when **the first indoor tennis court in the nation** opened in a new building in Brooklyn. The building was called the Heights Casino, but it was not a gambling establishment; it was an exclusive private club where members enjoyed squash and tennis. The club remains a fixture in Brooklyn Heights, but it now has a more open membership policy.

We've already hit two boroughs with tennis firsts. Now let's go to a third, Queens. That's where, in 1950, Althea Gibson became **the first Black tennis player to compete at the U.S. National Championship**, the precursor of the US Open. Although she didn't win the tennis title that year, she took the championship in 1957 and 1958. By breaking the racial barrier, Gibson opened the Queens courts to other Black tennis greats, including Arthur Ashe (whose name is now attached to the US Open's stadium) and Venus and Serena Williams.

(*See* Athletes in the Women Who Led the Way section for more about both Outerbridge and Gibson.)

Indoor Ice Rink

Is it possible to make enough ice for skating and to keep it solid when the temperature is above freezing—without benefit of electricity? Indeed it is, but it takes a lot of work.

London and Montreal boasted indoor ice rinks a few years before the United States. **The first indoor ice-skating rink in the United States** debuted in New York City on February 12, 1879. It was in Madison Square Garden—the first venue by that name, which, unlike most of the later ones, actually was at Madison Square. (*See* the site on Walking Tour 3.)

Making the ice was no simple matter. The first step was to lay a mile or so of pipes under the 16,000-square-foot floor. The pipes were filled with liquid ammonia, cooling the floor to thirty-two degrees. Then water was sprayed onto the floor and—presto!—it froze. The water spray continued until the ice was several inches thick, perfect for skating.

Hundreds of skaters took a spin on the ice that first day. Most wore masks and costumes, as this was a pre-Lent Carnival celebration. A band played, lights twinkled, and throngs of spectators cheered on the skaters. What an inauguration!

Golf

Golf, in some form, has been played in America since colonial times. The sport fell out of favor around the War of 1812 because it was a British import, and the Brits were the enemy. By late in that century, golf was making a comeback on this side of the Atlantic. Canadians (British subjects, of course) took up golf first, and then the game caught on in the United States. Clubs, in two senses of the word, were integral to the game—not just to swing at the ball but to play golf at all. That's because golf clubs— private groups of enthusiasts—created and maintained the golf courses.

One of those clubs was the Mosholu Golf Club of Riverdale, a section of the Bronx. Some members of the club wanted to have a somewhat wild area for a golf course, and they set their sights on nearby Van Cortlandt Park. That was municipal land, part of the city's park system. As such, the golf course could not be used exclusively by members of a private club but had to welcome all players.

The Van Cortlandt Park golf course was **the first public golf course in the United States**. Players teed off beginning on July 6, 1895. The next year, the Saint Andrew's Golf Club, one of the oldest in the country, organized and funded **the first public golf tournament** at Van Cortlandt Park. It was open to anyone, whether or not they belonged to a club. Fifty players competed.

The club members who had petitioned for the Van Cortlandt site probably had not anticipated that it would draw huge crowds. But it did, especially after public transportation made it easy to get to the course. By then, the original fifty-five-acre, nine-hole course had grown to a 120-acre spread with a full eighteen holes.

The Van Cortlandt course has been redesigned several times. It continues to draw golf enthusiasts, especially those who don't want to go far from the city to enjoy a round. Should they come with family or friends who don't play, the non-golfers will find plenty of other diversions. Van Cortlandt Park is the third largest park in New York City, and it offers playgrounds, hiking trails, running tracks, and fields for football, soccer, baseball, and even cricket.

INVENTION OF BASEBALL

The Baseball Hall of Fame is in Cooperstown, New York, about 200 miles north of New York City. That is Cooperstown's only connection to baseball. It is not the birthplace of the game.

Who said it was? Plenty of people. A common misconception is that Abner Doubleday invented baseball there in 1839. That cannot be true. Doubleday was enrolled then at West Point, and he never left the military academy from his first day in 1838 until graduation in 1842.

Rather, the credit for creating baseball goes to a New York City native named Alexander Cartwright. In September 1845, he organized a group of young men who, like himself, enjoyed playing ball in the open field at Madison Square. (*See* Madison Square on Walking Tour 3.)

Cartwright wrote down the rules of the game, which are similar to the baseball rules of today. The players called themselves the Knickerbocker Base Ball Club. On June 19, 1846, the Knickerbockers took a ferry across the Hudson River to another place they practiced, Elysian Fields in Hoboken, New Jersey. There they played **the first recorded baseball game** in history, against another team of New Yorkers. Despite having Cartwright on their side, the Knickerbockers lost with an embarrassing score of 23-1.

Because it was the setting of that baseball game, Hoboken claims to be the birthplace of baseball. Fuhgeddaboudit! The first game was played by two teams of New York City residents, and its rules and regulations originated in New York. (Hoboken may keep its claim to fame as the birthplace of Frank Sinatra, however.)

Initially, baseball was played on an open field. Then William Cammeyer, who owned an outdoor ice-skating rink in the Williamsburg section of Brooklyn and was looking for a way to extend his income-earning season beyond winter, converted the rink to a ballfield. He provided plenty of seats for spectators and enclosed the whole shebang with a fence. Union Grounds, as it was called, became **the first enclosed baseball park** with its opening game on May 15, 1862. Cammeyer did not charge admission for the opener. The regular fee of ten cents became twenty-five cents in 1867. The purpose of the price hike was not to increase Cammeyer's profits, although he didn't complain about the extra revenue. He upped the price to keep out rowdy, lower-class baseball fans for whom the higher fee would be burdensome.

BASEBALL UNIFORMS

In 1849, three years after playing the first recorded baseball game, the New York Knickerbockers donned **the first baseball uniforms**. They were simple attire: blue wool pants, white flannel shirts, and straw hats. The idea of a team uniform and team colors appealed to players and fans of this sport, which was rapidly becoming America's national pastime. Over the years, many modifications of the basic uniform occurred: the fabric; patterned cloth, such as stripes; collar treatment; socks in the team's colors; caps or helmets.

While the uniforms helped fans know which team was which, they didn't distinguish the individual players. In 1916, Cleveland tried putting numbers on players' sleeves, but that didn't help much. Then in early 1929, the New York Yankees had a brilliant idea. They announced that starting on the team's home opener, the broad backs of the uniforms would prominently display the players' numbers. Unfortunately, the opener was rained out, and Cleveland once again was the first team to take to the field sporting numbers, this time on their backs.

The players' numbers became as important as the colors and patterns of their uniforms. So important that when an outstanding player retired, so did his number. Just ten years after adding numbers to the uniforms, the Yankees were **the first baseball team to retire a number**: Lou Gehrig's number 4. Other teams followed over the years, permanently removing the numbers of the greats from their roster. A sport-wide number retirement occurred in 1997 when, fifty years after Jackie Robinson debuted with the Brooklyn Dodgers, his number 42 became **the first number retired from all professional baseball teams**. It remains the only number with this distinction. (*See* Jackie Robinson in this section for more firsts associated with him.)

In 1941, a few years before Robinson began playing with them, the Dodgers became **the first team to use a batting helmet**. The helmets were similar to baseball caps, but they had a hard lining. The move toward protective head gear had been underway for a good twenty years, ever since Cleveland player Ray Chapman was fatally hit in the head during a game against the Yankees.

It's hard to pin down when the baseball cap and jersey made the leap from the playing field to the bleachers. These days, the global sports apparel market is a multibillion-dollar business. When you put on a baseball cap with your team's logo or a shirt with your favorite player's number, thank the teams, especially the New Yorkers, that had a role in the creation of these wearable symbols of fan loyalty.

HOME RUN KINGS

When it comes to tallying up home runs, George Herman "Babe" Ruth holds some amazing records. In fact, he kept beating his own records.

In 1920, the new New York Yankee became **the first baseball player with more than fifty home runs in a single season,** smashing his record from the previous season (which hardly counts, because he played for the Boston Red Sox then); he topped his own record again in 1927 when he became **the first player with sixty home runs in a single season.** He earned the title "home run king" with a series of career milestones achieved between 1923 and 1934: he was **the first player to hit 200, then 300, 400, 500, 600, and finally 700 home runs.** The Yankees recognized that they had unusual talent and were not about to risk losing him. In 1922, Babe Ruth became **the first major league baseball player to earn a salary of $50,000.** He was one of the five players elected to the first class of the Baseball Hall of Fame. (*See* Baseball Hall of Famers in this section.)

Over the years, Babe Ruth's team, the New York Yankees, racked up more than its share of home run kings, including Lou Gehrig, Joe DiMaggio, Yogi Berra, Mickey Mantle, and Alex Rodriguez. After A-Rod's game on September 7, 2012, the Yankees became **the first club with six players who had hit 300 homers for the team.** The Bronx Bombers didn't stop at that. The 2016 Yankees were **the first team with three players who had 400 career homers**: Rodriguez, Carlos Beltran, and Mark Teixeira.

Like Babe Ruth, these home run kings often had notable firsts of their own. In 1936, Lou Gehrig became **the first baseball player with more than twenty grand slams.** Two years later, Gehrig became **the first pro to play in 2,000 consecutive baseball games.** He made such an impression on the game that when he was forced by illness to end his career in 1939, his number 4 became **the first uniform number to be retired.**

In 1936, the year Joe DiMaggio donned the Yankees uniform, the team went on to win the World Series—as it did the next year, and the year after that, and the following year too. Thus, DiMaggio was **the first athlete to be on a championship team in each of his first four seasons.** In 1941, he became **the first baseball player with a fifty-six-game hitting streak.**

What is it about the Yankees that attracts such great players? What will be the next first-time achievement of the team or of the individual players? Only time will tell.

JACKIE ROBINSON

Although Jackie Robinson is often credited with breaking the color barrier in professional baseball, that simply is not true. In 1884, Moses Fleetwood Walker played catcher for the Toledo Blue Stockings, making him the first Black professional baseball player. But racial prejudice reared its ugly head, and no African American made the cut again until Jackie Robinson joined the Brooklyn Dodgers in 1947. He was **the first Black major league baseball player in the twentieth century.**

Robinson enjoyed other undisputed firsts. At the end of that inaugural season, Jackie Robinson was **the first baseball player to be named Rookie of the Year.** In 1962, he was **the first Black player inducted into the Baseball Hall of Fame.** His performance throughout his career was so stellar that in 1997, fifty years after he first put on the Dodgers' uniform, the league chose his number 42 as **the first number to be permanently retired from baseball.** At this writing, it remains the only number with this honor.

Jackie Robinson was **the first baseball player to appear on a U.S. postage stamp,** in 1982. He was not the first Black man, however; that was Booker T. Washington, whose stamp came out in 1940.

On the field, Robinson turned a deaf ear to racist taunts. Off the field, he was an ardent supporter of civil rights. He was noted for saying, "There's not an American in this country free until every one of us is free."

(*See* the one-time home of Jackie Robinson in a Midtown hotel on Walking Tour 3.)

BASEBALL HALL OF FAMERS

When **the first class of the Baseball Hall of Fame** was announced in 1936, New York was disproportionately represented, with two of the five inductees. The honorees included Yankee great Babe Ruth (*see* Home Run Kings in this section) and Giants pitcher Christy Mathewson. Members of the Baseball Writers' Association of America cast 226 ballots in that inaugural year. The highest scorer was Ty Cobb, with 222 votes. Babe Ruth came in next, with 215 votes, and Mathewson garnered 205 votes.

No player ever received a nod from every Hall of Fame voter until 2019, when Yankees closer Mariano Rivera became **the first baseball**

player unanimously elected to the Hall of Fame. Each of the 425 voters, who qualified by a minimum ten-year membership in the Baseball Writers' Association of America, selected Rivera. Not only was it a unanimous vote; it occurred in the first year he qualified for consideration in the Hall of Fame.

Incidentally, before 2018, votes for the Hall of Fame were anonymous, unless the voter chose to reveal his selections. That left many people scratching their heads, wondering why some outstanding candidates didn't garner votes from everyone or repeatedly failed to make the cut. In an effort to increase transparency, votes are now made public. This change is likely to lead to more unanimous elections into the Hall of Fame.

WORLD SERIES MVPS

The New York Yankees have appeared in more World Series than any other baseball team, playing in about twice as many championships as the nearest rivals in the most-World-Series category. They've also had more World Series Most Valuable Players (MVPs) than any other team. Some of those games or MVPs were associated with notable firsts.

The first World Series MVP award was given in 1955. It went to Johnny Podres, who pitched for the Brooklyn Dodgers. Not the Yankees, who were the competitors in the championship series. Long-time rivals, the Dodgers and Yankees had faced off many times before, with the Yankees proving superior. Until game seven of the 1955 World Series, when Podres took the Brooklyn Dodgers' to their only World Series win.

Given that information, you can easily figure out who won the 1956 World Series, when the Dodgers and Yankees faced each other again. Game five in that series, played on October 8, entered the history books as **the first perfect game in the World Series**; it is still the only game with this distinction. The pitcher who achieved this rare feat for the Yankees was Don Larsen, who was MVP that year.

A strange coincidence occurred on July 18, 1999. It was Yogi Berra Day, and Don Larsen, long retired, threw out the ceremonial first pitch. That day, David Cone pitched a perfect game for the Yankees, only the fifteenth in regular-season baseball.

In 1960, Yankees second baseman Bobby Richardson was named World Series MVP. He was **the first World Series MVP from a losing team**. The Pittsburgh Pirates walked off with the championship that year. As of this writing, no other World Series MVP has been from a losing team.

Indoor Football

Have you ever sat wrapped in a blanket, with snowflakes falling around you, cheering on your favorite football team? Did you wish the game was in an indoor stadium instead?

While many people think that indoor football is a fairly recent concept made possible by retractable roofs, it's actually more than a century old. **The first professional indoor football game** took place on December 28, 1902, in New York City's Madison Square Garden. (*See* the site on Walking Tour 3.) The manager of the Garden at the time, Tom O'Rourke, decided to create a three-game championship playoff series, culminating on New Year's Day. He called it a World Series.

There was another big difference from a regulation football game, in addition to the inside venue. Rather, because of the venue. The field was one-third smaller than the standard football field. It was so small that one player ran into a wall at the start of the first game—the end of the game for him.

O'Rourke had the brainstorm for the indoor football series too close to the end of the year to get the top teams, but some players from those groups cobbled together squads just for the occasion. The first game, on December 28, was a showdown between two such teams: Syracuse, bolstered by three backfield players of the highly rated Watertown Red and Black, versus New York, which consisted not of players from the city or state but of players from Philadelphia's two stellar squads, the Phillies and the Athletics; they probably became "New York" because that's where the makeshift team was playing. Syracuse won the first game, 5-0, and proceeded to sweep the series against the other teams, including the hometown Knickerbockers. None of the opposing teams even scored.

Overtime in Football

It was almost as if sports promoter Harry Glickman had a crystal ball. In 1955, he asked the National Football League for permission to use sudden death should a particular upcoming preseason game end in a tie. The league had established tie-breaking rules in the 1940s, but they had never been used. Guess what! That preseason game, between the New York Giants and the Los Angeles Rams on August 28, 1955, actually was tied at the end of the fourth quarter. It became **the first overtime game in football.** The Rams won the toss to determine which team would start the overtime play and defeated the Giants in less than three and a half minutes.

Three years later, the Giants again played an extra-long game, **the first overtime championship game in football.** This time, New York was battling the Baltimore Colts at Yankee Stadium. The date was December 28, 1958, and the contest is known as "the greatest game ever played." Once again, the Giants lost, this time a little more than eight minutes into overtime.

Overtime was not good to the New York Giants in those games. But it did put the team in the history books as the only participant in both the first preseason and the first championship overtime games in American football.

Basketball

Boasting of hundreds of outdoor and indoor basketball courts, a New York City Parks website (nycgovparks.org/facilities/basketball) insists that "it's possible to find a game within walking distance of any location" and calls the city "the basketball capital of the world." Some people might dispute that; in fact, other cities also claim the title. Nonetheless, New York has had a couple of firsts in basketball.

In an era of segregated teams, the Harlem Rens were **the first all-Black professional basketball team;** that is, the players as well as the manager and owner, Robert Douglas, were Black. They played on a Black-owned court. When Douglas formed the team in 1923, he made arrangements with William Roach, owner of the Renaissance Ballroom and Casino, to use the Harlem space for practice and home games. ("Rens" is

a shortened version of the hall's name.) The Rens won the world championship in 1939, playing against the all-white Oshkosh All Stars.

Many baskets had been made since 1891, when a Massachusetts
man created the sport called basketball. But it is often said that **the first
basket** was scored in the first game in league history. The league wasn't
the National Basketball Association but its predecessor, the Basketball
Association of America. The date: November 1, 1946. The scorer: Brooklyn native Oscar "Ossie" Schectman, who was playing for the New York
Knickerbockers. The Knicks won the game against the Toronto Huskies
by two points.

With those hundreds of basketball courts in city parks and games a
short walk from anywhere, rest assured that New York City will achieve
more basketball firsts.

Toys, Games, and Other Diversions

THE LIST OF TOYS, GAMES, AND OTHER PASTIMES THAT ORIGINATED IN New York City is extraordinarily diverse. To name a few, toys for youngsters include such perennial favorites as teddy bears, Madame Alexander dolls, and Mr. Potato Head. Adults with a passion for words pass many an hour solving crossword puzzles and playing Scrabble. New York has been the birthplace of diversions for people at all levels of energy and derringdo, for those who like to stay at home and for those who prefer to play in fresh air. Sedate activities include card and board games. Like those games, bowling is another socially engaging pastime with New York roots. Thrillseekers can thank New York for introducing roller coasters. Young folks with a good sense of rhythm and agility enjoy Double Dutch jump rope. A twenty-first

One of the first teddy bears, created in 1903 by the Ideal Novelty and Toy Company in Brooklyn. It is now on display in the Smithsonian Museum of Natural History in Washington, D.C.

century innovation—the flash mob—has brought people together for no apparent reason. The broad array of toys, games, and other diversions created in New York is proof that residents of the city have always known how to have fun, in many different ways. (*See* the Sports section for more competitive individual and team games.)

BOARD GAME

Like so many things in early America, board games initially were European imports. **The first board game created and produced in America** was Travellers' Tour Through the United States. It was the 1822 creation of two brothers—no, not the Parker brothers, but Frederick and Roe Lockwood—who had a publishing business in New York City. (*See* the site on Walking Tour 1.)

Travellers' Tour was an educational game. The purpose was to teach the geography of this growing country, which then went as far west as the state of Missouri and the expansive Arkansas and Northwest Territories. Guided by a spinner (not dice, which were associated with gambling and vice), players followed a path around the board, naming cities and their population. The first person to reach New Orleans (population 10,000) was the winner.

The game apparently was a success. So much so that the Lockwood brothers created a similar game later the same year, this one taking players through Europe.

Note that the creator and producer of the first made-in-America board game was a publishing company, not a factory that could mass-produce the boards. A publisher or lithographer would have had the card stock and paper necessary to produce this type of game. Evidently, the Lockwoods didn't have proofreaders. The instructions had the apostrophe in "Travellers'," but the board lacked it; capitalization of "through" was also inconsistent. About that board. Printing presses of the day could use only one color of ink. Yet the publisher produced multicolored boards for Travellers' Tour, thanks to painstaking hand tinting.

These days, most American homes have at least one or two board games. Even with games available on all sorts of digital devices, old-fashioned board games remain much in demand. A twenty-first-century trend sometimes sees board games leaving the home for play at local game cafés and regional or nationwide game conventions or tournaments. Board games are becoming not just entertainment for family and friends but a way to connect socially in an era when many people prefer to engage with screens rather than with other human beings.

BOWLING

Near the southern tip of Manhattan is a park called Bowling Green. It is the oldest park in the city, dating from 1733, when the people of New York rented it for the sum of one peppercorn a year. Residents actually engaged in the sport of bowling there, that is, the English sport of lawn bowling, which is similar to the Italian bocce.

An obvious difference between colonial bowling and the modern version is that the former was an outdoor game. In 1840, **the first indoor bowling lanes in America** welcomed customers in New York City. Knickerbocker Alleys was a big hit, and soon other cities had indoor bowling lanes too.

The mid-1960s was the heyday of bowling, with about 12,000 alleys across the country. Subsequently, the term "multitasking" entered the language. With people having so much on their personal agendas that they felt they had to do several things at once, the desire for time-consuming leisure activity like bowling started to wane. By the end of the twentieth century, the number of bowling alleys in the United States fell to about 5,400, and it decreased to less than 4,000 by 2013. Alleys are trying to revive interest by adding gourmet fare and other attractions that appeal to a younger, upscale clientele.

ROLLER COASTER

Coney Island was already a favorite seaside resort where people could escape to the beach for a day or the whole summer, depending on their means. It already was famous for its hot dogs (*see* Hot Dog in the Food and Drink section). A carousel and a 300-foot-tall iron tower that had once been part of a world's fair were popular attractions. Then on June 16, 1884, something totally new came to entertain visitors: **the first roller coaster in America**. Called the Switchback Railway, it covered

600 feet and traveled at the, ahem, breakneck speed of six miles per hour.

The inventor of this thrill was LaMarcus Thompson. He was inspired by a ride he took on the Mauch Chunk Gravity Railway, a downhill track built to carry coal out of the mountains of Pennsylvania; it sometimes offered rides to people looking for adventure. Working off the roller coaster design plans of Richard Knudsen, who had a patent for what he called an inclined plane railway that he never actually built, Thompson tinkered until he was satisfied that he had something usable. The first roller coaster was born.

A ride on the Switchback Railway took all of a minute and cost five cents. The roller coaster consisted of two wooden tracks descending in opposite directions. Riders left their seats after the first descent and walked to the top of a fifty-foot tower to begin the second descent on the other track. Nobody seemed to mind the interruption, because they kept coming back for more. Within three weeks, the roller coaster had paid for itself.

These days, fans of roller coasters go to Coney Island to ride the Cyclone, which made its first heart-pounding trip in 1927. Like the Switchback, the Cyclone is a wooden roller coaster. It travels much farther and faster—2,640 feet of track covered at a speed of up to sixty miles per hour. The structure has twenty-seven elevation changes, including a sixty-degree drop. And the price? Well, let's just say that it's many multiples of that original nickel.

TEDDY BEAR

Nicknames of Theodore Roosevelt, the twenty-sixth president of the United States, make him sound like a tough guy: The Rough Rider, The Hero of San Juan Hill, The Lion, The Trust Buster. But he also had a softer, gentler side. Nowhere was this more apparent than in the story of an injured, 235-pound, captured black bear that he refused to shoot.

Roosevelt was known to enjoy hunting. In November 1902, he went on a hunting trip in Mississippi, accompanied by the governor and a guide, among others. The guide and his dogs managed to track and capture a bear, and he tied it to a tree until the president could finish it off.

But when Roosevelt saw the bear, he refused to shoot it, saying that killing a battle-weary, bound beast would be unsportsmanlike.

Newspapers throughout the country spread the story. Clifford Berryman, a political cartoonist, drew an illustration that appeared in the *Washington Post*. In the cartoon, the bear was a frightened cub, less than half the size of the president. Like the story itself, the cartoon spread near and far.

When Brooklyn candy store owners Morris and Rose Michtom saw the cartoon, they were deeply moved. To honor the president for sparing the animal, they quickly hand-made a stuffed bear, which they called Teddy's Bear, and displayed it in their shop window. Immediately, customers came in asking to buy the toy. Michtom wrote to the president, asking for permission to make and sell a toy bear with his name. The president agreed, adding that he doubted his name on the toy would make much difference in sales.

Theodore Roosevelt had many positive traits, but the ability to predict the future was not one of them. Teddy's bear was such a hit that the Michtoms turned it into a big business. In 1903, they founded the Ideal Novelty and Toy Company and manufactured **the first teddy bear**. Ideal soon became a leading toy and doll producer.

Incidentally, the Smithsonian Institution has one of the original teddy bears. Some sources indicate that it came from the Michtoms, others that it was a beloved plaything in the Roosevelt family.

GIN RUMMY

"Nearly everybody in the United States of America plays gin rummy. The little children in the street play it. Old broads play it. I understand there is a trained ape in the Bronx Zoo that plays it very nicely." New York story writer Damon Runyon put those words into the mouth of one of his characters, the Lacework Kid, in 1944. That was thirty-five years after another New Yorker (or perhaps a father-son duo) invented the card game.

The details are a bit sketchy. The acknowledged creator of gin rummy is Elwood T. Baker, a Brooklyn resident. He enjoyed playing cards and was good enough to teach whist. (And maybe also bridge? I said the details are a bit sketchy.) Baker was a member of the men-only Knickerbocker Whist

Club in Manhattan, and it was there that he fiddled around with other versions of rummy and similar card games to create gin rummy. One story alleges that his son was the co-creator; another story credits the younger Baker only with naming the game. Or did he? Most early references to the game call it gin poker or poker gin. Whatever it was called, the consensus is that **the first gin rummy game** was played in 1909 in New York City.

Despite what Damon Runyon wrote, gin rummy was not an instant winner. It didn't really catch on until the Roaring Twenties and the Depression. Gin appealed because, as Runyon suggests, anyone could learn it. Players didn't have to stay glued to their seats for hours; they could take a break and come back later to finish the game. That made gin rummy popular in Hollywood in the 1940s, when actors played it between takes. In the internet age, gin rummy has a big following among people who like their entertainment online.

Dolls

Sorry, Barbie. You can't take credit for being **the first full-figured fashion doll**. That was Cissy, a creation of Madame Alexander. Cissy came into being in 1955, four years before Barbie.

Cissy was not the first innovation of Madame Alexander. Her connection with dolls goes back much further, all the way to her childhood. Which is probably no surprise, because dolls are playthings of little girls. But her childhood association with dolls is unusual.

Beatrice Alexander Behrman—a.k.a. Madame Alexander—was born in 1895. Around the same time, her stepfather (the only father she ever knew), Maurice Alexander, opened **the first doll hospital in America** on Manhattan's Lower East Side, in the heart of the Jewish immigrant community. Because most residents of the impoverished immigrant enclave could barely afford to feed their families, they were not likely to pay to repair broken dolls (if their children even had dolls!). The doll hospital mended the fragile porcelain figures enjoyed by upper-class children. While these dolls awaited repair, Beatrice and her sisters enjoyed playing with them.

The young woman who grew up playing with broken dolls decided to create dolls that were more durable. She began sewing beautiful cloth dolls to sell in her father's business. In 1923, she opened her own business: the Alexander Doll Company. In the 1930s, Madame Alexander created **the first licensed dolls of popular characters**, including Alice in Wonderland, Scarlett O'Hara, and the four sisters of *Little Women*. Always experimenting with materials that would make dolls more realistic and enjoyable, Madame Alexander introduced **the first plastic dolls** in 1947, and this durable material became the standard of the doll industry. Alexander dolls' faces, bodies, and clothing won praise for their craftsmanship and attention to detail.

Throughout its successful history, the Alexander Doll Company kept many New Yorkers employed. At one point, it was the largest doll company in America. It was once one of the biggest employers in the Lower East Side and later in Harlem, where it moved in the 1950s. Production went overseas in the 1990s, but the Harlem facility remained open for about two decades as a small store, doll museum, and—harking back to the founder's childhood—doll hospital.

MR. POTATO HEAD

"Don't play with your food!" How many parents have chided their children with these words? Yet one New Yorker thought that playing with food might encourage children to eat their vegetables. His name was George Lerner, and he was the creator of Mr. Potato Head.

In 1949, Lerner made a deal with a cereal company to put silly plastic face parts into cereal boxes; this was the precursor of Mr. Potato Head. Kids were supposed to stick these plastic pieces into vegetables—potatoes, turnips, cucumbers, whatever. But the timing was bad. It was shortly after World War II, and the thought of wasting food so soon after the days of rationing did not sit well with most parents.

A few years later, Lerner struck another deal, this time with the Hassenfeld Brothers, whose company would soon become Hasbro. **The first Mr. Potato Head** appeared in 1952. The package included twenty-eight plastic facial features and accessories and a Styrofoam head, although children were encouraged to attach the pieces to real potatoes too. In the first year alone, more than one million Mr. Potato Head kits sold, thanks in no small part to a television commercial—**the first**

TV commercial for a toy. (*See* Television Commercials in the Media section.)

Over the years, Mr. Potato Head underwent several changes. A plastic potato replaced the Styrofoam in 1964. In 1987, the pipe disappeared in an effort to create a healthy role model. Mr. Potato Head in the original *Toy Story* movie had prominent eyebrows, and they have been features of the toy ever since. Incidentally, sales of Mr. Potato Head soared after the movie came out in 1995, recalling the TV ad's influence on the new product and providing further evidence of the marketing power of the media for products for youngsters.

CROSSWORD PUZZLE

I have to make a confession. I am an addict. I am addicted to crossword puzzles. I must have my daily fix: one to start the day and a couple of others later on. I was so happy to learn that my favorite pastime originated in my favorite city, New York.

The creator of the first puzzle was Arthur Wynne. He was working for the *New York World* when the editor of the newspaper asked him to come up with a new game for the paper's special Christmas edition. **The first crossword puzzle** appeared in the paper on Sunday, December 21, 1913. It didn't look like today's typical rectangle with black spaces between words. Rather, it was a diamond-shaped frame, and blank (not black) spaces between words formed a smaller diamond in the center. The numbering was odd too; a number appeared in the first and last square of each word, and the clues were numbered accordingly, such as 2-3 or 2-11. The numbering system made Across and Down headings unnecessary.

The original puzzle was called a word-cross. Readers of the newspaper enjoyed it so much that they begged for more, and their wish was granted on the next Sunday and the following one. On the fourth week, the typesetter accidently transposed the two parts of the name of the feature, and it became cross-word. Eventually, the hyphen disappeared.

For some time, the *World* produced the only crossword puzzles in town. They were a challenge to print, and other newspapers initially did not want to take on the burden. But circulation of the *World* kept going up up up, thanks in part to the puzzle feature, and other publishers realized they could sell more papers if they too had a puzzle. These days, most newspapers include at least one crossword as well as other puzzles, like Sudoku. Some newspapers feature special puzzle sections at the end of the year, reminiscent of the original crossword, I mean, word-cross.

The first book of crossword puzzles also was published in New York City. In 1924, two young men starting a publishing company, Richard L. Simon and Max Lincoln Schuster, paid the *World* $25 a puzzle for rights to reprint the newspaper's puzzles in book form. *The Cross Word Puzzle Book* sold for $1.35 and included a pencil. It was a runaway hit. Simon & Schuster continues to publish crossword books to this day—much to the delight of addicts like me.

SCRABBLE

If it weren't for the Great Depression, Scrabble might not exist. An out-of-work Queens architect, Alfred Mosher Butts, kept himself busy and mentally challenged during the Depression by creating a word game. He studied the *New York Times* and other publications to determine how many of each letter he should include in the game set. At this point, the game had tiles with letters but no board. It wasn't even called Scrabble, but Lexiko. Butts introduced the game to friends and family in 1933.

The early players enjoyed Lexiko so much that they urged Butts to get a major game company, like Milton Bradley or Parker Brothers, interested in his creation. Meeting with multiple rejections, Butts decided to manufacture the tiles himself. He sold them from his Queens apartment. Meanwhile, he kept tinkering with the game. In 1938, Lexiko became Criss Cross Words, complete with a board with premium squares for double and triple points. But the board game industry remained uninterested.

A decade later, when he was again gainfully employed as an architect, Butts met James Brunot, a game-loving entrepreneur. They refined the rules and gave the game yet another name: Scrabble. Trademarked in 1948, **the first Scrabble sets** came out fifteen years after the prototype Depression version, Lexiko.

Butts handed the reins to Brunot, agreeing to accept a royalty on sales. Initially, Brunot and friends cranked out the sets at the rate of twelve games an hour, working from an abandoned schoolhouse in Connecticut.

Slow as the production process was, enough games were in circulation by 1952 that more and more people were getting hooked. One of those Scrabble lovers was Jack Straus, the president of Macy's department store. He insisted his stores sell Scrabble. That's when the game really took off.

By 2017, more than 150 million Scrabble games had been sold. Three of every five American homes have a Scrabble set. Foreign language editions number in the twenties. Serious players can join Scrabble clubs and play in tournaments. The Depression baby has made it big time!

Double Dutch

I was never very good at jumping rope. So I am always amazed by Double Dutch. The jumpers—usually Black schoolgirls here in the city—have to go between the highs and lows of not just one but two moving ropes, and they often perform this feat while reciting rhymes or doing stunts such as handstands.

As the name implies, **the first Double Dutch games** likely came to this country in the 1600s, when colonists from the Netherlands settled in New York. Although the game varied in popularity over the next several centuries, city children practiced their skill at Double Dutch whenever they could find the time, a couple of ropes, willing rope turners, and space on the street or sidewalk.

Double Dutch went from a street game to a competitive sport in the 1970s thanks to two New York City policemen, David Walker and his partner Ulysses Williams. In those days, girls had few opportunities for organized sports. The policemen helped turn an activity the local girls loved—Double Dutch—into a tournament-level competition. **The first Double Dutch tournament** took place on February 14, 1974. Almost 600 middle-schoolers participated.

For many years, Double Dutch competitions took place at a very public New York City venue: the plaza at Lincoln Center. Before long, the competitive activity captured the world's attention. The International Double Dutch Federation, which David Walker founded, now has participants from thirteen countries. Males and females of any age and race can play, but girls generally outnumber boys.

Flash Mob

If you happened to be shopping for a rug at Macy's in Herald Square around 7:30 pm on a Tuesday in June 2003, you would have found yourself suddenly surrounded by hordes of people claiming to be shopping together for a "love rug." They were in and out in ten minutes (without making a purchase), having participated in **the first flash mob** ever. The flash mob was the brainchild of Bill Wasik, an editor at *Harper's Magazine*. He invited participants by a chain email from The Mob Project.

Wasik had tried to pull off the stunt two weeks earlier at a shop in Greenwich Village. Police got wind of it, and the flash mob was aborted. But Wasik did succeed six more times that summer and early fall, gathering a fun-loving mob in the early evening in places as diverse as the Grand Hyatt Hotel on 42nd Street, Central Park, St. Patrick's Cathedral, and a Midtown subway station.

Flash mobs quickly took to the streets of other cities around the world. Some crowds gathered and did nothing, but others engaged in harmless group activity. They danced, had pillow fights, or clapped (as they had for all of fifteen seconds at Wasik's third attempt, the one at the Grand Hyatt). Some flash mobs have convened to make a political statement. But not for too long; by design, flash mobs last only about ten minutes. If you get held up in traffic after receiving an email or text inviting you to the event, you may miss the chance to participate.

Transportation

NEW YORK CITY WOULD BE A MERE SHADOW OF ITSELF WERE IT NOT for its innovations in travel and its implementation of novel transportation systems. In the early days, the interest of this water-bound city was in shipping and in going beyond the water barriers, locally as well as nationally and internationally. Then attention shifted to moving the city's ever-growing populace across the ground—by mass transit, bicycle, car, and taxi. In the twentieth century, transportation achievements such as

Horse-drawn streetcar on Eighth Avenue (Central Park West), c. 1895.

highways and tunnels extended the metropolitan area, for all intents and purposes, beyond the city's geographic boundaries. The sky was no limit, literally. A few early aviation milestones took off from New York, and an aerial tram later opened the sky to commuters. Today, New York probably offers residents and visitors more transportation options than any other city in the world. It's one of the few places where a car is not necessary; in fact, fewer than half the city's households own cars. In transportation as in so many other fields, New York has been a leader, and its innovative approaches to moving people and goods have helped make it the great city it is.

STEAMBOATS

The early steamboats must have seemed like weird beasts, belching smoke as they traveled against the currents. So it's not surprising that the *Clermont*, the paddlewheel steamboat that Robert Fulton built in New York City with the help of Robert Livingston, was nicknamed "Fulton's Folly." Folly soon turned to fortune after the *Clermont*, **the first commercially successful steamboat,** set sail for Albany on August 17, 1807. "Folly" seemed an appropriate label when the engine stalled just after departure. Fulton had to tinker with it to get it going again. The 150-mile journey up the Hudson took thirty-two hours, which was much shorter than the standard trip. The commercial success on the return of that maiden voyage was minimal, with just two paying passengers. Yet in a matter of weeks, the trip between New York City and Albany occurred every four days, sometimes with close to 100 passengers.

Fulton did not invent the steamboat. That credit goes to John Fitch, who built steamboats in the late 1700s. In 1796, Fitch demonstrated his steamboat on the Collect Pond, a large body of water smack-dab in what was then the middle of Manhattan. Robert Fulton and Robert Livingston witnessed the Collect demonstration; according to some reports, they were actually on the vessel. (The Collect was drained a dozen years later. Court buildings dominate the area in present-day Lower Manhattan.)

Robert Livingston's brother-in-law, John Stevens, also was intrigued by the potential of steamboats. He launched **the first steam ferry service in the world** in 1811, sending a boat across the Hudson from New York

City to Hoboken, New Jersey. Commuter ferries made sense to Robert Fulton too, and in 1814 he established ferry service between Manhattan and Brooklyn. The twelve-minute ride solidified Brooklyn's reputation as a good place to live and led to the growth of America's first suburb, Brooklyn Heights. (*See* America's First Suburb in the Residences and Residential Areas section.)

Steamboats are pretty much a thing of the past, at least in the New York City area. But ferry service continues to connect the boroughs, islands of the city (including Ellis, Governors, and Roosevelt), and New Jersey. The ferries are pleasant alternatives to more crowded means of mass transportation.

Packet Ships

Crossing the Atlantic by ship was fraught with uncertainties from the day Europeans set sail for the New World. Would weather be a problem? What about pirates? Was there enough food on board? When would the ship set sail?

You'd think the last question wouldn't be an issue. But until 1818, predictable ship departures were a rarity. True, sailings were scheduled. But if a ship was not full, it might remain in port to take on additional cargo or passengers.

In 1817, the Black Ball Line began with a new mission: to set sail between New York and Liverpool, England, on a fixed schedule, regardless of how full the ship might be. The four ships in the initial fleet were called packets, because they carried mail in bundles or packets. A large black ball appeared on a sail of each ship in the fleet.

The first ship in a fleet crossing the Atlantic on a regular schedule left New York on January 5, 1818. The hold, not full after months of advertising the departure date, contained apples, flour, cotton, wool, and other goods. Eight passengers were aboard. The ship arrived in Liverpool on February 2. By then, a sister ship was well on its way from Liverpool to New York, exactly as scheduled. Soon the Black Ball Line was making two scheduled runs from each city every month and adding more sailing ships to its fleet. (*See* the site of the Black Ball Line's operation on Walking Tour 1.)

Before long, other shipping companies began to stick to a schedule. Manufacturers and merchants were happy, because they knew when they had to have their goods ready to ship and when merchandise would likely arrive. Immigrants appreciated the relatively inexpensive fare in the crowded steerage section. The packet ships also had cabins to accommodate wealthier travelers in better quarters.

In the Black Ball Line's first year, a crossing averaged twenty-five days to Liverpool and forty-three days to New York, when it was heading into the wind. The advent of the steamship later in the century cut the travel time in half and put the sailing packets out of business. One of the last companies to shut down was the granddaddy of them all, the Black Ball Line, which made its final crossing in 1878.

STREETCARS

In the 1820s, New York City was experiencing major growth, both in terms of geographic area and population. As the city spread out and more people worked farther from where they lived, mass transit became a necessity. Starting in 1827, New Yorkers could board a horse-drawn omnibus that ran along a set route on the cobblestone streets. Akin to a stagecoach, the omnibus could carry twelve to fifteen passengers.

Mass transit improved remarkably five years later with the introduction of **the first streetcar in the world** on November 14, 1832. The initial route was on the Bowery and Fourth Avenue between Prince Street and Union Square in Manhattan. Like the omnibus, the streetcar was pulled by horses. What distinguished it was that its wheels ran along metal tracks embedded in the pavement. As a result, the ride was smoother and faster—a whopping six to eight miles per hour! Streetcars (or trolleys, as they are sometimes called) also could accommodate more passengers. Because it was so efficient, the price of a trolley trip was just ten cents, compared with fifteen cents on the bumpier, slower omnibus.

Convenient as mass transit was, it had its drawbacks. The most glaring was that every one of those dependable workhorses produced about twenty-two pounds of manure every day, waste that piled up in the filthy city streets.

As new technologies to power trolleys—steam, cable, electricity—became available in the late nineteenth century, streetcars gained popularity not just in Manhattan and Brooklyn but in other cities throughout the globe. Streetcars fell out of favor in New York City in the early twentieth century. Faster elevated trains and subways became the preferred mode of mass transit. Cars began to outnumber horses. Buses replaced streetcars for surface movement of large numbers of people.

A relic of the streetcar era, oddly, is in the field of sports. The Brooklyn Dodgers baseball team got its name because pedestrians had to dodge the trolleys that crisscrossed the borough. These days, Brooklyn can boast of neither streetcars nor the Dodgers, but these one-time symbols of New York are popular in northern and southern California cities, respectively.

Scenic Rides

The diverse terms for roads often are descriptive. A driver pays a fare to use a toll road but not a freeway. Traffic on an expressway moves fast—except, ironically, during rush hour. And a parkway is a landscaped road that may be as scenic as the first syllable of its name.

The masters of park design, Frederick Law Olmsted and Calvert Vaux, coined the term "parkway." They saw this type of road as being purely for pleasure drives, without commercial traffic. Olmsted and Vaux envisioned a parkway system with landscaped roads connecting all the parks in an area. Eastern Parkway would lead to their great Brooklyn creation, Prospect Park. Ocean Parkway would go from there to Coney Island.

It didn't actually end up the way the parkway designers had planned. Today, Eastern Parkway and Ocean Parkway are both busy Brooklyn thoroughfares. Of course, when Olmsted and Vaux conceived the parkway system, horse-drawn vehicles plied the roads. Today, cars clog the parkways—making them anything but scenic.

Before the honking of impatient drivers replaced the neighing of carriage horses taking passengers for pleasure drives, Ocean Parkway became famous for its management of another form of recreational riding: bicycles. In 1894, **the first dedicated bike lane in America** opened on Ocean Parkway. Stretching five and a half miles, the bike lane was an updated version of an innovation of Olmsted and Vaux, who had used the concept of separation of traffic in Central Park and Prospect Park. In those parks, though, cyclists shared the paths with carriages or pedestrians. On Ocean Parkway, each had its own lane, shaded by trees along the dividing lines. The bike lane was created quite simply by dividing the pedestrian pathway so that both walkers and bikers had their own space.

The nineteenth century concept of parkways survived into the twentieth century, when the car became king of the road. In 1925, the Bronx River Parkway opened to traffic between that borough and Westchester County; it was **the first multilane, limited-access automobile road in America**. Many parkways followed, both in New York and in other parts of the country. The man behind many of the New York roads was long-time Parks commissioner Robert Moses. Unlike Olmsted and Vaux, for whom parks were the be-all and end-all, Moses felt the roads leading to them were at least as significant as the parks themselves.

AUTOMOBILE ACCIDENTS

Where there are cars, there may be accidents. Especially if drivers are reckless.

That was certainly the case on May 30, 1896, when several cars were participating in a "horseless wagon race" in New York City along Broadway. One of the drivers, Henry Wells of Springfield, Massachusetts, lost control and rammed into cyclist Ebeling Thomas. The biker, who was going in the opposite direction, suffered a broken leg. This is widely considered **the first automobile accident in America**. However, some claim that America's first accident occurred five years earlier in Ohio, when car inventor John William Lambert hit a tree root and crashed into a post; neither he nor his passenger was seriously injured. But without question, **the first car versus bike accident** was the Wells-Thomas affair.

The first fatal car accident in America occurred on the evening of September 13, 1899. Real estate dealer Henry H. Bliss had just gotten off the Eighth Avenue streetcar at 74th Street and was helping a lady friend off when he was hit by an electric cab. Bliss fell to the ground, and the cab ran over him. Although driver Arthur Smith was arrested, charges of manslaughter were dropped after witnesses reported that a large truck in the road had forced the cab to go close to the trolley. Incidentally, electric cars were common in those early automotive days.

TAXICAB

Although they never seem to be available when it's raining, taxicabs are so plentiful in Manhattan that yellow is the predominant color on the congested streets. The metered, motorized vehicle-for-hire was a German invention. **The first metered, gasoline-powered cabs in America** appeared on New York City streets on August 13, 1907.

Cabs existed long before then, but they were horse-driven hansoms. They had a little competition around the turn of the century from a new-fangled invention called the automobile. The Electric Vehicle Company operated cabs in New York City from 1897 until January 1907. An electric cab was involved in the first fatal auto accident (*see* Automobile Accidents in this section). Without a meter in the cab, drivers of horse-drawn or electric-powered vehicles could charge whatever they wanted. That's what led to the taxi being imported from Europe.

A New Yorker named Harry N. Allen became outraged when a hansom cab driver charged him five dollars for a brief ride of less than a mile. He decided to start a cab company that based fares on distance traveled, a practice already taking place in several European cities. A German invention called a taximeter made it easy to determine the distance and fare. That device suggested the name of Allen's new enterprise: the New York Taxicab Company. Allen imported a fleet of sixty-five gas-powered cabs equipped with a taximeter. He painted them yellow so they would be easy to spot from afar. In just a year, the fleet grew to 700 cabs.

The initial fare was fifty cents a mile. Although this was considerably less than the gouging fee that led Allen to start his company, it still was too steep for the average New Yorker. But that was a bargain by today's standards. At this writing, just getting into a cab costs two and a half dollars. Then the meter starts ticking, and the fare jumps up fifty cents for every fifth of a mile or every sixty seconds in slow or stopped traffic. Pile on a slew of surcharges—including rush hour, overnight, and the most recent congestion surcharge—as well as tolls on bridges and tunnels. And don't forget the tip. Cab rides are again becoming too steep for the average Joe.

UNDERWATER TUNNEL FOR CARS

The availability of automobiles meant that areas that once were a trek were now just a short drive away. For cities like New York that were surrounded by water, the challenge was having a road for that drive. Bridges over the water made that possible. Tunnels didn't seem like a logical solution, because they would retain exhaust from the cars. Leave it to a New Yorker to rise to the challenge and create **the first mechanically ventilated underwater vehicular tunnel** in the world.

That man was Clifford Holland, and his feat of engineering bears his name. The mile-and-a-half-long Holland Tunnel goes under the Hudson River and connects Canal Street in Lower Manhattan with Jersey City, New Jersey. The engineer erected two ten-story buildings on each side of the Hudson and placed eighty-four fans in them. Some of those fans are for back-up only, to be sure the ventilation system always works. Vents at the bottom of the tunnel funnel in fresh air, and ducts in the ceiling create the escape route for carbon dioxide. The air in the tunnel is completely replaced about every ninety seconds.

Holland did not live to see his masterpiece completed. He had a fatal heart attack when he was only forty-one years old. Three years later, in November 1927, the Holland Tunnel opened to traffic. The toll was fifty cents.

The tunnel toll is a lot more today. The exact fare depends on the size of the vehicle, the time of day, and the presence or absence of E-ZPass for payment. The toll can be as much as sixteen dollars for a car, a lot more for a bus or truck. One consolation: tolls are collected only when going into New York, not when leaving the city.

The Holland Tunnel was not the first underwater tunnel in the world. That honor goes to the Thames Tunnel in London, which opened in 1843. Given the year, that tunnel obviously was not built for cars. At just a fraction of the length of the Holland Tunnel, the quarter-mile Thames Tunnel posed little threat that those passing through it would be poisoned by noxious gas.

Early Aviation Milestones

Plane travel is so common these days that we seldom think of the daring men and women who flew where nobody had flown before. Two early aviators, although not New Yorkers, began their pioneering feats in New York.

The first was one of the brothers whose name is synonymous with early flight: Wilbur Wright. On September 29, 1909, he made **the first flight over water**, taking off from Governors Island, just off the southern tip of Manhattan, and circling the Statue of Liberty before returning to his starting point. He was so uncertain of the feasibility of this flight that he tied a canoe under the plane, just in case he made a premature splashdown. Thousands of boats, large and small, assembled in New York Harbor to witness the historic over-water flight.

Two years later, flights of fancy were starting to look more plausible, if only someone would rise to the challenge. Newspaper mogul William Randolph Hearst made one challenge appealing by offering a $50,000 prize to the first person to fly coast-to-coast in thirty days or less. Cal Rodgers took the bait, even though he had not spent much time piloting a plane. He took off from Sheepshead Bay in Brooklyn on September 17, 1911. Forty-nine days later—too late to collect the prize money, but not too late to earn the title of **first to complete a transcontinental flight**—Rodgers touched down in California. It was a miracle that he finished the 4,000-mile journey. The plane kept falling apart and crashing. Anticipating that the craft might not be sturdy enough for such a long and difficult journey, Rodgers had outfitted a train with spare parts, a repair shop, and mechanics, including the Wrights' mechanic Charlie Taylor; the train also carried the pilot's wife and mother. For much of his trip, Rodgers used the train tracks as his navigation guide. Rodgers spent eighty-two hours in the air; the rest of the time he was on the ground for refueling, repairs, and recovery from injuries sustained in his many crash-landings.

And we complain about the five to six hours to fly coast-to-coast today!

Charles Lindbergh's famous 1927 feat, the first solo nonstop transatlantic flight, doesn't merit inclusion in this book. Although described as a New York-to-Paris flight, Lindbergh departed from Roosevelt Field on Long Island, which is not part of New York City.

Automated Train

Driverless cars were the talk of the 2010s. Some fifty to sixty years earlier, it was driverless subways. Automated trains actually seem to make more sense than driverless cars, because trains go on a fixed track to a given destination; in other words, they travel an unchangeable path. But is a driverless train safe?

In the mid-twentieth century, after several years of testing and modifications to assure safety, the New York City transit system decided to give driverless trains a try. The line selected for **the first automated train in the United States** was a short subway run, the shuttle between Times Square and Grand Central Terminal. The automated train ran on track 4 and did not cross paths with any other train. Although it was fully automated, a motorman was on board for every ride from the maiden journey on January 4, 1962, until April 21, 1964.

Early on that April day, a fire broke out on track 3. The fire was so intense that it damaged the automated subway on the next track. Despite the popularity of the driverless train—riders often passed up the manually operated shuttle so they could ride the novelty—the transit company decided not to bring back the automated subway.

The two-year-plus run was more than a proof of concept. The feasibility and safety of automated trains were now certain. Today, driverless trains ride the rails in dozens of cities throughout the world. That includes New York, where the fully automated, driverless AirTrain links the terminals of JFK airport and connects to the city's subway system.

Aerial Commuter Tram

Back when the island in the East River about halfway between Queens and Manhattan's Upper East Side was known as Welfare Island, few people wanted to go there. After all, most people on the island, by design, were convicted criminals, extremely poor, or physically or mentally ill. By the 1960s, however, Welfare Island was almost a ghost town, and it seemed an ideal place for a bold experiment: a planned, middle-class community with a new name, Roosevelt Island. Because many of the residents would be working in Manhattan, they needed easy access across the river. While a subway was under construction, an aerial tramway began operating in 1976. It was **the first aerial commuter tram in the country**.

Today, residents and visitors have multiple options to reach Roosevelt Island. They can take the tram from Manhattan or a bus from Queens—once the only ways to get to the island, other than by car—or a subway or ferry from both boroughs. The tram remains a popular choice, in part because of the fantastic views of Midtown from high above the East River. About 6,000 people, in groups of up to 110, take the three-minute ride on most days.

As pleasant and efficient as this mode of mass transit is, decades passed before another American city decided to copy New York's innovative commuter method. In 2006, the Portland (Oregon) Aerial Tram began carrying passengers to a redeveloped area called South Waterfront. The tramways on both coasts have succeeded in transforming derelict spits of land into thriving communities.

Women Who Led the Way

MOST OF THE ENTRIES IN THIS BOOK DESCRIBE THE ACHIEVEMENTS OF men—not because they are more ambitious, capable, or creative, but because women historically have had fewer opportunities to showcase their talents and to pursue their hopes and dreams. This section singles out New York women who were pioneers in a variety of fields tradition-ally dominated by men: the military, medicine, business, sports, politics, and law. These women made their mark as early as the Revolutionary War period and as recently as the twenty-first century. Like so many other women, the people you read about in this section often had to overcome

The three women from New York City who have served on the Supreme Court, 2010. From left, Sonia Sotomayor, Ruth Bader Ginsburg, and Elena Kagan.

hurdles and harassment simply because of their gender. Some had to fight twice as hard against not just sexism but also racial, religious, or ethnic biases. These women who led the way embodied the true New York spirit, refusing to let senseless societal barriers stand in their way. May these trailblazers inspire future generations so that in the next 400 years as many women as men will be associated with firsts in New York City.

MILITARY SERVICE

Early in U.S. history, one New York woman made such an impression with her military service that the new Congress recognized her with a special honor. Margaret Corbin joined her husband during the Revolutionary War when he went to protect the northern end of Manhattan in the Battle of Fort Washington. When her husband was shot dead right before her eyes, she slid into his position and started firing a cannon. Before the battle was over, she was wounded so severely that she was unable to use her left arm for the rest of her life.

Her valor did not go unrecognized. On July 6, 1779, Congress awarded her a lifelong pension equivalent to half a soldier's pay, plus a suit of clothes to replace those ruined in battle. With these benefits, Margaret Corbin became **the first woman to receive a military pension from the United States.**

In the twentieth century, the area that she and her husband had defended so valiantly became a city park, Fort Tryon Park. Margaret Corbin received additional recognition at that time. The circle near the entrance and the park's long, steep drive are named for her. A plaque in the park calls Margaret Corbin "the first American woman to take a soldier's part in the war for liberty."

Consider making a visit to Fort Tryon Park. In addition to the memorials to Margaret Corbin, you'll find a lovely heather garden that is attractive year-round, great views across the Hudson River, and a branch of the Metropolitan Museum of Art, the Cloisters, which features medieval artifacts and tapestries.

Doctor

Elizabeth Blackwell was born in England and spent the last forty years of her long life there. Between the beginning and end of her life, though, she lived in the United States and achieved what no American woman had up to that time. Graduating from medical school at the top of her class in 1849, she became **the first woman doctor in the United States**.

Getting into medical school wasn't easy. Blackwell applied to many of the best schools in the country, and all of them rejected her because she was a woman. She was able to enroll in Geneva Medical College in upstate New York only because school administrators left the decision up to the students. Thinking it was a joke, they said, "Sure, let her come."

Armed with her medical degree, Elizabeth Blackwell moved to New York City to establish a practice. This was almost as challenging as getting into medical school! To attract patients, she gave lectures and wrote articles on women's health, hygiene, and the importance of physical exercise. In 1857, she opened the New York Infirmary for Women and Children to provide care for the poor. Blackwell also established the Woman's Medical College in conjunction with the hospital to train other female physicians. One of them was her sister Emily, who was the third woman doctor in America.

Elizabeth Blackwell died in 1910, at the age of eighty-nine. At that time, more than 7,000 American women were physicians. In 2019, nearly 360,000 women in America were practicing medicine, accounting for thirty-six percent of all physicians in the country. The percentage of female enrollees in medical school in the United States exceeded the percentage of males for the first time in 2017. Thank you for being a trailblazer, Elizabeth Blackwell!

Retail Executives

Women have always been the shoppers in the family. Yet throughout most of history, stores usually were owned and operated by men. Female employees, including relatives of the shop owner, tended to serve as clerks rather than as decision makers.

When Margaret Getchell moved to New York City in 1861, she took an entry-level clerk position at a three-year-old dry goods store called

Macy's. A former schoolteacher, Getchell was a whiz with numbers, and she soon was promoted to bookkeeper. She had lots of ideas about how to improve the business, and she often shared her thoughts with her boss, R. H. Macy himself. He was so impressed that he promoted her again, this time to superintendent, an executive position. That is how, in 1866, Margaret Getchell became **the first woman in an executive position in retail**. By 1869, Getchell oversaw 200 employees, who racked up a million dollars in sales a year. (*See* Department Stores in the Business and Commerce section for more about Macy's, and *see* the flagship store, which replaced the store where Getchell worked, on Walking Tour 3.)

Getchell's understanding of shopping, women, and female customers helped transform Macy's from an ordinary dry goods store to a full-fledged department store selling ready-made clothes, jewelry, toiletries, and household goods. She had ideas not just about what to sell but about how to lure customers into the store and into departments they had not planned to visit. She developed window displays to attract passersby and suggested that Macy's install a soda fountain for thirsty shoppers, placing it so customers had to walk through several departments on the way to refreshments.

Getchell married a Macy's employee, and they lived in rooms above the store. When her husband was promoted to partner, she was asked to give up her salary and agreed without a murmur. A company woman to the end, she continued to work for Macy's without pay while raising a family. She even ran the store for several months—while pregnant and not collecting a salary—when Macy and Margaret's husband were on a European buying trip. Would any woman do that today?

In the early twentieth century, another woman who eventually called New York City home made her mark in sales. Madam C. J. Walker, nee Sarah Breedlove, created a line of hair care products for Black women. She sold them personally, traveling around the country and giving talks and demonstrations. Her business was such a success that she became **the first Black female millionaire in America**. (For more about Madam C. J. Walker, *see* Millionaires in the Business and Commerce section.)

Brokerage Firms

In the mid- to late-1800s, Wall Street was very much a man's world. It came as a shock—a scandal, actually—when in 1870 two sisters, Victoria Woodhull and Tennessee Claflin, became **the first women to own a brokerage firm on Wall Street**. Initially, the curious came by to see if the business was for real. Within weeks, the sisters had a steady stream of clients—many of them women, from society wives to high-priced call girls with money to invest.

The sisters themselves were rather colorful characters. Before settling down to business, they supported themselves as spiritual advisors—the fortune-telling kind, not the religious type. Victoria Woodhull was twice divorced and a proponent of free love. A political activist, she advocated for women's rights and ran for president on the Equal Rights ticket long before women could vote. (*See* Presidential Politics in this section.) Tennessee Claflin was rumored to have had an affair with one of the richest men in America, Cornelius Vanderbilt. He provided financial backing when the sisters told him they wanted to open a brokerage house.

Although they owned a brokerage firm, Woodhull and Claflin did not own a seat on or become a member of the New York Stock Exchange. To own a seat, a broker had to go through a stringent review process, obtain sponsorship, and pay a substantial sum. The reward was also substantial, as membership enabled the broker to trade on the floor of the Stock Exchange. **The first woman to own a seat on the New York Stock Exchange** was Muriel Siebert, who obtained hers in 1967 after numerous rejections from would-be sponsors (all men, of course). For the next ten years, Siebert was the only woman, among more than 1,000 men, with a seat. In the 1990s, about nine percent of the traders were women. Since 2006, when the Stock Exchange switched from private membership to a for-profit entity, nobody—man or woman—can own a seat.

Recently, the statue of a young female, *Fearless Girl*, has been staring down the New York Stock Exchange. Her defiant pose—and the seemingly endless stream of girls and young women standing next to her for photos—may serve as a warning that women are poised to take a more prominent position in the brokerage world.

Athletes

You may know that Gertrude Ederle was **the first woman to swim across the English Channel**. But did you realize that she was a New Yorker? Born and raised in Manhattan, Ederle made the historic swim on August 6, 1926. She completed the feat in fourteen hours and thirty-one minutes, faster than the five men who previously had swum the channel. For this accomplishment, she was **the first woman to be honored alone (rather than with others) by a ticker-tape parade** in New York City's Canyon of Heroes. (*See* Ticker-Tape Parade in the Parades section.)

Just a few weeks later, Amelia Gade Corson became the second woman and **first mother to swim across the English Channel**. Born in Denmark, she had emigrated to the United States in 1919 and settled in New York City. She too was honored with a ticker-tape parade upon her return home.

Tennis is another sport with a you-may-know-but-did-you-realize story. You may know that the US Open takes place in the New York City borough of Queens every year toward the end of summer. But did you realize that a New York woman introduced tennis to the United States? The woman was Mary Ewing Outerbridge, a Staten Island resident. While vacationing in Bermuda in 1874, Outerbridge saw British army officers playing a game in which they used rackets to hit a ball to each other across a net. She returned to Staten Island with the game's equipment and created **the first tennis court in America** at the Staten Island Cricket and Baseball Club.

When you think of African American tennis players, the Williams sisters or Arthur Ashe probably come to mind. Before them, Althea Gibson, a Harlem resident, made history as **the first Black tennis player to compete at the U.S. National Championship and at Wimbledon**. She broke the racial barrier at the U.S. tournament in 1950 and at Wimbledon in 1951. Between 1956 and 1958, she won eleven major tennis championships. Although best known for her tennis prowess, Gibson was an athlete of many talents. In 1960, she was **the first Black woman to compete on the professional golf tour**.

(*See* Tennis in the Sports section for more about the game enjoyed by Outerbridge and Gibson.)

PRESIDENTIAL POLITICS

You may be surprised to learn that Hillary Clinton was not **the first woman to run for president of the United States**. That honor goes to Victoria Woodhull, who threw her hat in the ring for the 1872 election—nearly fifty years before women had the constitutional right to vote. Her running mate on the Equal Rights party ticket was the noted abolitionist Frederick Douglass. Woodhull was simultaneously treading where no woman had gone before in the business world. With her sister, she opened the first female-owned brokerage house on Wall Street in 1870. (*See* Brokerage Firms in this section.) Needless to say, Woodhull's presidential bid was unsuccessful.

A century after Woodhull's first foray into presidential politics, Brooklynite Shirley Chisholm became **the first Black woman to run for president** on a major party ticket. In the 1972 Democratic race, she earned 152 of the delegates' votes but bowed out after twelve primaries. Chisholm had already made history in 1968 when she was elected to Congress, **the first Black woman in the House of Representatives**.

Another New Yorker became **the first woman nominated for vice president.** Geraldine Ferraro, a congresswoman from the New York City borough of Queens, took the second-position slot on the Democratic ticket in the 1984 election. The presidential nominee was Walter Mondale, who was defeated by the popular incumbent, Ronald Reagan.

Back to Hillary Clinton. She was the first woman to win the presidential nomination of a major political party. But that doesn't earn her inclusion in this book. Although her husband opened an office in New York City's Harlem after his presidential term and she served as senator, she represented New York State (not City) and made her home in Chappaqua, a small town north of the city.

JUDGES

Only five of the 115 Supreme Court justices in the United States through 2020 have been women, and three of the five were New Yorkers. Not the first woman on the bench, however; Sandra Day O'Connor, who took a seat on the Supreme Court in 1991, hailed from Arizona.

Two years later, she was joined by Brooklyn-born Ruth Bader Ginsburg. A graduate of Columbia Law School, she returned as a faculty member, further solidifying her New York City ties. Ginsburg was **the first female Jewish justice on the Supreme Court**, but not the first Jew; that was Louis Brandeis, from Boston. When she died in September 2020, Ginsburg was **the first woman and the first Jew to lie in state at the U.S. Capitol**.

Sonia Sotomayor was the third woman appointed to the highest court in the land. Born and raised in the Bronx, she served as a judge in federal courts in New York before being named to the Supreme Court in 2009. She was **the first Hispanic judge on the Supreme Court**.

Elena Kagan joined her within a few months. A native of Manhattan, Kagan was **the first female Solicitor General of the United States**, but she held the post only for a few months before being named to the Supreme Court in 2009. By this time, all the Supreme Court "first" titles she would have fit had already been taken (first woman, first Jew, first New Yorker).

Female judges from New York also made history on lower courts. Deborah A. Batts was **the first openly gay or lesbian federal judge** when she took the bench of the U.S. District Court for the Southern District of New York in 1994; Sotomayor had previously served on this court. (Vaughn Walker, a federal judge in California, was appointed earlier, but he did not come out until after retiring in 2011.) Batts was the only openly LGBTQ judge in the federal court system for seventeen years.

Finally, when Rachel Freier won election for judge in a Brooklyn civil court in 2017, she became **the first Hasidic (a Jewish sect) woman elected to public office in the United States**. Not bad for a mother of six who was thirty years old when she began college.

Walking Tours

NOTE: Even if you can't take a walking tour, don't ignore this section. It has interesting stories about some of the buildings along the route, stories that would have cluttered the narrative about firsts in the main body of this book.

If you're like me, it's not enough to just read about a unique place; you want to see it with your own eyes. Unfortunately, that's not always possible for many of the firsts in this book. In some cases, I tried to pinpoint the exact address but was unable to do so. Other buildings for which I had exact locations have disappeared from the Manhattan landscape. That might also apply to some of the sites that existed when I wrote this, because New York is an ever-changing city.

The walking tours on the following pages focus on the firsts described in this book. I don't go into much detail and sometimes even avoid mentioning well-known places in plain sight. Therefore, the walks might be more interesting to New Yorkers, who have at least a nodding acquaintance with the major attractions of the city, rather than to tourists who want to see the highlights during their visit. I have selected areas where multiple innovations occurred and eliminated some of the more distant points in the vicinity, interesting though they may be. Some of the more remote points do appear, however, as Bonus Options. Other Bonus Options are not firsts but will appeal to some readers, especially tourists.

Because of the distances between points where firsts occurred, I have limited the tours to Manhattan. As it turned out, only four areas gave birth to a sufficient number of novel accomplishments to create good walking tours: the Financial District, from the southern tip of Manhattan north to about Fulton Street; Greenwich Village, from Astor Place on the east to Seventh Avenue on the west; Madison Square to Herald Square;

and Midtown in the 40s and 50s, within a few blocks either way of Fifth Avenue.

A note about typography in this section. Stops on the walking tours and firsts are in boldface. The non-bold wording in the stop's name is the present entity, if different, or the location. Walking directions are in italics.

Usually, the best place to stand to look at a building is across the street. That's why some of the stops are opposite the attraction. You might want to observe the top of skyscrapers from a few blocks away so you don't strain your neck, then go right up to the site to examine the details.

Whenever you find yourself walking several blocks to the next destination, make your own discoveries about New York City. You'll find something fascinating almost everywhere. Unless you're pressed for time, go into buildings along the route, and stop at the parks to enjoy New York's favorite pastime: people watching.

Hoping you'll enjoy such diversions, I haven't indicated how long the walks will take. Walking at a leisurely pace and pausing to read this text at each stop, you can probably do each walk, up to the Bonus Options, in fifty to seventy-five minutes. The main routes (not including Bonus Options and diversions of your choosing) range from one to two miles.

WALKING TOUR 1: FINANCIAL DISTRICT

(About one mile up to the Bonus Options)

Begin in front of 1 Broadway, across from Bowling Green Park (the oldest park in the city, where early residents enjoyed lawn bowling). Look down at the pavement.

1. Ticker-Tape Parades (on Broadway, starting in front of 1 Broadway and going north to City Hall)
More than 200 ticker-tape parades have traveled up Broadway. **The first ticker-tape parade** was on October 28, 1886, in honor of the dedication of the Statue of Liberty. Each parade is memorialized with a granite marker set into the sidewalk along Broadway on both sides of the street. You'll see more markers later when you return to Broadway.

As you cross Battery Place toward Battery Park, note the street sign for Broadway. In this area, because of the ticker-tape parades, it is nicknamed the Canyon of Heroes. As Broadway bends south, the name changes to State Street.

Enter Battery Park, and head toward the large round structure. You don't need to go all the way there unless you need a bathroom or want a good view of the Statue of Liberty in New York Harbor.

2. Castle Clinton/**Castle Garden** (inside Battery Park)

The land where Castle Clinton stands was once an island with this structure, a fortification built to protect the harbor leading up to the War of 1812; landfill subsequently connected the island to Manhattan. In 1824, when no longer needed for military purposes, the fort became an entertainment center named Castle Garden. This was **the first place Jenny Lind, "the Swedish Nightingale," performed in America,** in 1850. Five years later, Castle Garden was repurposed as **the first immigrant processing center in America**. It welcomed eight million immigrants over the next thirty-five years, after which Ellis Island took over. Castle Clinton, the current name, is the place to purchase tickets for ferries to the Statue of Liberty and Ellis Island.

Return to State Street (Broadway), and turn right (south). Walk two blocks south to Pearl Street, and cross the street. Stay on State Street, walking around the bend to the red-brick building.

3. **Shrine of St. Elizabeth Ann Seton** (7 State Street)

Elizabeth Ann Seton (1774-1821) was **the first American-born saint**. Her birth family, the Bayleys, lived in a building that no longer exists. The shrine building, next door to the Bayleys' home, was where James Watson lived; it dates back to 1793. Typical of the Federal-style homes of the era, it is the only building in this area from that period that is still standing.

Return to Pearl Street, by cutting through the plaza beside the shrine if you wish, and continue northeast on Pearl Street three blocks to Fraunces Tavern.

4. **Fraunces Tavern** (54 Pearl Street, at Broad Street)

In pre–Revolutionary War days, Samuel Fraunces operated a tavern here. At that time, taverns frequently served as meeting places, not just for eating and drinking but also for conducting business. On April 5, 1768, a group of businessmen met here and formed **the first Chamber of Commerce**. On December 4, 1783, George Washington bid farewell to his troops in the Long Room of the tavern. Later, several departments of the newly formed United States government made the tavern their headquarters.

Samuel Fraunces was born in the West Indies; he was probably Black. Renowned for his desserts, he so impressed America's first president that Washington hired him as his chief steward.

What you see here is not the actual tavern run by Samuel Fraunces, but a reconstruction. The building had been converted to a boardinghouse and was in bad shape when the Sons of the Revolution in the State of New York purchased it in 1904. They hired architect William Mersereau to restore the building to the way it might have looked in its heyday. It was pure guesswork, because no historic pictures were available. These days, Fraunces Tavern is both a restaurant and a museum with artifacts from its early days.

If you want, go into Fraunces Tavern to visit the museum or enjoy a drink or meal. Then cross both Broad and Pearl Streets, and walk along the wide sidewalk on Pearl Street almost to the next corner, Coenties Slip. Check out the plexiglass-covered areas over relics of colonial New York that were discovered during twentieth-century excavations. Continue north on Pearl Street another block to Hanover Square, noting the nineteenth-century buildings along the way. Turn left (west) at Hanover Square, perhaps stopping first to admire the little park (it's my favorite park in the Financial District). Continue two blocks on William Street, past Stone Street, to the triangular patch where William Street meets South William and Beaver Streets.

5. Delmonico's (56 Beaver Street, at William Street)
Delmonico's is considered **the first restaurant in America**. Other eateries preceded its opening in 1837. But this was the only freestanding eating establishment that offered choices, a printed menu, and fine fare. The restaurant began at a different building on this triangle. In 1890, architect James Brown Lord created the present structure.

As its high-class clientele moved farther north, so did Delmonico's. It had several homes before returning to the very location where it all began. It still serves its namesake steak. Delmonico's also professes to have invented lobster Newberg, baked Alaska, and **the first eggs Benedict**—dishes still on the menu—although some of these origin claims are disputed.

By the way, Delmonico's occupies only the ground floor of this building. Like many former office towers and commercial structures in the Financial District, the building now contains residential apartments on the upper floors.

Walk north on William Street (which turns here; watch the street signs) two blocks to Wall Street, and turn left (west). Pass the gilded Trump Building at 40 Wall Street (once the Bank of Manhattan, the tallest building in the world for a few months in 1930 until the Chrysler Building raised its spire). Continue to the corner of Nassau/Broad Street.

6. Federal Hall (26 Wall Street, at Nassau Street)

The correct name of the building with the many steps and columns is Federal Hall National Memorial. It replaced the previous building called Federal Hall, which was actually City Hall when New York was still a British colony. It was in that building that several historic firsts occurred.

In 1765, the Stamp Act Congress met at this site, uniting the colonies in **the first organized, peaceful, mass resistance** against British taxation. This gathering was one of the major events leading to the American Revolution. When the new nation, the United States of America, formed in 1789, City Hall underwent a hasty renovation to become Federal Hall. New York City was **the first capital of the United States**, and Federal Hall was the Capitol building. **The first Congress of the United States** met there and wrote the Bill of Rights. George Washington took the oath of office as **the first president of the United States**, standing on the balcony of the old Federal Hall at the spot where his massive statue, the work of John Quincy Adams Ward, now looks down on the street below.

Dating from the early 1700s, the old Federal Hall had seen better days by the time it became the first U.S. Capitol. It was razed in 1812. The current building, Federal Hall National Memorial, rose on this site thirty years later. It has had several lives. Built as the Custom House, it subsequently served as the U.S. Sub-Treasury from 1862 until 1920. It is now part of the National Park Service. You might want to climb the steps to visit exhibits recounting the history of the buildings on this site and to see bank vaults from the Sub-Treasury days.

As you leave Federal Hall, note the New York Stock Exchange on Broad Street (which is named Nassau Street north of Wall Street). As you continue west on Wall Street one block to Broadway, you'll see Trinity Church ahead, until 1890 the tallest building in the area. Turn right (north) on Broadway. As you walk north, look down for sidewalk markers commemorating ticker-tape parades, and glance up at the green-topped Woolworth Building ahead, the tallest building in the world from 1913 to 1929. The next building on the tour is the Equitable Building, between Pine and Cedar Streets (Pine is one block north of Wall; Cedar, two blocks). For the best view, cross at Broadway and Cedar, and observe the Equitable Building diagonally across the street from the edge of Zuccotti Park.

7. Equitable Building (120 Broadway, between Pine and Cedar Streets) The block on the east side of Broadway between Cedar and Pine Streets has been the site of two Equitable Buildings. The first, opened in 1870, was eight stories tall—too high for office workers to walk up. As a result, it was **the first office building with passenger elevators**.

After a fire destroyed that building in 1912, Equitable rebuilt on the same site. Big was again on the insurance company's mind. The massive structure that you see here was the largest office building in the world when it opened in 1915. Nobody would have complained about that had it been spread out over a larger area. But the hulk blocked the natural light for other buildings and cast shadows on the streets below. New Yorkers were so upset that they enacted **the first comprehensive zoning laws in the nation** the next year, restricting how high a building could go before setbacks made it possible for light to enter the area. The ruling resulted in skyscrapers that were wide at the bottom and tapered as they rose, creating the iconic New York skyline with tiered, wedding-cake-style buildings and distinctive narrow tops like those of the Empire State and Chrysler Buildings.

Equitable no longer occupies the building, which now goes by its address: 120 Broadway. It's a fashionable address for downtown office space.

If you want, relax for a while in Zuccotti Park, perhaps enjoying refreshments from a food cart here. Then continue north on Broadway. The street on the north side of Zuccotti Park is Liberty Street. Cross Broadway at Liberty. About halfway between Liberty and the next street, at 154 Broadway, two brothers issued **the first board game created and produced in the United States;** *the building where they worked in the 1820s is long gone. Continue another block and a half to John Street. Turn right (east) on John Street, and go a block and a half to the last official stop on this tour.*

8. John Street United Methodist Church (44 John Street, between Nassau and Dutch Streets)

John Street United Methodist Church is an active religious institution serving Financial District workers and residents. This building is the third Methodist church at this location. The first one, built in 1768, was called Wesley Chapel; it was **the first Methodist church in America**. The present church has exhibits on the lower level that recall life in New York in those early days; they are worth visiting.

This is the official end of the tour. If you want to explore more, continue with one of the two bonus options. Bonus Option A takes you east to sites where firsts occurred, although the structures themselves no longer exist. Bonus Option B takes you west to the site of the World Trade Center and the 9/11 Memorial. Both bonus options offer opportunities for shopping and refreshments. The sites for both options are several blocks away from the John Street United Methodist Church.

9. Bonus Option A

Continue east on John Street five blocks to Pearl Street, and turn left (north) on Pearl. Walk one block north to Fulton Street.

Pearl Street Power Plant (255-257 Pearl Street, near Fulton Street)

In 1882, Thomas Edison opened **the first central power plant** in the world at this location. The plant generated electricity for homes and businesses up to a mile away. Edison intentionally chose this location for the power plant because the area had a dense concentration of residences and workplaces. Within a year, the customer base grew from eighty-five to about 500 electricity-craving customers.

*At Fulton Street, turn right and walk east to enjoy the South Street Sea-port shops, restaurants, and vibe. Two blocks north of here, the Black Ball ships set sail from the East River beginning in 1818; they were **the first ships to cross the Atlantic on a regular schedule**. As you walk around the neighbor-hood, pay attention to the old buildings, some dating back nearly two hundred years to the time when New York was an active shipping center.*

10. Bonus Option B

From the John Street United Methodist Church, retrace your steps west back to Broadway. Cross Broadway, and go slightly north to Dey Street. Turn left on Dey Street, and continue west. One block away, on Church Street, is the space-age Oculus, which you can enter to go shopping. Or go a block farther, to the 9/11 Memorial Museum and outdoor 9/11 Memorial. Another block west is the upscale Westfield shopping mall, the domed structure ahead of you.

WALKING TOUR 2: GREENWICH VILLAGE

(About one and one-half miles up to the Bonus Options)

Begin on the east side of the pedestrian plaza at Cooper Square and Astor Place. Look at the large brownstone across the street.

1. Cooper Union for the Advancement of Science and Art (between Cooper Square and Third Avenue, Astor Place/St. Marks, and 7th Street) Industrialist, engineer, and innovator Peter Cooper opened his name-sake college in 1859 as a tuition-free institution of higher learning. The free education is just one example of Cooper's forward-thinking nature. Another example is visible at the roof. Do you see that round structure that looks like a broad chimney? It's actually **the first shaft for a passenger elevator**. Cooper had the architects include this shaft in 1853 so it would be ready for an elevator as soon as the new-fangled device became commercially available. But he guessed wrong about the shape, and the square elevator did not fit into the round shaft. Elevator inventor Elisha Otis created a round elevator just for this building. Students may still ride in it today. A big difference between present students and those of yester-year: since 2014, they have had to pay tuition.

You might want to go to the 7th Street side of the Cooper Union building. If it is open, go downstairs to the Great Hall. The huge auditorium has hosted public lectures by many famous people and those on the way to becoming famous. Perhaps the most noteworthy was Abraham Lincoln, at the time a relatively unknown contender for president of the United States. Many other presidents and presidential hopefuls have also spoken at Cooper Union.

Walk west across the pedestrian plaza so that Cooper Union is behind you, and cross Lafayette Street at Astor Place. Look back at the long, red-brick building to your right on the east side of Lafayette Street.

2. Public Theater/Astor Library (425 Lafayette Street, at Astor Place) When Joseph Papp opened the Public Theater in 1967 with *Hair*, the theater-going public was in a state of shock—not just because of the nudity but because of the music. *Hair* was **the first rock musical**, a major departure from the type of musicals that audiences were used to. Ever since that sensational opening, the Public has been one of New York's favorite off-Broadway venues.

The building that houses the Public began as the Astor Library, which opened in 1849. At least part of it did; two additions soon followed. Funds to establish the library came from the estate of John Jacob Astor, **the first multimillionaire in America**. When the building ceased to be a library, its extensive collection was not lost. Rather, the Astor Library, the Lennox Library, and the Tilden Trust merged to form the New York Public Library on 42nd Street in 1911.

Go north one short block to 8th Street, and turn left (west). Continue on 8th Street two blocks to Mercer Street. Turn left (south) on Mercer, and go two-thirds of the way down the block. Look at the ground floor of 291 Mercer, across the street in the red-brick apartment building.

3. Oscar Wilde Memorial Bookshop (291 Mercer Street) The ground floor of the large apartment building on this leafy Greenwich Village street has several commercial establishments. The one that opened in 1967 was the Oscar Wilde Memorial Bookshop, **the first gay bookstore** in the country. It was more than a bookstore; it was also a meeting place for gays and lesbians, many of whom lived in the Village. The bookstore moved out long ago. At the time of this writing, a dry-cleaning shop occupied the space.

*Continue on Mercer Street to the corner, and turn left (east) on Waverly Place. Walk one block on Waverly to Broadway, and turn left (north). One block north at Astor Place, look up at the top floor of 740 Broadway. That is where you'll currently find The Writers Room, **the first shared writing workspace in the country**. Continue three blocks north on Broadway to 10th Street.*

4. Grace Churchyard/**Fleischmann's Model Vienna Bakery** (Broadway and 10th Street)

Today you see a yard belonging to Grace Church at the corner of Broadway and 10th Street. In the late nineteenth century, Fleischmann's Model Vienna Bakery occupied the space. This was a posh neighborhood then, with A. T. Stewart and Wanamaker department stores attracting a steady stream of upscale shoppers, as well as customers for the bakery. But in the dark of night, a queue of have-nots formed, waiting for a handout from Fleischmann's. That was **the first breadline**, and it also was the origin of that term.

Shortly after the death of the bakery owner in 1904, Grace Church purchased the land to expand its yard. If you close your eyes and inhale deeply, maybe you can imagine a whiff of fresh-baked, yeasty treats from days past.

Turn left on 10th Street, and walk west three blocks almost to Sixth Avenue. The lovely block between Fifth and Sixth Avenues has been home to many writers and artists over the years and also reflects the architectural styles that were popular in the Village in various periods. Stop at the red-brick apartment building near the corner of Sixth Avenue on the north side of 10th Street.

5. Tenth Street Studio Building (45 West 10th Street, near Sixth Avenue)

For almost a century, starting in 1858, many artists lived in the Tenth Street Studio Building. They didn't just live there; they also worked there, because it was **the first building designed as a live/work space for artists**. One of the initial residents was Frederic Church, a leader of the Hudson River School of art, **the first American genre of painting**. Another early resident was the building's architect, Richard Morris Hunt, **the first**

American to study at the prestigious École des Beaux-Arts in Paris. In his residence/studio, Hunt started **the first architectural school in America**. Other resident artists over the years included John LaFarge, William Merritt Chase, and Winslow Homer.

The apartment building that you see here replaced the Tenth Street Studio Building in 1955. Actress Julia Roberts once owned a penthouse in this building.

Continue to Sixth Avenue, and look across the street at the red-brick building with the tall tower.

6. Jefferson Market Library/**Jefferson Market Courthouse** (425 Avenue of the Americas [Sixth Avenue], at West 10th Street)
This fanciful building dates back to 1877, when it served as a courthouse. It replaced the makeshift courtrooms above Jefferson Market, where area farmers sold their goods to city residents. The clock tower recalls the fire tower that loomed over the market, an essential lookout in the days when many structures were made of wood. One of the most notorious trials at the Jefferson Market Courthouse was that of Harry K. Thaw, who murdered famed architect Stanford White in a jealous rage in 1906 (*see* Walking Tour 3 for details about this crime). In 1927, Mae West was found guilty of obscenity here for the play *Sex*, which she wrote and performed. The Jefferson Market Courthouse functioned day and night for almost a dozen years, starting in 1907, for this building housed **the first night court** in the nation.

The courthouse complex became obsolete by the mid-twentieth century. Threatened with losing their beloved Victorian Gothic building, neighborhood residents rallied and saved the structure. It achieved a new life in 1967, when it became the Jefferson Market Library, a branch of the New York Public Library system. Eight years later, the Jefferson Market Garden, which neighborhood residents tend, blossomed on the site of the former women's prison that had been part of the courthouse complex.

Cross Sixth Avenue, and continue west one block on West 10th Street to Greenwich Avenue. Turn left (south), and walk to the next corner, admiring the Jefferson Market Garden along the way; go in to enjoy it if it's open. Cross Greenwich Avenue, and walk west on Christopher Street almost to Seventh Avenue three blocks away.

7. Stonewall Inn (53 Christopher Street, between Waverly Place and Seventh Avenue)

The rainbow flags at the Stonewall Inn hint at its connection to the LGBTQ community. In June 1969, a police raid at this gay bar led to days of protests. The Stonewall Rebellion, as the uprising was called, was **the first major event in the gay rights movement.**

Enjoy Christopher Park opposite the Stonewall Inn, and admire the white statues of two same-sex couples by sculptor George Segal. Exit on the opposite side of the park (Grove Street), and cross the street. Ahead is another small, triangular park, Sheridan Square. Take the street to the left of Sheridan Square, rather than West 4th Street on the right of that park. You won't see the name of the street you're on for a while. It is Washington Place, and it was on this street, between Sheridan Square and Sixth Avenue, where **the first gay pride march** *began in 1970.*

Go east on Washington Place to Sixth Avenue. Cross the avenue, and continue one block to Washington Square Park. If you don't plan to return here on Bonus Option A, you might want to visit the park now. Otherwise, make a left, and walk two blocks north to West 8th Street. About half a block before you get there, peek into MacDougal Alley, where you'll see carriage houses from the days when this alley contained stables for the wealthy residents north of Washington Square. On West 8th Street, turn right, and walk more than halfway to the next corner, Fifth Avenue.

8. New York Studio School /original home of the **Whitney Museum of American Art** (8 West 8th Street)

As her name suggests, Gertrude Vanderbilt Whitney belonged to the elite society of New York; she was born into the Vanderbilt family and married into the Whitney family. She also was a sculptor and a collector of art, especially the works of up-and-coming Americans. She amassed such a large collection of modern American art that she offered it to the Metropolitan Museum of Art. When the Met turned her down, she converted her Greenwich Village studio here on West 8th Street into a museum. Opened in 1931, the Whitney Museum of American Art was **the first museum dedicated to the works of living American artists.**

The Whitney Museum has had several homes since. It moved uptown, but now it is back downtown, at 99 Gansevoort Street. The current location is at the southern terminus of the High Line, **the first elevated linear park in America**.

After the Whitney left its 8th Street home, another art institution moved in: the New York Studio School of Drawing, Painting & Sculpture.

This is the official end of the tour. If you want to explore more, continue with one of the two bonus options. Bonus Option A takes you to Washington Square Park, the social heart of Greenwich Village, and beyond to a special café. Bonus Option B takes you north to Union Square. Both options provide an opportunity to relax in a popular park and perhaps sample tasty treats.

9. Bonus Option A

*Go to the corner of Fifth Avenue, and turn right (south). Walk south one block on Fifth Avenue, and enter the park through the Washington Square Arch. Take a seat on a bench, and enjoy the spirit that always fills Washington Square Park. When you're ready to leave, exit the park at the southwest corner (to the right of where you entered, all the way across the park; it has tables for playing chess). You'll be on MacDougal Street (not to be confused with MacDougal Alley, the carriage house lane you saw earlier). Walk one block south on Mac-Dougal Street beyond 3rd Street, and stop at Caffe Reggio (119 MacDougal Street), which served **the first cappuccino in America** when it opened in 1927. You'll find the original espresso machine on display inside. As you enjoy the signature drink or other refreshments, soak up the atmosphere that permeates the walls of this almost century-old café. Be sure to visit the funky bathroom. It gives new meaning to the term "water closet."*

10. Bonus Option B

From the New York Studio School, go to the corner of Fifth Avenue, and turn left (north). Walk north on Fifth Avenue six blocks to 14th Street. The avenue was lined with mansion homes in the 1870s, an era that Edith Wharton depicted in The Age of Innocence; *little remains of this period, so you have to use your imagination to picture it. At the corner of 14th Street, turn right and walk one block east to Union Square. The reviewing stand for **the first Labor Day parade**, in 1882, was here. These days, Union Square is famous for its greenmarket, held four days a week, where area farmers and food purveyors sell their produce, cheese, and baked goods to city dwellers. Kind of reminiscent of Jefferson Market in days past.*

Walking Tour 3: Madison Square to Herald Square

(About one and one-third miles)

Begin at the northeast corner of 23rd Street and Broadway, which is the south-west corner of Madison Square Park, or at the pedestrian plaza on the north side of 23rd Street between Broadway and Fifth Avenue. Look past the pedestrian plaza to the large building on Fifth Avenue.

1. Toy Center/**Fifth Avenue Hotel** (Fifth Avenue, between 23rd and 24th Streets)
The huge Fifth Avenue Hotel was the height of elegance when it opened in 1859. At that time, the Madison Square area was in the early stages of development, and it would soon become the place for fashionable New York society. The hotel's designers clearly anticipated this growth, because they outfitted the building inside and out with luxury. The many beautifully appointed public rooms attracted locals and visitors alike. One amenity drew particular attention, as this was **the first hotel with a passenger elevator**.

By the early 1900s, the area had become too commercial for the hoity-toity. The Fifth Avenue Hotel came down in 1908, replaced with a sixteen-story office building; that's what's there now. After World War II, it became the Toy Center, where toy makers and distributors had their headquarters. It is better known today as the home of its ground-floor establishment, Eataly.

Turn around and enter Madison Square Park.

2. Madison Square Park (between Madison and Broadway/Fifth Avenue, 23rd and 26th Streets)
Like Washington Square and Bryant Park, Madison Square Park was once the location of a potter's field (paupers' burial ground) when the population of New York City lived farther south. The formal park dates from 1847. Named for the fourth president of the United States, the park has been the scene of several firsts.

Before it became an official park, Alexander Cartwright and his pals used to play baseball on the open field. Cartwright wrote the rules of the game. The ballplayers, who called themselves the Knickerbockers, were one of the teams in **the first recorded baseball game** in 1846. The game wasn't played here but in Hoboken, New Jersey.

Many years later, in December 1912, a huge cut pine tree appeared in Madison Square Park. It was **the first outdoor community Christmas tree** in the nation. Thousands of New Yorkers from all walks of life gathered around the tree on Christmas Eve to celebrate the holiday. These days, the Star of Hope, a five-pointed white star on a tall white pole, commemorates the event. You can see it on the 23rd Street side of the park, about half-way between Broadway and Madison Avenue.

If you're hungry, stop at Shake Shack, a bit northeast of the Star of Hope. This is **the first Shake Shack in the nation**. Since opening in 2004, this Shake Shack has drawn crowds year round. That's rather amazing come winter as, true to the park venue, seating is al fresco.

Take some time to enjoy the park. When you're ready to leave, exit at Madison Avenue and 26th Street, diagonally across from where you entered.

3. New York Life Building/**Madison Square Garden** (26th Street and Madison Avenue)
People often ask why Madison Square Garden, the sports venue, is nowhere near Madison Square. It actually used to be. Twice, in fact. Both the first and the second Madison Square Garden occupied the space where the New York Life Building is now. **The first indoor ice-skating rink in America** was at the first Madison Square Garden (1879-1889). The second Garden (1890-1925) was the masterpiece of Stanford White, one of the great architects of the late nineteenth and very early twentieth centuries. Like the New York Life Building, it filled an entire square block. It offered an assortment of entertainment, including concerts, theater, sports, dining—easily as much variety as the present Madison Square Garden. Events that occurred there included **the first cat show in America, the first car show**, and **the first professional indoor football game**.

Scandal surrounded the second Madison Square Garden from the beginning. Atop the soaring tower was the figure of *Diana*, the Roman goddess of the hunt. It was the creation of Augustus Saint-Gaudens, the premier sculptor of the day and a friend of Stanford White. What's the scandal? *Diana* was **the first nude female statue** made in America. Even though her unclothed state could scarcely be detected from the ground, prudish New Yorkers made a big fuss about it.

The second Madison Square Garden is remembered not so much for the statue or for its architectural splendor but for the scandal surrounding the architect. He was quite a womanizer, usually going for much younger ladies. One paramour was Evelyn Nesbit, an actress and model whom Stanford White took advantage of when she was just a teenager. She must have mistaken sex for love, because they continued to see each other for a while. Eventually, she married a man named Harry Thaw. On June 25, 1906, Thaw followed White to the rooftop theater of his magnificent Madison Square Garden and shot him at point-blank range, killing the lothario architect. The subsequent trials—the first ended in a hung jury, despite the presence of plenty of eyewitnesses in the theater audience—kept the tabloids busy for years.

Walk two blocks east on 26th Street to Lexington Avenue. Stay on the right side of the street, across from the New York Life Building, and you'll notice a plaque between Park and Lexington indicating that the author Herman Melville lived on this block for almost thirty years. You'll then be walking beside the 69th Regiment Armory. Cross Lexington to get a good view of it.

4. 69th Regiment Armory (Lexington Avenue, between 25th and 26th Streets)

The massive armory building began to rise on this site in 1904, the handiwork of the architect sons of famed architect Richard Morris Hunt, who was **the first American to study at the prestigious École des Beaux-Arts** in Paris. Like father, like sons. This armory breaks from the medieval fortress style of previous New York City armories and gravitates toward the Beaux-Arts style.

The 69th Regiment, also known as the Fighting 69th, originally comprised Irish immigrants; it remains the city's only official Irish regiment. The building achieved National Historic Landmark status in 1996, not only because of its architecture and the Fighting 69th but also because it was the site of the 1913 Armory Show, **the first exhibition of modern art in the United States.**

The Armory Show was shocking to staid art lovers who were more familiar with classical styles. Do you suppose visitors to a different type of show a century later were equally shocked? For about a decade early in the new millennium, scantily clad ladies strutted here on the runway of Victoria's Secret Fashion Show.

*Cross Lexington to the Armory side, and turn north for a great view of the Chrysler Building, **the first building in the world taller than 1,000 feet.** (See the Chrysler Building up close on Walking Tour 4.)*

Walk north on Lexington Avenue to 27th Street, then make a left turn and return to Fifth Avenue three blocks west. As you walk by the New York Life Building, you'll get a feel for how the full-block Madison Square Garden dominated the area. Cross 27th Street.

5. Museum of Sex (233 Fifth Avenue, at 27th Street)
If you want a break, spend some time at the Museum of Sex. Opened in 2002, it is **the first museum in the United States devoted to human sexuality**. Europe already had sex museums.

Walk six blocks north on Fifth Avenue to 33rd Street. As you walk, admire the Empire State Building looming ahead. You may want to stop a block or so before 33rd Street to get a good view without stressing your neck as you look up.

6. Empire State Building/former site of the **Waldorf Astoria Hotel** (350 Fifth Avenue, between 33rd and 34th Streets)
The Empire State Building is so iconic that it literally is a stand-in for New York City. How often have you seen a picture of the Empire State Building and known immediately that the subject matter was New York?

Folks at the Chrysler Building weren't too happy to see the Empire State Building top off in 1931. It stole the title of tallest less than a year after the Chrysler Building had won the coveted title by snatching it less than a year after the Bank of Manhattan was declared the tallest. The Empire State Building had another title that could not be stolen: **the first building in the world with more than 100 stories**.

Those 100 stories in a building almost filling a city block were more a curse than a blessing in the early years. It was the Depression, and rent-paying tenants to fill the huge office tower were so hard to find that the edifice earned an embarrassing nickname: the Empty State Building. If it weren't for sightseers visiting the observation deck, the building would have been a vertical ghost town.

The Empire State Building is not the first boldface name to occupy this site. In the mid-1800s, mansions of two grandsons of John Jacob Astor, **the first multimillionaire in America**, were located here. Toward the end of that century, first one family member and then the other leveled their homes to build hotels, which they identified by names associated with the family; one was the Waldorf Hotel, the other the Astoria Hotel. Before long, the hotels became connected, both physically and in name. The Waldorf Astoria Hotel was world-renowned for its maitre d'hotel, Oscar Tschirky, who created several signature dishes: the Waldorf salad and, possibly, **the first eggs Benedict**. After the Waldorf Astoria moved uptown, making way for the Empire State Building, the new hotel became **the first hotel to offer room service**. (*See* the second Waldorf Astoria on Walking Tour 4.)

Turn left (west) on 33rd Street, and walk about half-way up the block past the end of the Empire State Building. The building at 33 West 33rd Street is the next stop.

7. Majors Cabin Grill (33 West 33rd Street, between Fifth and Sixth Avenues)

In the mid-twentieth century, a restaurant called Majors Cabin Grill was in this small structure in the shadow of the Empire State Building. A frequent patron was a businessman named Frank McNamara. He created the Diners Club card, **the first multipurpose credit card,** and introduced it here in 1950. That restaurant is long gone; at the time of this writing, a Chinese restaurant occupied the space.

Continue west on 33rd Street almost to the corner, where it intersects with Broadway and Sixth Avenue at Greeley Square.

8. Vedanta Society (54 West 33rd Street, between Fifth and Sixth Avenues)

There's not much to see here, but this address was the original home of the Vedanta Society. It was **the first Hindu group in America**, taking root in 1894.

Turn right at the corner, and continue north one block to 34th Street. Make a right (east) turn on 34th Street, and go a short distance to Herald Towers.

9. Herald Towers/**McAlpin Hotel** (50 West 34th Street)
The modern street-level façade of this residential behemoth disguises a century-old edifice, the McAlpin Hotel. It was the largest hotel in the world when it opened in 1912. The McAlpin had many amenities, including a Turkish bath, a special quiet floor for night-shift workers and others who had to sleep during the day, and another floor reserved for women and children traveling alone. It also was home to Jackie Robinson, the Brooklyn Dodger associated with many firsts. In 1947, Robinson became **the first Black major league baseball player in the twentieth century** and was **the first Rookie of the Year**. In 1962, he was **the first African American inducted into the Baseball Hall of Fame**. Twenty years later, he was **the first baseball player to appear on a U.S. postage stamp**. He was so unequaled that in 1997 his number, 42, was **the first number permanently retired from baseball**.

Backtrack slightly to the corner of 34th Street and Broadway. Cross to the triangular pedestrian plaza, Herald Square.

10. Herald Square (between Broadway and Sixth Avenue, 34th and 35th Streets)
Herald Square is named for the *New York Herald*, a newspaper that moved uptown from Newspaper Row to this area in the late 1890s. The *Herald* thrived on scandal and sensationalism, but it was also an innovator, engaging **the first foreign correspondents** in 1838. Founding publisher James Gordon Bennett later handed the reins to his son and namesake, whose behavior itself was rather scandalous. In a comparatively mild act, the junior Bennett won **the first transatlantic yacht race** in 1866.

Look across the street at Macy's department store.

11. Macy's (between 34th and 35th Streets, Broadway and Seventh Avenue)
This is the second location for Macy's. The flagship store has been at Herald Square since 1902.

Just a few years after R. H. Macy opened his previous store at Sixth Avenue and 14th Street, he hired **the first department store Santa**. In 1866, Macy promoted a female employee, making her **the first woman in an executive position in retail**.

The store you are looking at has two claims to fame in the first category. When it opened in 1902, it was **the first building in the world with modern escalators**. And in 2003, the rug department was the scene of **the first flash mob**.

This is the official end of the tour. If you want, go into Macy's or the Empire State Building to further explore some of New York City's most famous sights.

WALKING TOUR 4: MIDTOWN

(About one and three-fourths miles up to the Bonus Option)

Start on the south side of 42nd Street, about half a block east of Broadway. Look across 42nd Street at the ad-covered building in the triangular plot between Broadway and Seventh Avenue.

1. One Times Square/**Times Tower** (42nd Street between Broadway and Seventh Avenue)

When the *New York Times* moved into this tall, oddly shaped building on December 31, 1904, not much else was in this now-bustling area. The *Times* celebrated its new headquarters and the new year with a giant party. That was the origin of the annual New Year's Eve celebration in Times Square. Look up at the top of the building, and you'll see the famous crystal ball waiting for the one evening each year when it becomes the center of attention.

On November 6, 1928, all eyes turned to the Times Tower for a different reason. It was Election Day, and Times Square visitors saw the results as they had never seen them before. **The first electronic news ticker** flashed the outcome in bright lights wrapping around the fourth floor of the Times Tower: Herbert Hoover had won the election for president of the United States.

Despite its glorious past, the Times Tower is essentially a big billboard these days. Except on New Year's Eve, that is.

Walk one block east. Before crossing Sixth Avenue, look back at the ball atop the Times Tower. Then enter Bryant Park, and continue east almost to the stairs. Find a good place to take in the views.

2. Bryant Park (between 40th and 42nd Streets, Fifth and Sixth Avenues) This Midtown park has undergone many transformations, and it continues to change at least twice a year. It hosts a holiday market leading up to Christmas and an ice-skating rink throughout the winter, then it turns into a green, shady oasis from spring through fall—a popular refuge for nearby office workers. Your experience of Bryant Park will depend on when you visit.

This park was the site of **the first world's fair in America**, which ran between July 1853 and November 1854. The fair is often called by the name of the elaborate exhibition hall, the Crystal Palace. Across 42nd Street at Latting Observatory, Elisha Otis demonstrated **the first elevator safety brake** in conjunction with the fair.

From Bryant Park, you can get good glimpses of notable New York skyscrapers. Look to the south. The black building with the jagged gold top is now the Bryant Park Hotel (40 West 40th Street), but it was built in 1924 as the American Radiator Building, which is usually cited as **the first Art Deco building**. Doesn't it make you think of an old-time radiator now that you know its origin? Also to the south, the Empire State Building, almost half a mile away, fills the sky. It was **the first building more than 100 stories tall**. (*See* the Empire State Building up close on Walking Tour 3.)

Exit Bryant Park on the 42nd Street side, and stay on this side of the street. As you walk east past Fifth Avenue, be aware of what traveled beneath here in the 1960s: **the first automated train,** *carrying passengers between Times Square and Grand Central Terminal (just as the manually operated shuttle train does today). Also look up and see the Chrysler Building ahead.*

At the corner of 42nd Street and Madison Avenue, you have two choices. Most people will want to see the Chrysler Building up close. Continue east on 42nd Street two more blocks to Lexington, looking up at the ever-nearer Chrysler Building from time to time. Note the hubcap-like ornaments on the tower. You'll pass Grand Central Terminal, and you may want to visit the lower level for a bathroom or a bite to eat. But if you want a shorter walk and don't care to visit the Chrysler Building, turn left on Madison Avenue, and go four blocks north to 46th Street. Then turn right, and go two blocks east to Park Avenue. Turn left on Park Avenue, and continue north to 47th Street. Cross Park Avenue to look across the street, resuming the tour with stop 4 below (skipping stop 3).

3. Chrysler Building (405 Lexington, at 42nd Street)

The shiny, tapered top of the Chrysler Building seems to disappear when you see the edifice up close at street level. The building is a great example of the Art Deco style, which is apparent at the entrance and in the elaborate lobby. When the spire rose in 1930, Chrysler was **the first building more than 1,000 feet tall**, and it stole the recently won title of tallest in the world from a rival structure in the Financial District. In turn, the Empire State Building became the tallest less than a year later.

Admire the entrance up close, and go in to see the lobby. Then exit on Lexington Avenue, and turn right (north). Walk four blocks north to 46th Street. Turn left, and go west one block to Park Avenue. Turn right on Park and head toward 47th Street.

4. 250 and 270 Park Avenue (west side of Park, at 47th Street)

The building that used to be at 270 Park Avenue, between 47th and 48th Streets, was the Hotel Marguery, completed in 1917. It was **the first structure built on air rights**, over the tracks leading into Grand Central. All the buildings along Park Avenue were essentially erected on bridges over the tracks.

To get an idea of how the street might have looked in its heyday in the 1920s and 1930s, before the steel and glass structures took over, look at 250 Park Avenue, between 46th and 47th Streets, but ignore the modern entrance. Now picture one building after another in similar fashion lining both sides of the street.

Continue walking north on Park Avenue, but cross Park no later than 49th Street to get a better view of the Waldorf Astoria.

5. Waldorf Astoria Hotel (301 Park Avenue, between 49th and 50th Streets)

Like the Hotel Marguery, the Waldorf Astoria Hotel made its initial mark on Park Avenue when elegant hotels catered not just to travelers but to long-term guests. The Waldorf Astoria was **the first hotel to offer room service**, something travelers take for granted these days.

This is the second Waldorf Astoria Hotel. The first was on Fifth Avenue and 34th Street, where the Empire State Building is now. (*See* the site on Walking Tour 3.) That hotel also appealed to the high society of New York, and its famous Chef Oscar kept guests pleasantly surprised with new creations, including, appropriately, the Waldorf salad. He may have served **the first eggs Benedict**, although the origin of this dish is disputed.

The Waldorf Astoria Hotel on Park Avenue closed in 2017 for a major renovation. The new Waldorf Astoria combines a high-end hotel and luxury condominium residences. This mixed use is actually quite similar to the operation of previous apartment hotels, except now the permanent residences are owned rather than rented.

Continue north on Park Avenue two blocks to 51st Street. Turn left (west) on 51st Street, and note the small storefront two doors past the corner.

6. Just Salad (320 Park Avenue, but entrance is on 51st Street)

This unassuming spot was the home of **the first Just Salad**, which opened in 2006. Although other outlets in this New York–based chain offer seats for customers, this one is clearly carryout only for area office workers.

Continue walking west on 51st Street two blocks to Fifth Avenue. Turn right, and walk one block north on Fifth Avenue to 52nd Street. Cross both Fifth Avenue and 52nd Street, and continue west to the Paley Center. Just before you reach this stop, you may pass a brownstone adorned with painted, cast-iron statuettes of jockeys, at 21 West 52nd Street. This is the site of the famous 21 Club, a popular speakeasy during Prohibition that continued to attract celebrities and New Yorkers on expense accounts until it closed during the coronavirus pandemic; its future at the time of this writing was uncertain.

7. Paley Center for Media (25 West 52nd Street, between Fifth and Sixth Avenues)
The head of CBS, William S. Paley, opened the Museum of Broadcasting about two blocks away, at 1 East 53rd Street, in 1975. The institution took a new name—the Museum of Television & Radio—and this new home shortly after his death in 1990. Now the institution is called the Paley Center for Media, renamed in memory of its founder. By whatever name, it is **the first museum of radio and television**. If you want, go in to attend a public screening, to watch a favorite TV show, or to listen to a taped radio broadcast from the museum's vast collection.

Continue a bit west, then turn right into the mid-block park. Walk all the way through to 53rd Street. In front of you is MOMA.

8. Museum of Modern Art (MOMA) (11 West 53rd Street, between Fifth and Sixth Avenues)
This was once Rockefeller territory. John D. Rockefeller, Sr., **the first billionaire in America**, had a townhouse about two blocks away, on 54th Street off Fifth Avenue. John D. Rockefeller, Jr., and his wife Abby Aldrich Rockefeller, who was cofounder of MOMA, owned a townhouse at 11 West 53rd Street. In 1932, when the fledgling MOMA, **the first museum of modern art in America**, needed a home, the Rockefellers gave it their townhouse. Obviously, the building has changed, but the address of the museum has remained the same.

Spend some time at MOMA, if you wish, or return here after the next stop, the official end of the tour. To reach it, turn left on 53rd Street, and go west to the corner, Sixth Avenue. Turn right on Sixth Avenue, and walk three blocks north to 56th Street. Cross 56th Street, turn right (east), and proceed to Benihana.

9. Benihana (47 West 56th Street, between Fifth and Sixth Avenues)
Most Americans were not familiar with Japanese cuisine in 1964, when a young immigrant from Tokyo opened **the first Benihana** at this location. After a few rocky months, a favorable review from a restaurant critic enticed customers to give Benihana a try. The fare was good, but the real draw was the entertainment—chefs chopped up food in front of guests, grilled it at their table, and tossed it to them. Soon business was so brisk

that the owner opened another restaurant in New York. Benihana went national and then global, proof that if they like it in New York, they'll like it everywhere.

This is the official end of the tour. If you still have energy, you might want to return to the Paley Center or MOMA for a museum visit. Or continue north to explore the Bonus Option: Central Park.

10. Bonus Option: Central Park

Next to Benihana you'll see a block-long pedestrian arcade. Enter it, and enjoy the sculptures on display there. Exit on 57th Street, and turn left. Walk west to the corner, which is Sixth Avenue. Turn right, and walk two blocks north on Sixth Avenue, which ends at Central Park.

Central Park is my favorite place in all of New York City. I could write a book about it, but I'll leave you to explore it on your own.

Central Park claims several firsts. Created in the mid-nineteenth century, it was **the first planned public park in America**. In 1890, **the first starlings in America** were intentionally set free in Central Park. And in 1970, **the first gay pride march** ended in Central Park's Sheep Meadow, about six blocks north of where you'll enter the park.

Appendix: Beyond Manhattan

Most of the entries in this book occurred in Manhattan. But each of the five boroughs and some islands that are part of New York City were the scene of pioneering achievements. Below is a list of people, places, and events, in no particular order, associated with firsts in New York City locations other than Manhattan.

BROOKLYN

Brooklyn Heights

- First suburb in America
- First indoor tennis court in America
- First Hasidic (a Jewish sect) woman elected to public office in America serves in civil court here

Dumbo

- First precut foldable cardboard boxes

Brooklyn Navy Yard

- First sweeteners in single-serving packets

Crown Heights

- First museum in the world designed specifically for children
- First Chabad (Lubavitch) Jewish community in the U.S.

Flatbush

- First universal bank-issued credit card

Brownsville

- First teddy bear
- First birth control clinic in the United States
- First Darul Islam group in the U.S.

Williamsburg

- First Giglio feast in America
- First enclosed baseball park
- First building with air conditioning
- First general museum about food and drink

Coney Island

- First hot dog stand
- First frozen custard
- First roller coaster
- First escalator

Bensonhurst

- First Sbarro

Sheepshead Bay

- First transcontinental flight took off from here

Green-wood Cemetery

- First statue of a physician in America relocated here

Ocean Parkway

- First dedicated bike lane in America

Brooklyn Bridge

- First suspension bridge in the world with steel cables

Williamsburg Bridge

- First all-steel suspension bridge

Manhattan Bridge

- First suspension bridge based on deflection theory

Ebbets Field

- First televised professional baseball and football games

Brooklyn Dodgers

- First team to use a batting helmet
- First World Series MVP

Jackie Robinson

- First Black major league baseball player in the twentieth century
- First baseball player named Rookie of the Year
- First Black player inducted into the Baseball Hall of Fame
- First player whose number was permanently retired from baseball
- First baseball player to appear on a U.S. postage stamp

Shirley Chisholm

- First Black woman in the U.S. House of Representatives
- First Black woman to run for president on a major party ticket

QUEENS

Forest Hills Gardens

- First garden city in the United States

Jackson Heights

- First radio commercial, for Hawthorne Court apartments
- First Scrabble game created here

Jamaica

- First closed-circuit TV home security system

Woodside

- First television commercial, for Queens-based Bulova Watch Company

Astoria

- First movie museum in the United States
- First Bareburger

Althea Gibson

- First Black tennis player at the U.S. National Championship and at Wimbledon

Geraldine Ferraro

- First woman nominated for vice president of the United States

The Beatles

- First rock concert in a stadium

BRONX

Yankees

- First baseball team to retire a number
- First club with six players who hit 300 homers for the team
- First team with three players who had 400 career homers
- First televised World Series

- First perfect game in the World Series
- First losing team with a World Series MVP

Babe Ruth

- First baseball player with more than fifty and later sixty home runs in a single season
- First player to hit 200, 300, 400, 500, 600, and 700 home runs
- First baseball player with a salary of $50,000
- First group of Hall of Fame member

Lou Gehrig

- First baseball player with more than twenty grand slams
- First professional baseball player to play in 2,000 consecutive games
- First baseball player to have his number retired

Joe DiMaggio

- First athlete on a championship team in each of his first four seasons
- First baseball player with a fifty-six-game hitting streak

Mariano Rivera

- First baseball player unanimously elected to the Hall of Fame

Giants

- First overtime championship football game, at Yankee Stadium

Van Cortlandt Park

- First public golf course in America
- First public golf tournament

Bronx River Parkway

- First multilane, limited-access automobile road in America

Häagen-Dazs

- First superpremium ice cream

DJ Kool Herc

- First hip hop event

Sonia Sotomayor

- First Hispanic judge on the Supreme Court

STATEN ISLAND

Sailors' Snug Harbor

- First home for retired seamen in America
- First old-age home in America

Staten Island Cricket and Baseball Club

- First tennis court in America

Incinerator

- First high-temperature, mixed-refuse municipal incinerator in America

GOVERNORS ISLAND

- First garbage incinerator in America
- First flight over water took off and landed here

RANDALL'S ISLAND

- First televised college football game

ROOSEVELT ISLAND

- First aerial commuter tram in the country
- First residential high-rise passive house

Appendix: New York City Firsts by Year

1612 First brewery in the New World
c.1614 First male of European descent born in America
1632 First commercial brewery in America
c. 1634 First Double Dutch games
1654 First Jews and Jewish congregation in America
1670 First brewery started by someone born in America
1730 First synagogue in America
1736 First public hospital in America
1751 First public cricket match in America
1762 First St. Patrick's Day parade
1765 First peaceful, organized, mass resistance in America
1766 First Methodist congregation in America
1768 First chamber of commerce in America
1770 First performance of Handel's *Messiah* in America
1779 First woman to receive a military pension from the United States
1789 First capital of the United States
1789 First U.S. Congress
1789 First president of the United States sworn in
1800 First recorded murder trial in the United States
1801 First secular philanthropy in America
1807 First commercially successful steamboat
1811 First steam ferry service in the world
1814 First suburb in America
1818 First ship in a fleet crossing the Atlantic on a regular schedule
1821 First patent for dry cleaning
1821 First Black person to receive a U.S. patent

1822 First board game created and produced in America
1823 First printing of "A Visit from St. Nicholas"
1824 First purpose-built tenement in America
1825 First uniquely American genre of painting
1825 First Hudson River School artist
1827 First African American newspaper
1827 First Episcopal seminary
1832 First streetcar in the world
1833 First successful penny newspaper
1833 First home for retired seamen in America
1833 First old-age home in America
1834 First modern sewing machine
1835 First marble statue made in America
c. 1835 First baby carriages made in America
1837 First restaurant in America
1838 First performance by a Black man in a minstrel show
1838 First American newspaper with foreign correspondents
1840 First indoor bowling lanes in America
1843 First American performance of Beethoven symphonies No. 3 and No. 7
1844 First international sporting event
c. 1845 First tap dancing
c. 1845 First multimillionaire in the United States
1846 First recorded baseball game
1846 First department store in America
1848 First push stroller for young children
1848 First building with a cast-iron façade
1849 First safety pin
1849 First woman doctor in the United States
1849 First baseball uniform
1849 First public bath in America
1850 First American to study at the École des Beaux-Arts in Paris
1850 First time Jenny Lind sang in America
1853 First hotel with a bathroom in every suite
1853 First hotel with a honeymoon suite

1853 First world's fair in America
1853 First shaft for a passenger elevator planned
1854 First elevator safety brake
1855 First immigrant receiving center in America
1857 First passenger elevator in the world
1857 First commercial toilet paper
1858 First building designed as a home and workspace for artists
1858 First architectural school in America
1858 First planned public park in America
1858 First YWCA in the United States
1859 First hotel with a passenger elevator
1861 First photographs of an American war
1862 First enclosed baseball park
1862 First cocktail recipe book
1862 First department store Santa
1866 First sanitary (health) code in the nation
1866 First woman in an executive position in retail
1866 First transatlantic yacht race
c. 1866 First musical comedy
1870 First apartment building in America
1870 First office building with passenger elevators
1870 First woman-owned brokerage firm on Wall Street
1871 First hot dog stand
1871 First corrugated cardboard
1872 First woman to run for president of the United States
1873 First illustrated daily newspaper
c. 1874 First Manhattan cocktail
c. 1874 First tennis court in America
1875 First American cardinal
1876 First formal legal aid society
1879 First precut foldable cardboard boxes
1879 First indoor ice-skating rink in the U.S.
1880 First publication of an actual photograph in a newspaper
1880 First English muffin
1881 First residential co-op in America

1881 First world performance of Tchaikovsky's Piano Concerto No. 2

1881 First electrified residence

1882 First central power plant in the world

1882 First Labor Day parade

1882 First electric Christmas tree lights

c. 1883 First breadline

1883 First suspension bridge in the world with steel cables

1884 First roller coaster in America

1884 First luxury apartment building

1884 First residential building with a service elevator

1885 First garbage incinerator in America

1885 First U.S. performance of some Wagner operas

1886 First ticker-tape parade

1886 First settlement house in the United States

1888 First photographer to use flash powder to shoot dark scenes

1888 First American to convert to Islam

1890 First starlings in North America

1891 First nude female statue made in America

1891 First statue in the world lit by electricity at night

1893 First Islamic newspaper in the United States

1893 First world performance of Dvorak's *From the New World* (Symphony No. 9)

1894 First Hindu group in America

1894 First dedicated bike lane in America

1894 First statue of a physician in the United States

c. 1894 First eggs Benedict

1895 First cat show in America

1895 First doll hospital in America

1895 First public golf course in the United States

1896 First public golf tournament in the United States

1896 First automobile accident in America; first car versus bike accident

1896 First ice cream cones

1896 First escalator

1896 First chop suey

1896 First newspaper comic strip
1899 First ice cream sandwich
1899 First museum in the world designed specifically for children
1899 First fatal car accident in America
1900 First automobile show
1902 First building with air conditioning
1902 First private residence with a structural steel frame
1902 First house with multiple Otis elevators
1902 First building with modern wooden escalators
1902 First independent Young Women's Hebrew Association
1902 First school nurse
1902 First professional indoor football game
1903 First teddy bear
1903 First raid on a gay bathhouse
1903 First Giglio feast in America
1903 First municipal playground in the United States
1903 First all-steel suspension bridge
1904 First indoor tennis court in America
1904 First Jewish museum in America
1905 First pizzeria in the United States
1907 First night court in the nation
1907 First metered, gasoline-powered taxicabs in America
1908 First high-temperature, mixed-refuse municipal incinerator in America
1909 First garden city in the United States
1909 First gin rummy game
1909 First flight over water
1909 First suspension bridge based on deflection theory
1910 First public radio broadcast
1910 First world performances of some European operas
1911 First transcontinental flight
1912 First Oreos
1912 First outdoor community Christmas tree in the United States
1913 First exhibition of modern art in America
1913 First crossword puzzle

1914 First time the term "birth control" appeared in print
1914 First Reuben sandwich
1916 First comprehensive zoning regulations in the country
1916 First birth control clinic in the United States
1916 First billionaire in the United States
1917 First structure built on air rights
1917 First textbook for school nurses
1919 First frozen custard
1919 First Black female millionaire in America
1920 First Ahmadiyya Muslim mission in America
1920 First donut machine
1920 First baseball player with more than fifty home runs in a single season
1922 First radio commercial
1922 First major league baseball player to earn a salary of $50,000
1922 First Reconstructionist (Jewish) congregation
1922 First bat mitzvah in the world
1923 First all-Black professional basketball team
1923 First baseball player to hit 200 home runs
1924 First Art Deco building
1924 First book of crossword puzzles
1925 First multilane, limited-access automobile road in America
1925 First movie theater with modern air conditioning
1926 First woman to swim across the English Channel
1926 First woman to be honored alone with a ticker-tape parade
1926 First mother to swim across the English Channel
1926 First Feast of San Gennaro in America
1927 First high-rise residential complex in the world
c. 1927 First Lindy Hop danced
1927 First baseball player with sixty home runs in a single season
1927 First cappuccino in America
1927 First mechanically ventilated underwater vehicular tunnel in the world
1928 First electronic news ticker (zipper) in the world
1929 First modern art museum in America

1930 First building in the world taller than 1,000 feet
c. 1931 First Kelly tool for forcible entry by firefighters
1931 First building in the world with more than 100 stories
1931 First museum dedicated to works of living American artists
1932 First hotel in the world to offer room service
1932 First apartment project in the country to receive federal funding
1934 First baseball player to hit 700 home runs
1935 First low-income public housing project in the United States
1936 First class of the Baseball Hall of Fame, which included two New Yorkers
1936 First baseball player with more than twenty grand slams
c. 1937 First licensed dolls of popular characters
1938 First pro to play in 2,000 consecutive baseball games
1939 First televised college baseball game
1939 First televised professional baseball game
1939 First baseball team to retire a number; first uniform number to be retired
1939 First athlete to be on a championship team in each of his first four seasons
1939 First televised professional football game
1939 First televised college football game
1940 First televised college basketball game
1940 First Chabad (Lubavitch) Jewish community in America
1941 First television commercial
1941 First baseball team to use a batting helmet
1941 First baseball player with a fifty-six-game hitting streak
c. 1943 First club to feature bebop
1943 First store with a Black Santa Claus
1946 First universal bank-issued credit card
1946 First American named a saint
1946 First basket scored in league play
c. 1947 First abstract expressionist
1947 First Black major league baseball player in the twentieth century
1947 First baseball player to be named Rookie of the Year
1947 First plastic dolls

1947   First West Indian Day Carnival and parade
1947   First televised World Series
c. 1947   First sweetener in a packet
1948   First Halligan bar for forcible entry by firefighters
1948   First long-playing record
1948   First Scrabble sets
1950   First multipurpose credit card
1950   First Black tennis player to compete at the U.S. National
        Championship
1951   First Black tennis player to compete at Wimbledon
1952   First Mr. Potato Head
1952   First television commercial for a toy, targeting children
1954   First Neo-Dada artists
1955   First weekly alternative newspaper in America
1955   First full-figured fashion doll
1955   First overtime game in football
1955   First World Series MVP
1956   First perfect game in the World Series
1956   First Sbarro
1957   First artificial sweetener in a packet
1958   First Puerto Rican Day parade
1958   First overtime championship game in football
1960   First automated teller machine
1960   First superpremium ice cream
1960   First Black woman to compete on the professional golf tour
1960   First World Series MVP from a losing team
1962   First automated train in the United States
1962   First Darul Islam group in the United States
1962   First U.S. president at a dedication of a housing development
c. 1962   First pop art exhibitions
1962   First Black player inducted into the Baseball Hall of Fame
1964   First group of the Five Percent Nation (Islam)
1964   First Benihana
1965   First TGI Fridays
1965   First singles bar

1965 First pocket park in the nation
1965 First Salute to Israel parade
1965 First rock concert in a stadium
c. 1965 First world performance of contemporary works by American composers
1966 First group exhibition of minimalism
1966 First Hare Krishna group in America
1966 First closed-circuit TV home security system
1967 First rock musical
1967 First official group in America for LGBTQ college students
1967 First bookstore in America devoted to books by and about gays
1967 First woman to own a seat on the New York Stock Exchange
1968 First exhibition of earth art
1968 First Black woman in the House of Representatives
1969 First major event in the modern gay rights movement
1970 First federally subsidized housing for artists in the U.S.
1970 First dances for gays and lesbians at any school
1970 First gay pride parade
1972 First Black woman to run for president on a major party ticket
1973 First support group for parents of gay people
1973 First hip hop event
1973 First General Tso's chicken served in America
1974 First Double Dutch tournament
1974 First support group for bisexuals
1975 First American-born saint canonized
1975 First venue in America featuring punk rock
1975 First museum of radio and television in the world
1976 First aerial commuter tram in the country
1977 First pasta primavera
1978 First shared writing workspace in the country
1982 First company in the nation to offer domestic partner benefits
1982 First baseball player to appear on a U.S. postage stamp
1982 First Dominican Day parade
1983 First person to win Grammys for both classical music and jazz

1983 First opera company in the United States to use supertitles

1984 First Brazilian Day parade

1984 First woman nominated for vice president of the United States

1986 First naturally occurring retirement community–supportive services program (NORC-SSP) in the country

1987 First Cosmopolitan cocktail

1988 First movie museum in the United States

1993 First female Jewish justice on the Supreme Court

1994 First openly gay or lesbian federal judge

1997 First jazz work to win a Pulitzer Prize

1997 First number retired from all professional baseball teams

2002 First museum in the United States devoted to human sexuality

2003 First flash mob

2003 First Persian parade in the United States

2004 First venue in the world specifically designed for jazz

2004 First Shake Shack

2006 First Just Salad

2009 First female Solicitor General of the United States

2009 First elevated linear park in the United States

2009 First Hispanic judge on the Supreme Court

2009 First Bareburger

2012 First baseball club with six players who had hit 300 home runs for the team

2012 First Giving Tuesday

2013 First cronut

2013 First general museum about food and drink

2016 First baseball team with three players with 400 career homers

2017 First residential high-rise passive house in the world

2017 First Hasidic woman elected to public office in the United States

2019 First baseball player unanimously elected to the Hall of Fame

2019 First museum in the U.S. dedicated exclusively to posters

2020 First woman and first Jew to lie in state at the U.S. Capitol

2021 First U.S. president impeached twice

2021 First U.S. president whose impeachment trial occurred after he left office

Photo Credits

Page 1: https://commons.wikimedia.org/w/index.php?title=File:Madison_Square_Garden_Diana.jpg&oldid=187768401. Photographer unknown.

Page 9: Adapted from Chrysler Building, New York City, c.1930. loc.gov/item/2004673267. Photographer unknown.

Page 15: https://commons.wikimedia.org/w/index.php?title=File:A._T._Stewart_1870.jpg&oldid=466458230. Photography by Wurts Brothers.

Page 25: https://commons.wikimedia.org/w/index.php?title=File:Supper_at_Delmonico%27s,_New_York_1898.jpg&oldid=477312338. Illustration by Albert E. Sterner.

Page 42: https://commons.wikimedia.org/w/index.php?title=File:Equitable_Building_(Manhattan)_(3).JPG&oldid=505339358. Photograph by Elisa Rolle.

Page 52: https://commons.wikimedia.org/w/index.php?title=File:Elisha_OTIS_1854.jpg&oldid=525749183. Creator unknown.

Page 65: https://commons.wikimedia.org/w/index.php?title=File:Stonewall_Inn_5_pride_weekend_2016.jpg&oldid=505863192. Adapted from photograph by Rhododendrites.

Page 71: https://commons.wikimedia.org/w/index.php?title=File:Jacob_Riis,_Lodgers_in_a_Crowded_Bayard_Street_Tenement.jpg&oldid=510313466. Photograph by Jacob Riis.

Page 82: The Miriam and Ira D. Wallach Division of Art, Prints and Photographs: Picture Collection, The New York Public Library. "A beautiful representation of the New York Crystal Palace." The New York Public Library Digital Collections. 1853. https://digitalcollections.nypl.org/items/510d47e0-ccbb-a3d9-e040-e00a18064a99. Wood engraving: John William Orr. Artists: William Wade and Samuel Wallin.

Page 92: The Miriam and Ira D. Wallach Division of Art, Prints and Photographs: Print Collection, The New York Public Library. "Interior of Niblo's Opera House, New York City" The New York Public Library Digital Collections. https://digitalcollections.nypl.org/items/510d47da-238d-a3d9-e040-e00a18064a99. By John William Orr.

Page 102: https://commons.wikimedia.org/w/index.php?title=File:NixonTicker TapeParadeNYC1960.jpg&oldid=355907358. Photograph by Toni Frissell.

Page 109: Image by Howard Ho. Posted on Pixabay.

Page 115: https://commons.wikimedia.org/w/index.php?title=File:Sukkot_in_ Union_Square.jpg&oldid=473373282. Photograph by Rebecca Wilson.

Page 128: The Miriam and Ira D. Wallach Division of Art, Prints and Photographs: Photography Collection, The New York Public Library. "Studios, 51 West Tenth Street, Manhattan" The New York Public Library Digital Collections. 1938. https://digitalcollections.nypl.org/items/510d47d9-4f77-a3d9-e040-e00a18064a99. Photo by Berenice Abbott for the Federal Art Project.

Page 144: The Miriam and Ira D. Wallach Division of Art, Prints and Photographs: Picture Collection, The New York Public Library. "The Labor Exchange —interior views of the office at Castle Garden, New York." The New York Public Library Digital Collections. 1868-08-15. https://digitalcollections.nypl.org/items/510d47e1-0f55-a3d9-e040-e00a18064a99. Illustration by Stanley Fox.

Page 155: The Miriam and Ira D. Wallach Division of Art, Prints and Photographs: Photography Collection, The New York Public Library. "Lou Gehrig, George Herman [Babe] Ruth and Tony Lazzeri" The New York Public Library Digital Collections. 1927. https://digitalcollections.nypl.org/items/510d47d9-bb22-a3d9-e040-e00a18064a99. Adapted from a photograph by Underwood and Underwood.

Page 169: https://commons.wikimedia.org/w/index.php?title=File:Teddy_bear_early_1900s_-_Smithsonian_Museum_of_Natural_History.jpg&oldid=524649004. Photo by Tim Evanson.

Page 180: Library of Congress. Horse-drawn streetcar no. 148 of a New York City system, c. 1895. loc.gov/item/2004667717. Photo originally copyrighted by Loeffler.

Page 191: https://commons.wikimedia.org/w/index.php?title=File:O%27Connor,_Sotomayor,_Ginsburg,_and_Kagan.jpg&oldid=516883828. Adapted from photo by Steve Petteway, photographer for the Supreme Court of the United States.

Index

billionaire in United States, 20
Black female millionaire, 20
central power plant in the world,
  19, 205
chain restaurant start-ups (Sbarro,
  Benihana, TGI Fridays, Shake
  Shack, Just Salad, Bareburger),
  23–24 (*See also specific restaurant
  names*)
chamber of commerce, 16–17
credit cards, 20–21, 216
department store in America, 17
department-store Santa and Black
  Santa, 18, 121, 218
electrified residence in the world, 19
millionaires and multimillionaires,
  19–20, 194, 207, 216
shared writing workspace, 22
singles bar, 24
woman in executive position in
  retail, 18
women retail executives, 193–94

Cabrini, Frances, 120
cabs (metered, gasoline-powered), 186
Caffe Reggio, 31, 211
Cammeyer, William, 161
capital of the United States, first,
  44, 203
cappuccino, first in America, 31, 211
cardboard, firsts, 58–59
cardinal (Catholic), first American,
  118–19
Carrier, Willis, 60–61
Cartwright, Alexander, 160–61, 212
cast iron façade, first, 10–11
Castle Garden/Castle Clinton, *144*,
  148–49, 201
cat show in America, first, 84, 213
Catholicism. *See* religion
CBGB club, 101

Cecchini, Toby, 39
Central Park, *109*, 110–11, 223
Chabad (Lubavitch) Judaism, *115*,
  124–25
chain restaurant start-ups (Sbarro,
  Benihana, TGI Fridays, Shake
  Shack, Just Salad, Bareburger),
  23–24
chamber of commerce, 16–17
Chase, William Merritt, 133, 209
Chelsea co-op, 135
Chinese food in America (chop suey,
  General Tso's chicken), first, 29
Chisholm, Shirley, 197, 226
Christmas, firsts, 120–22, 213
Christopher Street Liberation Day
  March, 69, 106. *See also* Stonewall
  Inn
Chrysler Building, *9*, 12, 13, 215,
  216, 220
Churchill, Lady Randolph, 38
Claflin, Tennessee, 195
classical music, firsts, 96–97
closed-circuit television (CCTV)
  home security system, 64
Cobb, Ty, 164
cocktails, firsts (Manhattan and
  Cosmopolitan), 38–39
Coit, Stanton, 151
Cole, Thomas, 2–3
comedy, musical, first, 95–96
comic strips, first newspaper, 75–76
commercials, first
  radio, 78
  television (and aimed at children),
    80–81, 175–76
Cone, David, 165
Coney Island, 26, 33, 57, 172, 225
Congress, first U.S., 44, 203
co-op apartments, first, 135–36
Cooper, Peter, 16, 56, 206

ABOUT THE AUTHOR

Laurie Lewis is a freelance writer and editor who moved to New York from the Midwest in the mid-1980s. After being a volunteer tour guide in Central Park for eleven years, Lewis became a licensed NYC tour guide and began Take a Walk New York, which offers scheduled and private tours of New York City. She is the author of the award-winning book *What to Charge: Pricing Strategies for Freelancers and Consultants.*